PENGUIN BOOKS

THE GREEKS

James Pettifer was born in 1949 in Hereford and was educated at King's School, Worcester, and Hertford College, Oxford. He has travelled extensively in Greece and the Balkans, reporting on events for the *Independent*, the *Scotsman*, the *World Today* and many other publications in Britain and abroad. He is a member of the Royal Institute of International Affairs. He is also a regular broadcaster and commentator on the Balkan countries on radio and television. He is a Senior Associate Member of St Antony's College, Oxford.

D0315742

PENGUIN BOOKS

Published by the Penguin Group
Penguin Books Ltd, 27 Wrights Lane, London W8 5TZ, England
Penguin Books USA Inc., 375 Hudson Street, New York, New York 10014, USA
Penguin Books Australia Ltd, Ringwood, Victoria, Australia
Penguin Books Canada Ltd, 10 Alcorn Avenue, Toronto, Ontario, Canada M4V 3B2
Penguin Books (NZ) Ltd, 182–190 Wairau Road, Auckland 10, New Zealand

Penguin Books Ltd, Registered Offices: Harmondsworth, Middlesex, England

First published by Viking 1993
Published in Penguin Books 1994
1 3 5 7 9 10 8 6 4 2

Copyright © James Pettifer, 1993
All rights reserved

The moral right of the author has been asserted

Printed in England by Clays Ltd, St Ives plc

Except in the United States of America, this book is sold subject
to the condition that it shall not, by way of trade or otherwise, be lent,
re-sold, hired out, or otherwise circulated without the publisher's
prior consent in any form of binding or cover other than that in
which it is published and without a similar condition including this
condition being imposed on the subsequent purchaser

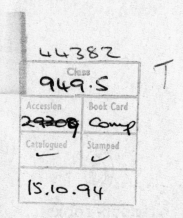

44382

Class
949.5

Accession
29308

Book Card
Comp

Catalogued

Stamped

15.10.94

JAMES PETTIFER

THE GREEKS

THE LAND AND PEOPLE SINCE THE WAR

PENGUIN BOOKS

For Richard Seaford

ὄλβιος ὅστις τῆς ἱστορίας ἔσχε μάθησιν

happy is he who has the understanding of inquiry

– Euripides

Contents

Part Three NEIGHBOURS AND MINORITIES

List of Plates

The bitter mountain war: Greek troops in the Devoli Valley in Albania in 1941 (*Dimitrios Harissiadis*)

Anti-fascist resistance: ELAS andartes. Their style draws on the klephtic tradition, the heroic bandits resisting foreign occupation (*King's College, London*)

Wartime starvation in Athens: the famine claimed over a hundred thousand victims (*Dimitrios Harissiadis*)

For a while, national unity: right-wing EDES resistance leader Zervas with a young ELAS fighter (*Topham Picture Source*)

Liberation: a demonstration in Athens in October 1944 (*Dimitrios Harissiadis*)

After years of resistance and civil war, fighting as a way of life: Democratic Army leader, Markos Vafiades

The terrible price: relatives identify bodies after a massacre near Piraeus (*Dimitrios Harissiadis*)

The British protectorate: Churchill and Eden with Archbishop Damaskinos, Regent of Greece, in February 1945 (*Dimitrios Harissiadis*)

List of Maps

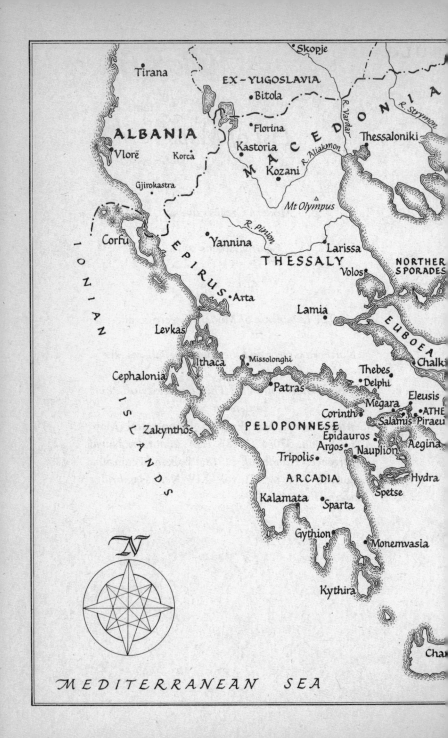

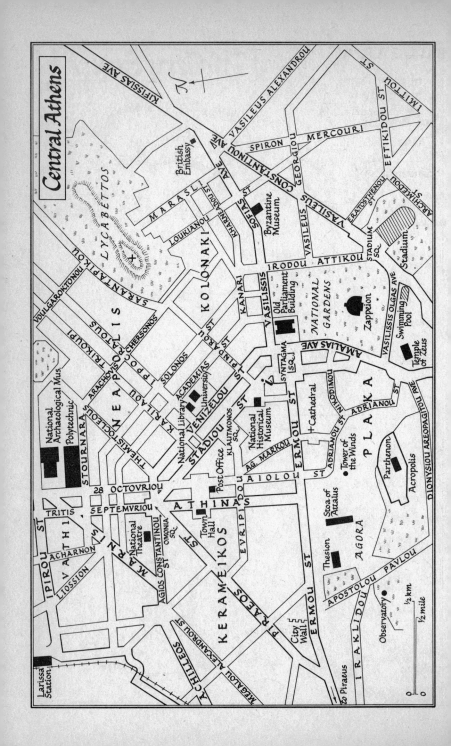

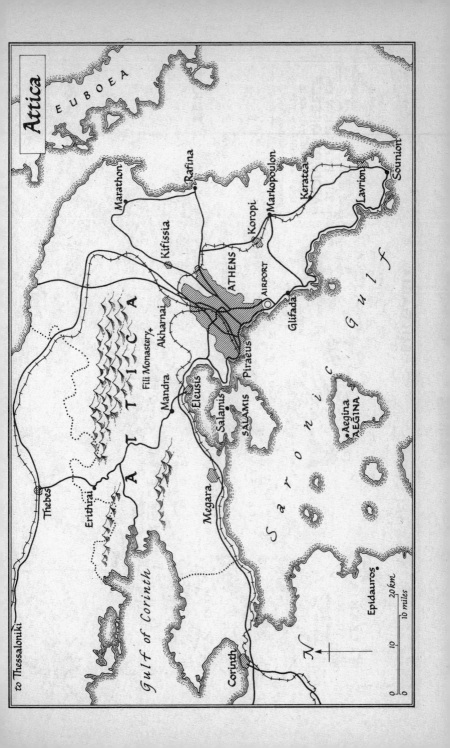

Attica

EUBOEA

ATTICA

Thebes

to Thessaloniki

Gulf of Corinth

Erithrai

Marathon

Kifissia

Fili Monastery +

Akharnai

Mandra

Megara

Eleusis

Salamis

SALAMIS

Corinth

Rafina

ATHENS

Piraeus

Koropi

AIRPORT

Markopoulon

Glifada

Keratea

Lavrion

Sounion

Aegina

AEGINA

Saronic Gulf

Epidauros

N

0   10   20 km
0   10 miles

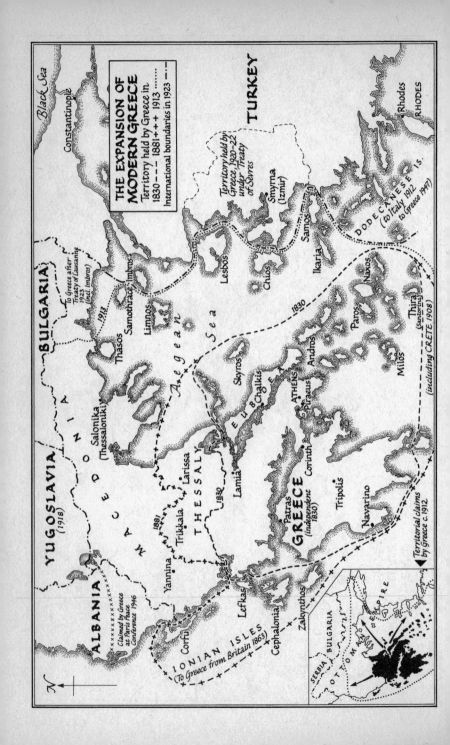

THE EXPANSION OF
MODERN GREECE
Territory held by Greece in
1830 ----- 1881+++ 1913 ....
International boundaries in 1923 -----

Black Sea

Constantinople

TURKEY

BULGARIA

To Greece after
Treaty of Lausanne
1923
(incl. Imbros)

Territory held by
Greece, 1920-22
under Treaty
of Sèvres

Smyrna
(Izmir)

Samos

Imbros

1913

Samothrace

Lesbos

Thasos

Limnos

Chios

Ikaria

DODECANESE IS.
(to Italy 1912
to Greece 1947)

YUGOSLAVIA
(1918)

Salonika
(Thessaloniki)

Rhodes

RHODES

A e g e a n

S e a

1830

ALBANIA

M A C E D O N I A

Skyros

Naxos

Paros

Andros

Thira
(Santorini)

Claimed by Greece
at Paris Peace
Conference 1946

Yannina

1881

Trikkala

Larissa

THESSALY

1830

Lamia

Chalkis

E U B O E A

ATHENS

Piraeus

Milos

(including CRETE 1908)

Corinth

Patras

GREECE
(independent
1830)

Tripolis

Navarino

Corfu

Lefkas

IONIAN ISLES
(To Greece from Britain 1863)

Zakynthos

Cephalonia

Territorial claims
by Greece c. 1912

N

SERBIA

BULGARIA

OTTOMAN EMPIRE

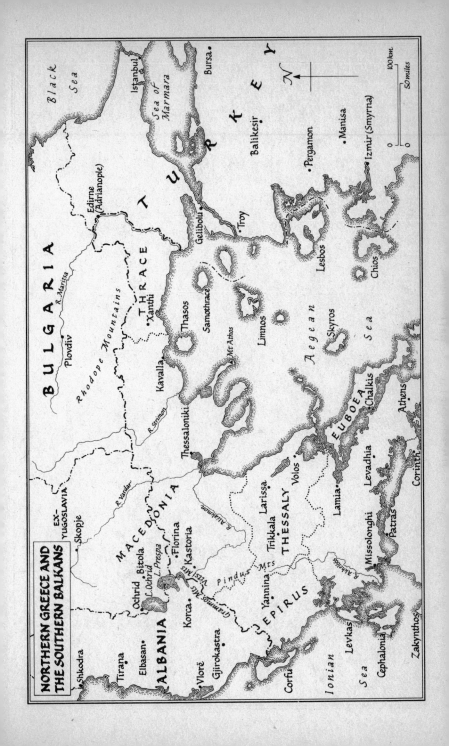

NORTHERN GREECE AND
THE SOUTHERN BALKANS

EX-
YUGOSLAVIA

Skopje

BULGARIA

Plovdiv

Rhodope Mountains

R. Maritsa

Edirne
(Adrianople)

Istanbul

Black
Sea

Sea of
Marmara

Bursa

T U R K E Y

Balikesir

Pergamon

Manisa

Izmir (Smyrna)

100 km.

50 miles

Gelibolu

Troy

Lesbos

Chios

THRACE

Xanthi

Thasos

Samothrace

Mt Athos

Limnos

Skyros

Aegean

Sea

R. Vardar

MACEDONIA

Florina

Bitola

Ochrid
L. Ochrid

L. Prespa

Vitsi Mts

Kastoria

Korca

Pindus Mts

Grammos Mts

Yannina

EPIRUS

ALBANIA

Shkodra

Tirana

Elbasan

Vlorë

Gjirokastra

Corfu

Ionian

Sea

Levkas

Cephalonia

Zakynthos

Kavalla

R. Strimon

Thessaloniki

R. Aliakmon

Larissa

Trikkala

THESSALY

Volos

Lamia

Missolonghi

Patras

R. Akheloos

Levadhia

Challis

EUBOEA

Athens

Corinth

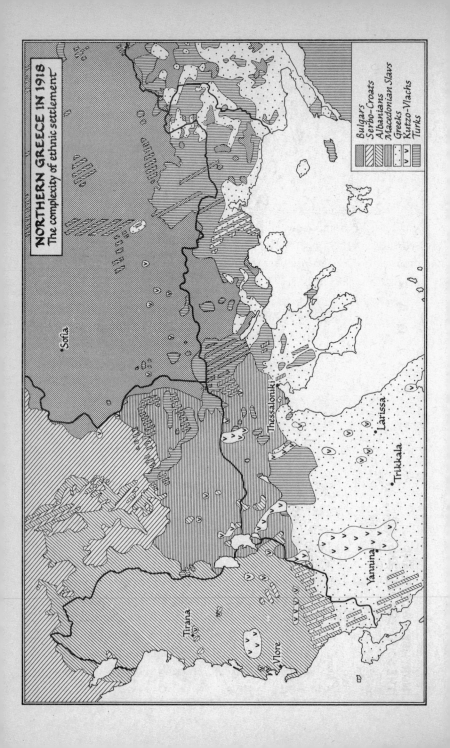

NORTHERN GREECE IN 1918
'The complexity of ethnic settlement'

Bulgars
Serbo-Croats
Albanians
Macedonian Slavs
Greeks
Kutzo-Vlachs
Turks

•Sofia

Thessaloniki

•Larissa

•Trikkala

Yannina•

Tirana

Vlore

Acknowledgements

There are so many books about Greece – Ancient, Byzantine or modern, on some aspect of Greek life or history – that anyone writing another must have an almost infinite number of debts, conscious and unconscious, that are difficult to repay. But always the most important must be to the Greek people themselves, invariably prepared to talk about their private concerns with strangers, and whose hospitality and warmth are legendary.

I would like to thank my friends and colleagues who have helped in so many ways – with advice, information, practical assistance, documents, controversy about the Balkans, seminars, talks in kafenia and articles in newspapers – in particular, Dr Thomas Adams, Alexandros Alexiou, Nicos Aroditis, Neal Ascherson, the late Nicholas Ashford; Frank Barrett, Antony Beevor, Nora Beloff, Anita Bennett, John Bothwell, Gerald Butt; Professor Averil Cameron, Bob Campbell, Nicholas Canellos, Pantelis Caracabassis, Dr Paul Cartledge, Debbie Cavanagh, Christopher Cviic, Nigel Clive, Professor Richard Clogg, Patrick Cockburn, Colonel Edward Cowan; Ilias Damas, Richard Davy, Andrew David, Judy Dempsey, Dr Rauf Denktash, John Dew, Peter Doherty; Nicholas Egon, Dr Jonathan Eyal; Jamie Ferguson, Robert Fisk, Arthur Foss, Dr Daniel Franklin; Jane Gabriel, Soteris Georgialis, Phil and Elli Gooden, Charles Gray, Imogen Grundon, Mesut Gunser; Stavros, Dimitris and everyone at the Hermes, Sir Reginald Hibbert, Christopher Hitchens, Lucy Hodges, Harry Hodgkinson, Kerin Hope, Barry Hutchinson; Nicholas and Jill Jacobs; Michael Kaser, Jonathan Keates, Ani King-Underwood, Haris Kyriakides; Paddy Leigh Fermor, Jenny Little; Neal Malcolm, Andrew Marshall, Professor

Laurence Martin, Nikos Mavroyenneas, Liam McDowall, Charles Meynell, Andy Michealides, Dr Edwina Moreton; Assan Navathchkov; Professor Sir Dimitri Obolensky, Richard Owen, Ozker Ozgur; Dr Nicos Papadakis, Jeanne Pettifer, the late John Pettifer, Dr Michael Prest, Yannis Putos; Liz Routier; George Savvas, Lindy Sharpe, Taki Sirianos, Helena Smith, Phillipos Spiropoulos, Geoffrey Stern; Dennis Taylor, Peter Thompson, Roger Trapp, Nicos Tsarapatsanis, Dr Stavroula Tsinorema; Miranda Vickers; Rory Watson, Robert Winder. Mistakes and the inevitable over-simplifications of the many complexities of Greek life, history and society over the last fifty years are my own responsibility.

My special thanks go also to Dr Lisa French and Dr Guy Sanders of the British School in Athens – and to the staff of the school – for their hospitality and use of library facilities; the staff of the British Embassy in Athens and Vice-Consulates in Greece; the Greek National Tourist Office in London; members of the Greek and Greek-Cypriot communities in London; the Anglo-Hellenic League; the Friends of Democracy in Greece; the Royal Institute of International Affairs at Chatham House; the Turkish Consulate-General at Komotini; the staff of the British Library; the staff of the Bodleian Library and St Antony's College library, Oxford; Larry Laurence and the *Independent* library staff; the staff of the Turkish Embassy in London; friends in Albania who helped me understand the world of Greeks living there: Sokol Gjoka, Arben Ruka, Shaban Murati and Shqelqim Beqari; Maria Hyteri and her staff at the Greek government press office in Athens, especially Rhena Spanou; Kenneth Barnett at the King's School, Worcester, who first taught me Greek literature; and Hieromonk Ambrose for his hospitality and assistance in the monastery at Fili.

I must also thank my agents at Curtis Brown, Natasha Fairweather and Peter Robinson, for their involvement with the conception and development of this book, my editors, Eleo Gordon and Mary Omond, who have been sources of continual assistance and patient understanding, and Susan Rose-Smith for her expert picture research.

Finally, I remember with gratitude Sue, Julia and Alexander, who over the years have put up with irregular absences, frequent travel, hikes up precipitous slopes, the none-too-clean decks of ferry-boats, Athens on hot summer days – and without whose help this book could never have been written.

Athens, April 1993

Introduction

Ever since the fall of the Greek mainland to Roman invaders, well before Christ was born, Greece has had a dual identity: Historia and Mythologia, the real and the imaginary. The home of civilization – of much of what is most important in European culture – or just a small country of limited political importance stretching from south-east Europe into the Mediterranean, a country rich in associations but poor in terms of crops, industries and business institutions.

The Mythologia, the traditional images – the sea, the mountains, the Parthenon, the islands, the strange-looking letters of the written language – are overwhelmingly strong, but images is all they are. They simplify reality, but they also obscure it. Even when the Romans annexed Greece, it was a country with a very long and complex history. And a great deal has happened since; the complexity has increased, the simple stereotypes become ever more misleading.

The events that have made Greece as it is today stretch back thousands of years, but in some aspects they have a more contemporary resonance than the remote past of other countries. This book explores something of what has happened in Greece in the last generation or so, reaching back into history to try to illuminate the present, particularly the revival of the Balkan conflicts. So while this is emphatically not a history book nor a book about politics as such, a good deal of both are essential.

The Greeks, inventors of politics as we know them, are among the most political people in the world. Greek history since the Second World War has run the full gamut of extremes of political experience: from the Civil War to an authoritarian democracy, then to a military dictatorship and back to a fuller democracy. At least twice Greece has almost gone to war with its old enemy, Turkey. None the less it is still possible to find elderly Greek people who remember their childhood under Turkish rule, the strange sense of some Turks as 'gentlemen', but with memories of real oppression mingled with those of the direct mail service to the Sublime Porte – the most important event in remote communities in the mountains of northern Greece.

This Greece is largely unknown to the millions of holidaymakers who visit the country every year, or to the businessman who makes a hurried trip to Athens or Piraeus. The great majority of visitors go to islands which have recently evolved differently from the rest of the country – and only to a few islands at that, mainly Corfu, Crete and Rhodes, which have been developed for mass tourism. The traditional images of sun, sand and sea do seem to approximate to a complete reality here, but in winter even the most tourist-trap islands are another world, with the people living in an entirely different way.

Although, in a political sense, Greece is a highly centralized country, more like France than England, where decisions about anything important are taken in Athens, it is also strongly regional, and loyalty to the place where you were born or grew up is overwhelmingly strong. Geography is the dominant factor here, as it was in antiquity when the country was divided into a myriad collection of city states, usually on bad terms with each other. The sea may be pictured in holiday brochures but mountain and valley have often mattered more in history. The saying goes that the sea unites the country, the mountains divide it. Most of mainland Greece is mountainous and communications are still bad in some areas. Until the 1950s metalled roads were unusual outside the main routes and many villages could only be reached on foot or by mule. It took until 1972 for every Greek community to have electricity.

The sheer diversity of the country needs to be borne in mind from the green deciduous forests of the north-west highlands, with as much rainfall as parts of Wales, to the open rolling plains of Macedonia and Thessaly, with little fields of tobacco and pepper plants, and the wooded, remote fastnesses of the Rhodope mountains next to the Bulgarian border, haunt of the brown bear and the griffon vulture. These are landscapes of the far north, hardly Mediterranean in what is Europe's most Mediterranean country. Then there are the great provincial cities, many, like Thessaloniki and Volos, infrequently visited by tourists, but with an economic vibrancy and freedom from the ever-present febrile political atmosphere of Athens. There are the large islands near Turkey like Samos and Lesbos, traditional strongholds of the Left; the Italianate architecture of the Dodecanese; the Ionian chain, with cricket played in Corfu; remote islands with a few hundred inhabitants; domestic popular islands near Athens like Aegina; bare little rocks with only a few birds, lizards and tortoises; the military strongholds of Lemnos and Samothrace facing Turkey. And, above all, there is the great diversity of the central and southern mainland itself: from the bustling cosmopolitan city of Patras, business-oriented and westernized, to the sleepy, sensual towns of the southern Peloponnese, like Kalamata and Gythion, where the colours are so bright in the summer sun and where the silky warmth of life makes it difficult to believe that the Turks ever left the country. And within each region and sub-region hundreds of villages, each one different and with a unique economy and history, have traditional districts in Athens where their young people go to live and seek their fortunes in the great labyrinth at the top of the Saronic Gulf. And there are Greeks from so many foreign parts: the refugees from the Black Sea coast; those home from Australia and Canada; political migrants from the old Eastern Bloc; sons and grandsons of those the Turks expelled from Smyrna; descendants of families who did important jobs in every city where the Ottoman foot trod; Cypriots who know London like the back of their hands; well-to-do elderly men from the Greek and Cypriot business settlements of the West African coast; people from long-established Greek communities in Argentina and Uruguay – the list is very long. Beneath the apparent homogeneity of Greek life and the stereotypes on every Greek street – little old ladies in black, men in short-sleeved blue postmen's shirts bent over the backgammon table – there is a people of extraordinary richness and diversity.

The great ancient historian Momigliano said that any fool could write contemporary history, and I have no intention of trying to do so, especially given the complexity of Greek society and social experience in the last fifty years. To present a picture of contemporary Greece, and how it has been formed by the period of history since the Second World War, I have tried to illustrate what seem to me to be the most important elements in that history through the places and people I know and love and where perhaps some of the deeper historical forces can be sensed. Chapters are linked to particular places or regions that seem to exemplify the issues. For example, the beginning of the book, which goes into the War, and the Civil War and its aftermath, is focused on northern Greece, on what are still remote regions. Then for the 1950s and 1960s the scene moves to Athens, with the mass migration of Greeks as the capital grew into its present form. And the chapter on agriculture and the rural economy is partly set in and around Messenia – and so on. There are statistics, but only those that really seem needed. For instance, to say that tobacco was the mainstay of the northern Greek economy before the War and is now much less important appears to me sufficient.

Any volume of this kind is bound to be out of date as soon as it is written and this is specially true of the last part of the book where I explore what appear to be future options for the Greeks. The Balkan crisis, so far moving inexorably southwards from the former Yugoslavia, will affect Greece in fundamental ways, impossible to predict. But, whatever happens, an understanding of the recent past is important, even within the context of the rather gloomy aperçu that as well as never forgetting their history the

Balkan countries never learn from it, or Saki's comment that more history is produced in the Balkans than can be consumed locally.

For convenience I have referred to the prospective new state of Macedonia, or the Republic of Skopje, as Macedonia. This does not imply any view on the increasingly vexed question of recognition, or what name the new state should have, but is used only insofar as the territory concerned still occupies what was known as the socialist republic of Macedonia, within what used to be Yugoslavia. This Yugoslavia was, of course, the second Yugoslavia, and a third Yugoslavia has now been formed, comprising Serbia and Montenegro – although it has not generally received international recognition. Although this usage may not please some Greek readers, it seems essential here to be precise about the nature of the geographic entity concerned. I hope I have made clear, in the chapter on archaeology, where the work of Professor Manolis Andronikos at Vergina is discussed, and in the chapter on the re-emergence of the Macedonian question itself, enough of the evidence for the Hellenism of Macedonia for readers to come to their own conclusions. I would also add that my usage is concerned with geography and history, not with politics, in as much as they can be legitimately separated. It is known, for instance, that one of the reasons why the ancient Romans hesitated before making Macedonia into a Roman province was because of the difficulty of delineating satisfactory borders.

Part One

FROM CIVIL WAR TO DEMOCRACY

1. Origins: Epirus and the North

12 October 1944   LIBERATION

At the beginning it was all joy and love. Down from
the mountains came the partisans to be wept over
and embraced. The prisons were opened. Families
were reunited. The Greek flag flew alone once more
over the Acropolis. But soon, so soon, came a feeling
of vague uneasiness. The partisan army had marched
to Athens to join in the rejoicing, but outside the
city it stopped. Why?

– Melina Mercouri, *I was Born Greek*

Few foreign visitors go to Epirus, few Greeks for that matter.
Seen from Corfu, across the narrow straits, the mountains of
north-west Greece are remote, yet these are only coastal
mountains, not those of Alpine scale and grandeur – the
Grammos and Vitsi ranges on the inland border with Albania,
brutal walls of limestone and granite marking the boundaries
of northern Greece. In Epirus, fifty years ago, wolves and
bears were still common and traditional dress was worn by
shepherds. After a brief period of prominence in Byron's time,
when the region was the seat of despotic, glamorous Ali
Pasha, the diamond of Yannina, with a huge harem and
armed retinue, and who, under the Turks, ruled a vast, wild
domain stretching from Arta in the south to Berati in Albania,
Epirus sank into primitive obscurity. It was one of the last
parts of Greece to be liberated from the Turks; they did not

leave their grim fortress at Yannina until 1913. Today, the city is quiet, a respectable regional capital, with fine metal workers and its great lake still full of eels, carp, trout and tench. The reeds stretch for acres, teeming with dark blue dragonflies and different varieties of frogs. It is difficult to associate Yannina with nationalist passion or the blood-drenched years of struggle against Ottoman rule. But a walk on Ali Pasha's island in the middle of the lake soon reminds the visitor of history. Here the great enemy of the Turks met his end; here the eyes of every saint in the beautiful frescoes on the walls of Philanthropian monastery have been gouged out.

Epirus is dense forest; the only significant relic of ancient Greece is the theatre and the oracle at Dodona – wintry Dodona, Homer called it. Olives grow only in the most sheltered coastal areas; the trees are deciduous on the lower slopes. Epirus is also music, the deep bubbling rumble of the Epirot clarinet. The empty forest roads pass occasional logging camps and timber mills, all a very long way from Athens.

For the citizens of that city, it is the Wild North rather like the Wild West; an Athenian would no more consider living there than a Cockney move to a rain-sodden blanket bog in Wester Ross. When the Epirots emigrate, many go to Canada; it is not difficult to see why – just as those from the hot plains of Laconia and Messenia go to Australia.

But modern Greece was born among these forests as much as in the streets around Syntagma. Olivia Manning caught it exactly in *The Balkan Trilogy* in the passage where a hotel porter in 1940 Athens gives an account of the Greek troops' heroic fight in the beech woods:

The old porter, who waited in the hall with the news, enacted for the Pringles and other foreigners the drama of the encounter. He stumbled about to show how the Italians had been blinded by snow then, drawing himself up, eyes fixed, expression stern, he showed

how the Greeks had been granted miraculous penetration of vision
by Our Lady of Tenos ... The evzoni captured the heights of
Ochrida in a snowstorm ... the Greek women, who had followed
their men, climbed barefooted up the mountainside to take them
food and ammunition.

The porter is a modern Homer; the teller of epic tales, but
where the legend is also pure history. Ancient and modern
military heroism coalesce in these remote woods. When Olivia
Manning wrote, it was the heroism of a united nation, when
even the dictator Metaxas, who seized power in 1936 and
abolished parliamentary democracy, had to resist the Italian
forces sweeping down through the Drin valley from Albania.

But in a very Greek reversal of fortunes, a profound echo of
the reversals of ancient tragedy, it was in these same northern
woods that the final, excruciating and bloody encounters of
the Civil War were fought in 1949. In the Grammos mountains
inland, remnants of the left-wing Democratic Army retreated
to Yugoslavia and Albania under bombing by the US-advised
airforce, the first use of napalm.

The history – or at least attempts to write the full history –
of those nine years of turmoil and pain under occupation and
through the Civil War is only just beginning to be written in
Greece, fifty years of silence and propaganda is being broken.
The political rights and wrongs are opening up to rational
discussion by historians and commentators; the files on
participants were consigned a couple of years ago to the
furnaces of the Athens public incinerator by the then coalition
government in an act intended to promote national reconcilia-
tion. But the Civil War lives on as an important background
element in their psychology however much Greeks of all
political persuasions would often like to forget it.

Some of the outlines are clear: the criminal, almost unbelievable mistakes of the EAM leadership which threw away what

could have been majority support for a left-wing government over much of Greece at the end of the War against a background of betrayal by Stalin at Yalta; the atrocities both sides committed and the lethal damage to the social structure chronicled, from the point of view of the Right, by Nicholas Gage in *Eleni*.

But whatever the conclusions of historians, and the bitter exchanges between Right and Left over what really happened, the economic and social consequences were as terrible as they always are in civil wars. In Greece these were principally rural depopulation – the collapse of the traditional village way of life in some places – mass emigration to the cities (Athens in particular) and political exile in distant lands.

This legacy was perhaps not easy to foresee when the Axis forces first swept down from the north into Greece, following the same routes as all previous invaders from the Slavs of the Dark Ages onwards. But the irresistible desire of the Greek people for freedom saw the flag of resistance raised in the mountains and the cities, and among militant trades union organizations in cities like Volos and Patras. It was a lonely struggle against a determined and ruthless occupier. Reprisals against villages suspected of supporting the resistance were severe and, as the history of similar movements elsewhere in Europe shows, local loyalties were strained to breaking-point. With the background of recent Greek history, the inter-war political turmoil and the weakness of democratic institutions, it was not surprising that what had begun as the necessary use of military force by the resistance acquired a dynamic of its own and led to prolonged civil war. Our images of these years have been formed by the many memoirs and histories written by British officers attached to the various resistance groups and usually parachuted in by SOE from Cairo. They found themselves in a world with a genuinely heroic dimension – the popular struggle against the Germans and Italians, often against overwhelming odds in the early days – but also a world of dark intrigue and Byzantine political complexity as the different political forces shaped up to fight over Greece's future after defeat of the Axis. As elsewhere in Europe, many of the most efficient resistance groups were Communist-led; the tension between the immediate military objectives of the resistance and long-term political needs of the western powers became overwhelming. In simple terms this meant Greece was effectively a British Protectorate in 1945.

The National Liberation Front (EAM) and its military wing, the National Popular Army of Liberation (ELAS) were by far the most effective anti-German forces in the country. Both were ultimately controlled by the Greek Communist party (KKE). British policy was to restore the monarchy and right-wing government, and the leaders of the resistance were invited to Cairo in an attempt to secure unanimity among guerrilla leaders and politicians. After a series of manoeuvres of infinite complexity, this plan, and its formal expression, the Lebanon agreement, collapsed. The liberation of Greece, however, was proceeding apace and by October 1944 Athens and Piraeus had been liberated, with EAM the effective government of most of the country. But British forces, under General Scobie, landed in Athens soon afterwards and played a major part in dispossessing EAM. The seeds of future tragedy were sown and whatever legitimate motives the British forces may have had in attempting to enforce order in the chaos of Athens, the reality to many Greeks was that they were protecting collaborators and fascists from popular justice and attempting to determine the political future of their country.

It is worth remembering just how materially devastated Greece had become in 1945. The Paris Reparations Conference estimated the cost of war devastation at $8,500 million. One quarter of all buildings had been destroyed, along with over two thousand villages, three quarters of all merchant ships, two thirds of all motor transport and nine tenths of all railway rolling-stock. All larger road bridges had been demolished, huge areas of olives, vines and agricultural land were ruined, and hundreds of thousands of people were on the brink of starvation.

The British may have believed that the army could impose order and that democratic government would re-emerge under the monarchy but the wounds went too deep. Society was too divided and shattered for anything more than a truce to be possible. Between 1947 and 1949 the last bitter battles were fought out: the Democratic Army leadership of Markos Vafiades established an effective guerrilla army that operated without hindrance in much of northern Greece with considerable support from the peasantry but was unable to take any of the major towns held by government troops vitally assisted by US air power. The final offensive in the Grammos mountains was controlled by a joint US–Greek general staff, symbolic of the underlying political realities that were to dominate Greece for the next thirty years. General Papagos, who was commander-in-chief of the national army, became political leader of the country soon afterwards. This would never have happened without American support under the Truman Doctrine from 1947, following Britain's withdrawal from the fray.

The last stand of the Democratic Army on Grammos, a heroic fight against hopeless odds, has been a powerful symbol for the Left. Greece is a profoundly Orthodox country and Orthodoxy is very much a church of martyrdom. The Civil War supplied both sides with numerous real martyrs, good people who died for what they believed in, symbols to justify their social and political attitudes.

Although these events took place fifty-odd years ago, and Greece has experienced both military dictatorship and left-wing populist democracy since then, they are in a way where the story should begin and end. Without the wounds of the Civil

War, so many only partially healed, the intermittent turmoil and febrile atmosphere of Greek life cannot be understood. But many people, even now, may strongly disagree with this outline of events. According to the extreme Right, for instance, or some of its apologists, the peasants never, ever, voluntarily helped the ELAS guerrillas and the British army never protected Axis collaborators, and so on. In the view of some hardliners on the Left, Stalin never betrayed the Greek Communists, the ELAS men never stole so much as a chicken throughout the Civil War, and so on. The issue that generated most controversy, and still does today, was the Communist removal at the end of the Civil War of twenty thousand Greek children for education in the 'socialist' countries. While the subject is still emotive, and there are those alive who took part in the events, it is unlikely that the real reasons of those involved – and what took place – will be established. When the Left knew it was losing the Civil War, children were sent abroad for reasons of their own safety if government troops were thought to be about to enter left-wing villages to take reprisals on the inhabitants – as had sometimes happened. Nobody, for instance, sees any anomaly now that children from the Catholic areas of Northern Ireland were sent to Brittany during the Troubles, or from the East End of London to the Cotswolds in the Second World War, or that Jewish children left Nazi Germany – all for reasons of safety.

But there are well-documented cases of children being taken against the wishes of their parents to make up the numbers. Independent Red Cross witnesses interviewing children in exile in the 'socialist' countries at the time did not find widespread evidence of coercion, although it was claimed that they had been hoodwinked by the KKE. As elsewhere in the Civil War, what happened undoubtedly varied very much from place to place. What is not in doubt has been the enormous propaganda value of the episode to the Right. This persists, at least among the older generation in Greece, to the present day in a society which prizes the family unit above all and where small children are the most honoured members in it.

At the end of the Thirties the population of Athens was just over one million people. Greece was still a predominantly rural society where agricultural methods had changed little since antiquity. Many areas, such as Crete and huge tracts of the wild mountains in the north, in Thrace and Macedonia, had only recently become part of the modern state after the Turks finally relinquished territory before the First World War. Until then brigandage had been endemic and many areas were only nominally under the control of Athens, *de facto* under local chieftains from traditionally powerful families. Central authority in Athens was weak, to say the least, and Greeks who had emigrated in large numbers from poor rural areas since the end of the nineteenth century did not find much change on their return.

The founders of ELAS, such as Aris Velouchiotis, had been seen as successors of the old brigand leaders, men of the mountains, who had taken up the national cause when it seemed lost in Athens – then, as sometimes later, viewed as a corrupt middle-class city under foreign control. The resistance and political struggle for a new socialist Greece had begun in small communities that many members of pre-war Greek governments would scarcely have heard of – like Karpenissi, Velouchiotis's base in central Roumeli. The defeat of ELAS in the Civil War was not simply a defeat for Communism but a defeat for an older Greece, the anarchic world of pre-capital-ist kinship ties and a primitive sense of local democracy and nationality.

Apart from anything else, the Right stood for a kind of modernization, the integration of Greece into a modern technological world with its foreign investors and new factories, and a powerful central government in Athens which would legislate for Greece to become a modern western democracy.

The history of Greece since the Civil War has been, in essence, a struggle between these two worlds. Both sides can claim victory in a sense. For example, the Right can, and does, trumpet success that Greece is a member of NATO and the European Community, has remained within the western orbit since 1945, and so on. On the other hand, it could be said to have failed, in reality – even if the victory of the Right in the Civil War has determined the formal institutions, the reality of political development has been very different. The most obvious manifestation of this failure has been the suspension of democracy itself for some years.

Greek politics are a potential quagmire; the country has an increasingly fragile, some might say derelict, economy; the fabric of many aspects of social life are in decline; adherence to the West has only been achieved by long periods of very partial democracy when major political parties were banned and honest men served years in gaol for their beliefs; a pattern of endless foreign interference in domestic politics became apparent, mainly by the United States; and there were several years of brutal military dictatorship.

After the Civil War there was stability of a kind. The old cliché is true: the war was won with dollars as much as guns, and the integration of Greece into the new economic world of the 1950s proceeded apace. A new commercial ethos grew in middle-class life and the cities were a hubbub of new building with many of the dispossessed from the villages finding jobs in the construction industry. But although on the surface Greece became another small part of a Western Europe dominated by the United States, underneath many facets of life had not changed.

Agriculture stagnated and crops that had been the mainstay

of the economy, such as tobacco, declined. Shipping boomed, with the Fifties seeing the consolidation of Very Rich Greeks – the Niarchos, Onassis and other shipping dynasties – as international figures of folklore, but little of their vast wealth found its way back to Greece. Piraeus started its long decline as a commercial port as ship sizes increased and dwarfed its capacity.

Mass tourism did not start to become a decisive economic or social factor until the Sixties' advent of package tours and cheap flights, so the economic level of many islands continued to be dependent on subsistence agriculture and remittances from abroad.

A consistent picture emerges of a country with a pattern of uneven and arrested development, a producer of agricultural products that are mostly in decline, like currants, or already in oversupply in Europe, such as wine, without the transport or industrial infrastructure to produce anything the world might need. Although investment in new industries grew – the establishment of a modern petrochemical industry in the Gulf of Corinth, for example – the owners of the new installations were frequently foreign and much of the wealth generated left the country.

The norm for business of any kind was still the small family enterprise, which had the advantage of preserving native craft traditions in industries such as leather and woodwork, but was hopelessly incapable of withstanding international competition. The single most important growth industry of the Fifties worldwide – motor-vehicle manufacturing – was completely non-existent in Greece. An economic dependence on outside forces was established with profound consequences for the development of the country and for democracy itself.

There has always been the belief in Greece that behind every leading politician is a foreign boss pulling the strings of his puppet as in a shadow play. Sometimes, as with Metaxas, who was beholden to Mussolini's Italy in the late Thirties, this was so. It goes with the general Greek belief that their country is the centre of the political world and that outside powers are always seeking to control it, an idea that can aid both Right and Left. It was very damaging, for instance, that the Communist party in the Civil War was manipulated by Stalin, and that Papagos in the early Fifties was considered a tool of the White House.

Despite all the dollars and propaganda, the American writ did not really run very far outside Athens. As soon after the Civil War as January 1950 new elections were held under the 1946 system of proportional representation that showed a distinct swing away from the Right towards the Centre, and created a situation where no single party could command a majority in parliament. After four doomed governments collapsed, elections were held in November 1952 under a new, and basically unfair, electoral system designed to eliminate the smaller parties. Civil-war-soldier General Papagos was duly installed as leader of the first stable government for many years. This stability had been bought at a high price, reinforced by later reforms of the system in 1956 which excluded many strands of opinion from parliament by arbitrary manipulation of electoral boundaries, with a bizarre mix of different systems for different areas of the country, and by deliberate gerrymandering and under-representation of traditional left-wing areas such as Thessaly and western Macedonia.

But the Centre and Left revived and after Papagos's death in October 1955 the figure of Constantine Karamanlis became increasingly central with the establishment of his new party, the National Radical Union. It campaigned for new elections under a fair electoral law. The essence of politics in these years, in domestic terms, lay in the struggle of these moderate and responsible forces to obtain fair representation – and their underlying failure to do so. The old Right was always grossly over-represented in parliament and in all sorts of positions in Athens that were ultimately dependent on, and answerable to, foreign powers – the USA mainly – rather than responsible to the democratic institutions in Greece itself.

So the new prosperous middle class that grew in these years suffered from a terrible insecurity. In far too many cases, wealth and position seemed to depend on foreign money or political patronage rather than on hard work or ability. A dependent economy was created at every level: from the remittances of sons in Australia that elderly parents might receive every month in rural Arcadia – sent by men who, if the family had the 'wrong' political colour, could never get a job in the village – to the mixture of legitimate foreign investment and local bribes that came to many members of the Athens élite.

And politics continually intruded, most forcefully in the shape of the Cyprus problem. Just when the national question appeared to have been solved, the Greek Cypriots sought independence, then union with Greece, and drove what were designed to be complaisant Athens governments into open conflict with Britain and the United States. In their handling of the Cyprus question, the Papagos and Karamanlis governments frequently appeared to Greeks to be acting as agents for the major western powers rather than for the Greeks of Cyprus. The Athens governments could never ignore the Cypriot demands for *enosis* (union with Greece) even if they wanted to, and the long struggle of the Cypriots for independence gradually eroded much of the foreign policy credibility of the Greek governments of the Fifties and early Sixties, and made many ordinary Greeks take a more critical attitude to Britain and the United States.

And although the figures tell an optimistic story of these years, with high growth rates and a large increase in GDP and employment, it was a very fragile economic miracle. It involved the virtual abandonment of large rural areas in Epirus, Thrace and many parts of Macedonia to economic collapse, where the inhabitants of villages without sewerage or electricity had living standards lower than in many parts of the Third World. As the distinguished historian C. M. Woodhouse has pointed out, in commenting on the war years when he had been attached by SOE to the Greek resistance, the élite of Athens knew and cared as little about this rural world as they did about Tibet. The sprawling growth of the Athens basin with its accompanying unplanned industrial development laid the foundations for the Attica environmental crisis today. The political culture was unhealthy where the Communist party and other left-wing groups were still officially banned, and where the commitment to democracy was still skin-deep.

The chickens began to come home to roost as a better-educated population in the new cities, tired of the fortress mentality that had developed through the Cold War, looked to take the western rhetoric seriously, so that in addition to security from Communism, protection from ill-health and want in old age was sought, as well as the decent schools and facilities that for many years had been provided by the public sector in western countries. In short the Greeks wanted a welfare state or at least some of the basic elements of one.

Against this background, support for the Centre and Left grew. The election of 1961 was a watershed in that the level of gerrymandering and intimidation from the Right reached such levels that the whole process was called into question by many people who by no stretch of the imagination could be called stooges of the Left. Perhaps as many as a hundred thousand illegal votes were cast by the Right in the left-wing stronghold of the Athens region, and in the rural areas there were widespread and well-documented cases of violent intimidation of voters by the extreme-right Security Battalions, an anti-

Communist militia with roots in the Civil War period. In one
electoral district 206 gendarmes were alleged to have used the
same address. The virtual monopoly of power enjoyed by the
Right, with the backing of their foreign allies since the mid
Thirties, could now only be maintained by the most outrage-
ous manipulation of democracy itself. It was subsequently
claimed that a NATO-inspired plan called Operation Pericles
had been put into operation to fix the elections for the Right.
George Papandreou, the centrist leader who had suffered most
from the electoral corruption, blamed the whole fraudulent
process on the palace and broke off all contacts with the King.
It was the beginning of a loss of confidence in the democratic
process that was to culminate in the colonels' coup six years
later.

Tension was increased in May 1963 by the murder of
Grigorios Lambrakis, a left-wing deputy in Thessaloniki. His
extreme-right murderers were subsequently shown to have
had close links with the Thessaloniki police. The murder
demonstrated, above all, that there still existed an extreme-
right-controlled paramilitary apparatus, mostly consisting of
ex-Security-Battalion men, with strong links with the United
States, that would if necessary use violence against the Centre
and Left if they showed any signs of winning power by
democratic means. But in the aftermath of the murder, the
Centre and Left continued to advance and in the November
1963 elections, much fairer than two years previously,
Papandreou's Centre Union emerged as the largest party, with
the extreme-left United Democratic Left, largely a front for
the still-banned KKE, holding the balance of power.
Karamanlis left Greece to begin what was to be an eleven-year
exile, and after yet another election in the following year
Papandreou emerged with undisputed power. But real and
effective power was elusive, as he soon discovered: many
appointments were in fact made by foreign interests or the

palace – or both. Although some worthwhile reforms, mainly of the educational system, were made before his government was engulfed in the major political crisis of July 1965, little structural change had been attempted. Greek democracy and the nation were to pay a heavy price for this failure in the years ahead.

The labyrinthine moves that led to the colonels' coup and the end of democracy in 1967 had many causes. On the Left it has been conventional to ascribe the whole process as a conscious attempt by the United States, the CIA particularly, to subvert the democratic process; on the Right the coup had its apologists at the time among those who saw Greece slipping towards chaos and probably Communism, and the colonels restoring 'order'. The memory of the Civil War was still strong in many western capitals and, in the early days, led to the colonels being given the benefit of the doubt by some commentators and foreign politicians who should have known better. But what is more important is that the coup was only able to succeed – and the colonels establish a viable regime that lasted for some years – because of very serious deficiencies in the existing democratic culture, or the absence of it in many respects.

The violence, the use of torture, the judicial murder of political opponents, detention on prison islands like Amorgos and Makronisos – they had all been part of the script in the Civil War. When the same play was enacted in the late Sixties, the Greek people knew what to expect.

Ritual plays a large part in Greek life, whether in the beautiful customs of the Orthodox Church, the small courtesies of the home or of the taverna, or in the nature of greetings that are offered to friends. With Greek politics since the War, there is sometimes a sense of a terrible ritual being repeated, the same people being locked up again. The distinguished poet Yiannis Ritsos spent time on Makronisos in his youth in the Civil War only to return there under the colonels' junta in the Sixties, meeting again, as he has written, many of his friends as he set foot on this grim rock off the south-east coast of Attica.

Yet there have been many improvements over the same fifty years; the average Greek is better housed and has more material wealth than wartime generations could have dreamt of – even if health and social services still lag behind comparable countries in Western Europe. The unique beauty of land and sea remain, along with the variety of flora and fauna in the regions, and the warmth, generosity and humanity of the people.

Many important new discoveries have been made about the ancient civilization, the inexhaustible spiritual font of western culture. The scattered diaspora communities of Greeks have flourished, with many people of Greek origin, such as US Vice-President Spiro Agnew rising to the highest positions in their adopted countries a generation after their families arrived as desperate and penniless refugees.

Greeks are, in a real sense, the descendants of Odysseus, wanderers over the sea who return home, even if only to a burial place. As Cavafy wrote:

> Ithaka gave you the marvellous journey.
> Without her you wouldn't have set out.
> She has nothing left to give you now.
>
> And if you find her poor, Ithaka won't have fooled you.
> Wise as you will have become, so full of experience,
> You'll have understood by then what these Ithakas mean.

Cavafy lived in a Greek community in the Egyptian city of Alexandria, a world of Greek merchants and traders. But his homosexual milieu was not the world of other diaspora Greeks. More typical was John Sakellaridis, mastermind behind the Egyptian cotton industry and pioneer developer of new growths of cottons; or Hercules Voltos, the first classifier of fine cottons; or Demetrius Cassaveti, founder of one of the largest Alexandrian trading houses which opened a London office as early as 1837.

Many twentieth-century Alexandrians have done just as well, although whether the legacy of Hellenism has been carried on quite as traditionally is open to doubt. The key element of Greekness, at nearly all times in history, has been use of the language. The original definition of barbarian was simply that of someone who did not speak Greek. There are disturbing signs of a decrease in the use of the language in Canada, the United States and Australia today, linked to an increasing secularism in the communities and the declining influence of the Church.

Herodotus, the founder of history, wrote that 'poverty is the inheritance of Hellas from old'. While this has been true for most of the population, through all periods of history, the years since Common Market membership have tended to obscure his observation. Though now it may be becoming more relevant again, as Greece slips to the bottom of the league in the EC in relation to the size of its debts, lack of growth in the economy, rising unemployment, and so on.

President Karamanlis, speaking at an important government function in the summer of 1991, observed that despite Greece's problems there were no threats to the democratic order within the country as in the past. The fact that such a statement is made at all is important. It is, of course, true, on the face of it – although few coup plotters ever announce themselves before they seize the radio station, any more than the colonels did in 1967. For although the Greeks invented democracy, it has been peculiarly difficult for them to make it work in a modern industrial society.

2. The End of the Monarchy: A New Democracy?

κτανθεὶς τὸν κτείναντα κατέκτανον ἀλλ' ὁ μὲν οὐδ' ὥς
ἤλυθεν εἰς Ἀΐδην· αὐτὰρ ἔγωγ' ἔθανον.

Though killed I killed the killer; but even so he
didn't go to Hades; it was I who died.

        – Riddle from the Delphic Oracle

At the moment the King of Greece lives in exile in southern
England, a familiar figure who is part of the royal circle. It is
perhaps difficult to see him as a fundamentally divisive person
although he is the son and grandson of very controversial
men; a book about one of his recent ancestors is called
Constantine – King and Traitor. Yet the current ex-monarch
appears to us to be harmless enough and, with the revival of
interest in monarchy in the Balkans and in Eastern Europe, it
might seem possible for him to return to his throne.

But any actual prospect of King Constantine's return to the
royal palace in Athens is remote. Most Greeks – in overwhelming majorities according to all recent opinion-poll evidence –
do not want their monarchy back. The reasons lie in the events
of the Second World War and the Civil War and where opposition to the monarchy was suppressed in the quasi-democratic
Fifties and re-emerged under the junta, although the monarchy
had been in an unstable position many years before.

Always seen as a foreign imposition by most Greeks, the
German-influenced Glücksburg dynasty in the twentieth century
had suffered extraordinary vicissitudes ever since King

George was assassinated by a Macedonian in Salonika in 1913, followed by the unfortunate efforts of his son Prince Constantine to keep Greece neutral during the First World War, his subsequent abdication in 1917 and flight from a small port in Euboea to Swiss exile.

His successor, King Alexander, lasted in power for just three years, dying of blood-poisoning after being bitten by a pet monkey. After a chaotic inter-regnum King Constantine returned to Athens, only to abdicate, again, after the catastrophic defeat of Greek forces in Asia Minor in September 1922. George II succeeded him but was also soon forced into exile, later to return after the abortive military rising in 1935. The whole process seems to represent some slightly odd game of snakes and ladders, with too many snakes.

After a period of collaboration with the Metaxas dictatorship in the late Thirties, exile was again the fate of the monarchy during the Second World War. Largely thanks to the obsession of Churchill in aiding his restoration, the King returned to the palace – with the Greeks, as always, deeply divided on the issue. The impression is of a monarchy, whatever its other qualities, which has been a symbol of foreign interference in Greek political life and which has needed a fast car running on the gravel for when the patience of the Greek people ran out.

But all their previous difficulties pale into insignificance compared with the train of events that began with the political crises of the late Sixties and the colonels' *coup d'état*. After the death of King Paul, a gloomy but not deeply unpopular figure, at least compared with some of his predecessors, the young King Constantine assumed the throne, very much under the influence of his mother, Queen Frederika. She was a domineering figure with her own web of palace contacts and a côterie of extremely reactionary advisers. Her instincts were inherently anti-democratic and some might say anti-Greek, at least as far as the traditional political élite was concerned.

The centrist government of George Papandreou was viewed with scarcely disguised contempt from the palace, and the Prime Minister's attempts to secure the appointments of officers loyal to the government in the highest ranks of the armed forces were made more and more difficult. The monarchy acted without regard for the normal constraints on the institution in any parliamentary democracy – a problem common to Greek monarchs going back to the nineteenth century. Relations between monarchs and the elected politicians had usually been bad from the era of Constantine's grandparents when the great republican Prime Minister Eleftherios Venizelos had been unifying the modern state. Much of his time, as a Cretan republican, was spent at loggerheads with the royal family, who, quite rightly, felt him to be a rival for national fame and affection. During the nineteenth century the monarchy had been seen as a bastion of German influence in Greece, in view of its Bavarian origins. This continued until the First World War, in an open form, with Greece taking the side of Germany in the intense rivalry between Britain and Germany in the Balkans between 1911 and 1914. Few of the Glücksburg line seemed to possess any notion of the needs of the country or any sense of political tact. Most royal politics have been of, or around, the extreme Right, and time and again this led to conflict between the Greek national interest and that of the monarchy. At a more basic level the actual institution seemed to inhibit the development of democracy itself and act as a focus for authoritarian tendencies.

So it was not surprising when, at the end of the War, with the country torn by the Civil War and the attempted socialist revolution, it took strong support from Churchill to secure the restoration of the monarchy, against the advice of Roosevelt and most of the Allied political leaders, and the artificial creation of a pro-monarchist faction of the Greek army in Egypt. Yet again, foreign patrons were required to keep the

Greek King on the throne. As long ago as 1935 George II had only been able to return to power after an openly rigged referendum when 98 per cent were supposed to have voted for the monarchy and only 2 per cent against. In the September 1946 re-run there was massive evidence to show vote-rigging and intimidation on a scale to produce the result that Churchill and the Right wanted. The Allied Mission for Observing the Greek Elections concluded in a secret report that 'the conditions necessary for holding a fair plebiscite did not exist in several parts of Greece', and many other contemporary observers felt that without the 'white terror' against the Left in 1945–6, and monarchist control of the police and armed forces, the people would have voted overwhelmingly for a republic.

On 21 April 1967 when tanks rolled into Athens and democracy was snuffed out, a unit of armoured vehicles also surrounded the King's country house at Tatoi outside Athens. Whatever else, the colonels were nationalists, and even at this early stage in their coup they sensed a centre of power outside national parameters that needed to be controlled. In the early days of the junta the King's private secretary, Brigadier Michael Arnaoutis, who still runs his London office today, was arrested. But although he was quickly released, the palace made no attempt to rally the Greek people to defend democracy. In the stunned confusion of Athens, the King was seen to compromise with the junta, a course which many feel was recommended to him by the Central Intelligence Agency bureau chief in Athens who is generally believed to have had foreknowledge of the coup. Whatever the details of events, this error led to the irresistible conclusion by the great majority of Greeks that the monarchy and a functioning democracy were once and for all irreconcilable.

Worse was to follow for Constantine in the next few years under the colonels' regime. After early compromises had destroyed any possibility of the palace being seen as the defender of democracy, or as anything other than the enemy of the Left and Centre, the royal relationship deteriorated with the colonels themselves, demolishing whatever remaining mass support the monarchy had among Rightists.

The junta officers seem to have been divided about the role of the monarchy. There was little respect for the King himself but the actual institution was seen to have a useful symbolic value as Constantine began to identify himself with some of the junta's policies. But his movements were strictly controlled, especially in terms of international contacts, and any remaining independence the palace had was reduced mainly by regular purges of staff from all important state institutions. Ominously the junta decided to bring in a new constitution with the clear indication that the role of the monarchy was open to question. The colonels were ungrateful for the real gift Constantine brought them – diplomatic recognition – when he swore them in as the legal Greek government.

But events outside Greece were to have a decisive influence on the future of both the junta and the monarchy. The outbreak of the Six Day War between Israel and the Arab states had brought many diplomatic gains to Greece as a valued member of NATO. In a key decision the United States ended the arms embargo that had been imposed in the early days of the coup. This was counterbalanced by the failure of General Grivas in Cyprus to overthrow the island's first president, Archbishop Makarios. Grivas was a close ally of the colonels, an extreme right-winger who had been a veteran of the wartime Security Battalions, an illegal pro-fascist militia. He sought *enosis*, the complete union of Cyprus and Greece, and the expulsion of Turkish influence from the island.

The King had been shocked by this failure and he seems to have begun to understand, at last, that the colonels' regime was inherently unstable and that it was never likely to lead to progress in Greece. So Constantine began to conspire to overthrow the junta but without any real basis of political support to enable him to do so. An inept coup attempt was organized in November 1967 (of which the junta was well forewarned), based on support for the monarchy among army units in northern Greece. But in mid December, after units loyal to the junta took over the 3rd Corps HQ at Komotini, the King and his family took refuge in Western Europe where the Queen miscarried her baby in January. It was a disastrous end to Constantine's rule. Pro-junta elements in the upper reaches of the Church announced that he had 'deserted his duties' and swore in junta-supporter General Zoitakis as Regent. The United States stopped wavering between palace and junta and hardened its support for the colonels. With hindsight those few months ended the monarchy in Greece more effectively than the Greek Communists and their allies had ever been able to.

The official position of the monarchy remained unchanged during the rest of the junta's regime in that the King was free to return if he wanted, but Constantine would not do so without progress towards the restoration of constitutional government, preferring exile. But the junta lasted longer than the King expected. When Constantine fled, the colonels had several years in power left, and during that time the monarchy, having destroyed its own (always limited) political base by the disastrous misjudgements of the first six months of the colonels' rule, began to seem increasingly marginal to the new generation who had turned sharply to the Left while fighting for democracy, and who were inclined to see the whole institution as fatally compromised.

A further problem for Constantine was the intermittent series of conspiracies among pro-monarchist officers in the armed forces, especially the traditionally monarchist navy. These were ineffectual and served only to convince the junta leaders, especially Papadopoulos, that the whole institution should be abolished. After the abortive naval mutiny of May 1973 Papadopoulos declared that Constantine was deposed and he proclaimed the establishment of a 'presidential parliamentary republic'. This was ratified in a bogus plebiscite in which Papadopoulos himself was the sole candidate for the presidency, at a time when he was also Premier, Minister of Defence and Education and Minister of Government Policy. When the Cyprus crisis had driven the junta from power in 1974, organized support for the King had been almost completely destroyed outside the ranks of diehard royalists. In some parts of Greece, such as the Peloponnese, which had always been a traditional centre of royalist feeling, there were many individual monarchists but no organized political movement of any substance to campaign for Constantine.

In the referendum on the future of the monarchy in December 1974, 69 per cent voted for abolition, a remarkably similar proportion to the last reasonably fair test of opinion on the constitution – the 1924 vote – when 70 per cent voted for a republic and 30 per cent for the monarchy. Only in the traditional royalist areas of the southern mainland was there a substantial vote in favour of the King but even here, in the monarchist stronghold of Lakonia, the figure was only 40 per cent.

So Constantine Karamanlis was left in undisputed charge of the country in 1974 with the onerous task of cleansing the body politic of the abuses of the junta period and of modernizing the political system so that Greece could join the full European family. After the dignity of his long period of exile, the old Macedonian succeeded markedly in his main objectives. The Left was integrated into normal political life with the legalization of the KKE, and the whole atmosphere of government was quite different from the earlier periods of his premiership. Perhaps the most important legacy from this time was not the fact of EC membership, for it is clear now that many of the underlying problems of Greece have been much less affected by this fact than the original proponents of membership thought, but the modernization of the Right. The leading figures of the junta were rapidly put on trial and given long gaol sentences, and the United States was quick to learn that its unforgivable backing of the Turkish invasion of Cyprus in 1974 would incur a heavy long-term cost when Karamanlis withdrew Greece from the military command structure of NATO

But there was much that could not be changed easily, even if Karamanlis had really wanted to. The New Democracy party itself was still really only a vehicle to project his leadership and there was little democracy in its internal life. Many traditionalists remained in leading positions at all levels and found it hard to adapt to the new political environment. In particular there was a notable drying up of traditional largesse from the United States and a sense of the end of an era. The energy that was put into the new relationship with the EC was a strong factor in the changes as well. Karamanlis was a creature of the post-civil-war consensus, but it seemed to mean increasingly little to the young generation radicalized by the junta.

There was also much unfinished business from the junta period that contributed to the growth of the new Panhellenic Socialist party (PASOK), which was to dominate Greek political life in the next decade. A central figure in the anti-monarchist rows of the late Sixties had been George Papandreou's son, Andreas. He had been a left-wing student in Athens in the late Thirties but had gone into exile after getting into trouble with Metaxas' secret police. He spent all the War and Civil War years in America where he had a distinguished career as an academic economist. When he returned to Greece, he immediately took up a leading role in his father's party and it was clear that life in the USA had done little to change his Marxist outlook. The founding declaration of PASOK in 1974 is worth quoting in part as it expresses so clearly the revulsion against the United States after the years of the junta.

The seven medieval years that have passed with the black military dictatorship constitute no more than an especially harsh expression of the dependence of Greece on the imperialistic establishment of the USA and NATO.

Greece has been transformed into an advanced nuclear outpost of the Pentagon so as to serve the military and economic interests of the great monopolies more effectively. The state apparatus, the armed forces, the parties, the trade unions, the political leadership of the country have been undermined so as to make possible the imposition of a foreign-inspired military dictatorship. The military dictatorship was imposed to cut short the march of our people towards popular sovereignty and national independence . . .

Whatever the strengths and weaknesses of PASOK over the years, the party could always draw on a great reservoir of resentment against the United States and NATO, a feeling which was to dominate Greek foreign policy throughout the next decade. Although Karamanlis was seen as a man of great integrity and strength, someone who despite his age and intellectual orientation was capable of changing his views in the light of experience, he was in the last analysis perceived as the Americans' man in Syntagma Square, someone with a history in the Cold War that prevented him from taking them on, on Greece's behalf, when this was necessary. Andreas Papandreou was very different. He knew the United States extremely well and exactly how to probe the weaknesses of the Pentagon and of the American Presidents. He was also that archetypal figure in Greek life, the wanderer who had returned from abroad rich in experience, someone who would be able to put Greece on the international map. His charismatic personality, his warmth, his love of whisky and of attractive women endeared him to a wide section of the voters. Greek politicians, especially party leaders, are not allowed to be worthy. An important element in the public image of Prime Minister Constantine Mitsotakis is his talent as a dancer and no election campaign passed without his skill being shown on television.

The years of the late Seventies were spent in building up the basic organization of PASOK and in taking over the votes of the traditional centrist parties, which by the election of 1981 had been consigned to political oblivion. Until PASOK came on the scene, Greek political parties had little stable organization or pattern of internal democratic life at any level. Most parties did not outlive their founders and most were loose coalitions of prominent individuals around a single leader. Although elements of this continue to the present day, PASOK was new in that it had a coherent pattern of rank-and-file organization, and a constitution that in theory at least allowed the membership a substantial role in the inner life of the organization. This was particularly important in rural areas where, despite the party's anti-EC rhetoric, much support came from small farmers who had benefited from EC membership. Papandreou in essence built a coalition in these years, based on non-privileged groups, with a strong populist element. Although some PASOK supporters considered themselves to be Marxist socialists, many did not but nearly all shared a sense of grievance against the narrow stratum of the really rich who with their international contacts, Swiss bank accounts and houses abroad were, and still are, held by the lower-middle class to be responsible for most of the ills of the country. In the late Seventies New Democracy was not able to completely distance itself from the image of this élite, although the reality of their support for the party, or lack of it, is complex. In financial terms, the old business aristocracy was, and is, very important for New Democracy and the Right. Substantial quantities of money are collected, mainly at election time, among ship-owners in London, for instance. But how far this translates itself into any very active influence over policy is difficult to evaluate. In many cases Greece itself is not so important for their business activities; they may not be officially resident in the country and most of their capital is not invested there.

What is certainly clear is how far Greek nationalism was harnessed by PASOK, in a way central to Papandreou's rise to power. The Karamanlis governments of the late Seventies were continually stalled on major foreign policy questions such as Cyprus and in relations with the USA and Turkey. Whatever else the junta had done, it exploited a climate of popular nationalism among many sections of the lower-middle class that had outlived the colonels and became an important factor in the PASOK era. Although at the time the economic arguments for EC accession seemed overwhelming, there were always 20–30 per cent of the voters against full membership – even in the years of the high tide of EC optimism between 1974 and 1979. Although there is a serious commitment to internationalism among most better-educated Greeks, further down the educational and social scale xenophobia is common and the excesses of the tourist industry have added to this, with the foreigner seen as something of a figure of ridicule to be milked for marks or dollars, and certainly not considered a source of superior culture. Cynics might say that the same psychology has dominated Greece's financial relations with the European Community at an economic level.

So the election of PASOK in 1981 marked a watershed not only in that the post-civil-war consensus had finally broken down but that the transfer of power to what was on the surface a militantly left-wing party was orderly and took place without complications. The election campaign had been intense and dramatic even by Greek standards, and it seemed

as though the country as a whole accepted that the new
political force must be given a fair chance. But the economic and
social foundations of the society that 'our Andreas' started to
govern were as inherently insecure as many of his predecessors
had found. The roots of many of the problems faced by
PASOK lay in the immediate past.

3. A European Destiny? Greece and the European Community

Once tyrant Love put aside his bow, his torch,
And took up an oxherd's rod. With pouch on back,
He'd harnessed and yoked himself a tough pair of
  steers
And was ploughing and sowing Demeter's
  wheatfields
When, looking up, he called on Zeus, 'Give me
  good harvest,
Or I'll yoke my plough to Europa's bull.'

– Moschus, c.150 BC

Although they were in power less than twenty years ago, the Greek colonels' regime seems more distant. Some of them are alive, old men. One or two, like Colonel Papadopoulos, are still in prison, their death sentences commuted but with life imprisonment still meaning life. Lesser fry are at liberty, living in obscurity. Occasionally they surface, mostly in local feuds such as the prolonged effort of the local authority on the Saronic Gulf island of Poros to deprive the Papadopoulos family of its land.

Looking back, the colonels' very existence seems bizarre. Similar regimes in Europe, the dictatorships of Franco and Salazar, were leftovers from pre-war days in countries without strong democratic traditions. But, in Greece, what appeared to be a full democracy had been usurped, torture had returned as part of daily life and the rule of law had disappeared – all in the name of anti-Communism, but without any evidence produced, then or since, to support the colonels' claim that the KKE was planning an armed insurrection to take power in Athens.

Documents of the time seem strange. In a secondhand bookshop in Athens recently, I found a brochure produced by the Piraeus Port Authority, promoting the port as a haven of peace and industrial tranquillity under the junta, with rows of happy dockers applauding their employers at meetings, and, quite unbelievably, sitting drinking milk during their lunch-breaks. The posed photographs and forced smiles of those involved had all the lack of conviction of Soviet propaganda films of the 1930s, a kind of special emptiness about the content.

It is easy to forget it all, to dismiss the junta as an aberration without any basis in modern Greek life. Greeks love conspiracy theories and the junta has perhaps been subject to them more than anything else in recent Greek experience. But conspiracy theories disguise the fact that nasty historical phenomena can have real popular support. In most kafenia it is possible to find someone who looks back to the period with sympathy, sometimes with nostalgia.

Mr Tsanboutsis is one of these people. Sitting staring across the Bay of Messenia, with his little moustache and Brylcreemed hair, he looks like a retired army NCO. In fact he is a local landlord and keen amateur artist. For him, the colonels brought 'order', although it is difficult to establish what, if anything, they changed in Mantinea. Greeks of all persuasions have very strong subjective identifications with their political leaders and often talk of them as personal friends, even if the closest they have been to them is a hundred yards from a balcony during a whistle-stop speech in a general election campaign. Mr Tsanboutsis clearly feels the colonels were people like himself, doing their best for Greece. And the torture and human rights violations?

'Communist propaganda. Half of Athens is controlled by the Communists.'

He reaches for his ouzo at the thought of the leftist bureaucrats and newspaper editors. One of the bases of the junta's support was in the provinces, in towns that had long been traditional rivals of the capital, a very considerable time indeed in a stronghold of pro-dictatorship feeling like Sparta. The colonels were provincial men who had taken the traditional route into the Greek army officer class as provincial boys without family means or background. Even when they rose to the top of the army, many harboured grudges against the very senior officers. It was perhaps not unexpected that they got on so badly with the King. It is quite easy in Greece to rise from the working class to what, in a sociological sense, would be regarded as the lower-middle class in other countries. It does not cost much to rent a shop or a workshop, but it is difficult to go further without substantial family resources or a powerful patron. Bank credit is often difficult to obtain and mortgages were rare until recently. In these economic realities are the roots of the clientistic relationships that so bedevil Greek political and economic life. To be a client can be an unsatisfactory experience for those so convinced of their ultimate equality.

Inside the Mr Tsanboutsises of Greece is a seething cauldron of resentment and frustration, a genuine sense, often, of unfulfilled talents and a strong pessimism about a different social order offering anything better. And there is always the danger of slipping back down the social scale if a mishap affects the family business or if political disorder breaks out. It is surprising that there are only one or two potential dictators in each kafenion, not more.

Ironically Mr Tsanboutsis fell foul of 'order' through

'disorder' in his personal life. An artist, he fell in love with
one of his models and seduced her. This became public
knowledge through the girl's outraged mother and he was
duly arrested under the anti-adultery law and sentenced to
nine months in gaol – one of the last people in Greece to be in
trouble for this particular offence.

The ideology of the junta, of nationalism and bigoted
Christianity, had reached its limit in Cyprus. The support
given by the colonels to the ultra-rightists in Cyprus, and
the Turkish invasion, brought them down. In the atmosphere
of democratic renewal ex-Prime Minister Karamanlis returned
from exile to form a democratic government in 1974. All
parties, including the two Communist parties, were legalized,
so ending the KKE's ghetto existence since 1947.

The central achievement of these years was the integration
of Greece with Western Europe through the Common Market
and the stabilizing of a pluralistic political system. Most
shades of political opinion welcomed the application for full
membership (apart from the pro-Moscow Communist party),
although how far anything fully European has penetrated the
political culture outside the Athens élite is an open question.
The Community was seen as a source of capital and privileged
access to a huge market for Greece, an incentive for foreign
investment by the business community and for more progressive social and economic policies by the non-Communist Left.
The EuroCommunist KKE-Interior and other independent
Leftists welcomed membership because the Community was
seen as a progressive counterweight to American domination
of Greece at a time when the United States was bitterly
unpopular because of the CIA's role in the coup and dictatorship, and the subsequent US support for the Turkish invasion
of Cyprus in 1974.

Most of all, membership was welcomed by the professional
politicians and diplomats because it meant that Greece as a

small country had, in theory at least, an equal voice with the European giants like Germany and France and could make this voice heard more effectively on the international stage. The Community provided a significant number of well-paid jobs for the upper reaches of the bureaucracy, soaking up graduate unemployment and no doubt benefiting Greece.

Dramatic changes were forecast in many areas of Greek economic life: large-scale industrial restructuring, a boom in manufacturing exports, massive inward investment, particularly from Germany, and so on. Few of these have actually taken place in the ways envisaged. There was undoubtedly an immediate upheaval in the pattern of Greek imports, which involved EC producers taking over substantial market shares in many sectors where they had only been marginally represented. Cars were an obvious example and American imports disappeared almost overnight after a significant presence in the Fifties and early Sixties.

The predicted boom in Greek-manufactured exports to the EC countries never materialized. Many Greek companies were unable to compete openly in the EC with their larger and much better financed and equipped northern competitors. They continued to trade in niche markets or stuck to customers in Eastern Europe or the Middle East where they were not subject to the same competitive pressures. Little major industrial restructuring happened, with long-established patterns of growth or decline continuing as before. Traditional industries, where foreign investors had always had a presence, such as the food and drink sectors, continued to thrive, while whole new areas, such as the electronics industry, passed Greece by. One of the long-term effects of EC entry was to place a question mark over the future of some major installations in sectors where years of under-investment had meant that Greek firms were unable to compete. These became the notorious 'loss-making state firms'; the PASOK government had made investments in privately owned firms with the laudable object of protecting jobs but found that the process demanded an increasingly expensive public subsidy.

Greece had, of course, been involved in an Association Agreement with the EC since 1962, and by the time application for full membership was launched tariffs on imports of manufactures of EC origin had already been abolished for 66 per cent of imports, while for the remaining 34 per cent tariffs had been lowered by 44 per cent. What is perhaps most important for the non-specialist to understand is that throughout this period, and up to the present, Greece has been plagued by a substantial balance of payments deficit and that the financing of this deficit has generally been the central economic issue facing all Greek governments. Greeks have been consuming more than they produce for many years and they have relied on 'invisible' earnings from industries such as shipping and tourism to bridge the gap.

The position steadily worsened in the 1980s and today no less than 21 per cent of Greek government income is taken up with financing the national debt in its various forms. Whatever the details of the arguments about the exact effect of EC membership on Greece – and some of the economic issues are open to debate with specialists differing in their conclusions – it is an irrefutable fact that EC membership has primarily been a political and national security benefit to the country. But although it has made financing the current account deficit easier, and given Greek governments access to large amounts of loan capital that might not otherwise have been available, it has not brought about a fundamental change in economic orientation or eased serious problems.

A major problem, both for Greeks and foreign investors, has been the valuation of the drachma since the end of the Civil War. After drastic reform of the foreign exchange and international trade system in 1953, Greece maintained a policy that linked the drachma firmly to the US dollar until 1973 when the fixed parities system broke down under the impact of the first oil crisis. During much of this time the dollar's value fell and that of the drachma with it, but this was compensated for by large American subventions to Greece.

In more recent years the pattern remained the same and the Cyprus-inspired military mobilization brought particular difficulties in 1975 and 1976. In the next three years the currency followed the dollar down and in 1980 it was uniformly depreciated against all major currencies. Again, in January 1983, it was devalued by 15.5 per cent across the board. Inflation remains obstinately high, at 16 per cent in 1992, and it has been well above the Community average for many years. Those who predicted an integration of Greece with the economies of its northern partners have been sadly disappointed. One of the major problems for the country in the near future may be its integration in the Single European Market after 1992 when many remaining tariff barriers will disappear. It is still the intention of the government to join the European Monetary System.

As long ago as 1953 authors from the Royal Institute of International Affairs commented in a publication that 'Since 1947 the Greek economy had depended in the fullest sense of the word on American aid. It would probably be an exaggeration to say that all the major decisions on economic policy had been taken by the American missions. But it was certainly true that until the end of 1952 no Greek government was in a position to take the lead.' In many senses this remained true although now the financial masters of Greece are in Brussels or in the IMF and World Bank missions supervising the development of the economy in Athens.

How this situation is viewed is one of the keys to understanding the Greek attitude towards their society. To some on the Right it is no more and no less the sort of position the majority of European countries found themselves in at the end of the War, except that Greece was in a worse state than many after nine years of occupation and Civil War. The starvation in Athens in the winter of 1943 alone killed over a hundred thousand people. So it has taken longer for Greece to put itself back on its feet, and the attitude is that it only needs everyone to work a little harder and all will be well. For others, principally the political Left, the situation is a symbol of Greece's lack of independence; to change things for the better demands social and economic transformation.

It was out of this dilemma that the Greeks began to reject the solutions of the political Right and Centre and to prepare for the days of Andreas Papandreou and PASOK after the general election of 1981. Europe had on the whole turned to the Left in the Sixties and early Seventies, but when Greece had begun to do so the junta period intervened and almost all social, economic and political change was frozen. When the junta fell in 1974 there was a logjam of raised social expectation but once the excitement of EC entry had passed, and its promised transformation of Greek life – apart from agriculture – had not on the whole occurred, the Centre had little to offer.

The overwhelming appeal of Andreas Papandreou and PASOK was that the party had an explanation for this state of affairs, a radical reversal of most of the political assumptions that had guided Greek governments since the end of the Civil War. Instead of seeing itself as a western state, Papandreou encouraged Greece to see itself as part of the world affected by underdevelopment, close to the Third World and sharing many of its interests. But there was also an important social agenda for PASOK which helped to bring Greece towards the norms of a secular northern European state. Adultery was abolished as a crime, divorce by consent was introduced and civil marriage was legalized despite the strong opposition of the Church.

More controversial were the opening of Greek doors to political refugees from the Civil War who had spent long years of exile in Eastern Europe, and the moves to challenge the hegemony of professional associations, such as the medical, over their spheres of influence. The professional classes in Athens had long enjoyed freedom from most forms of tax collection and earned very high salaries by comparison with their European counterparts. One of the key social objectives of PASOK in its efforts to create a 'European' society was to try to bring a national health service into being against the entrenched opposition of professional groups.

How far 'Europe' has affected the basis of Greek life in other ways is debatable. Most Greeks never travel there, partly because it is still extremely expensive to do so, given the chronic weakness of the drachma, and partly because the tradition has not established itself. If they do travel it is likely to be to one of the great centres of the diaspora where they have relations, such as Melbourne, one of the largest Greek cities in the world. Popular Greek culture is still affected by American films and little is known of, say, French or German life apart from the accounts, often not flattering, of those who have worked there as *gastarbeiters*. It is quite arguable that there was more French or English influence in Greece a hundred years ago than there is now. Many moderate-sized Greek provincial towns, like Sparta or Nauplion, for instance, were designed on French models. Germany is still deeply suspected because of war crimes committed during the Axis Occupation and although German tourists proliferate throughout Greece they are tolerated mainly for their money. It was a landmark in 1991 when Chancellor Kohl attended the fiftieth anniversary celebrations of the Battle of Crete, but old fears and prejudices die hard. The other southern European countries in the EC, Spain particularly, are seen as rivals for increasingly hard-to-come-by regional and Mediterranean agriculture aid funds and there is little sense of solidarity with them.

Most Greeks, of whatever political persuasion, do not feel that fellow Community members understand the central question of Greek foreign and security policy – their relationship with Turkey. While Cyprus has gone off the boil, with a distinct impression that the issue no longer has the power to move Greek public opinion as it once did, Turkey remains absolutely central to the Greek consciousness of the world. Greeks find the Western European habit of bracketing the two countries especially irritating as Greece has a population of only nine million and Turkey one of nearly sixty million, and also because of Turkey's strategic position, a very privileged place in the inner councils in NATO and in Washington. In terms of human rights Greeks feel bitter that their country went through a severe process of trials and public investigations after the junta, whereas the Turkish military have never been brought to book for crimes committed during the army regime of the early 1980s when the late Turkish president, Turgut Ozal, was a military-sponsored politician.

The Turkish application to join the EC has been a source of friction in Brussels, insofar as all Greek governments since the end of the dictatorship have said that they would veto Turkish entry. Cynics might comment that Germany would beat them to it as Turks would be entitled to work in Germany if Turkey became a full member. It is ironical that it is possible to go to a Greek-owned supermarket in Munich opposite the BMW factory, packed with Turkish goods and shoppers, all from the same working-class diaspora of guestworkers going back to the Sixties and Seventies. But that world is dead now and Western Europe has turned against further immigration as jobs become scarcer with ever more immigrants from the newly free countries of Eastern Europe in search of employment with hard currency wages.

So although the head of Greece is firmly in Europe – with the sources of Common Market cash, political influence on a quite disproportionate scale for a small country and all sorts of international spin-offs – outside the Athens élite the heart may not be. Hellenism is a universal creed in terms of spreading Greek culture abroad and people from an inaccessible village on the Black Sea coast or from a suburb of Lagos visiting Athens are much more important than some fellow 'European' whose only link with Greece is a European Community passport. Some of the greatest and most influential Greeks this century have come from the diaspora, the poets Seferis and Cavafy and the businessman Onassis. Although there is a genuine pride at being seen as important to Europe and as the well-spring of European culture, Greeks are ultimately answerable to the Greek world and to no other and it is up to other nations to understand this. One of the most energetic proponents of this approach in the present generation, if perhaps an ultimate failure, was Andreas Papandreou.

The view in most western capitals was that the Greek position of being the odd man out during the years of final confrontation with the Soviet Union was an irritant, or a stupid eccentricity, or both. But now that period has passed, and the future may be seen in a different light. The nationalist path that PASOK followed in many ways prefigures the other growing nationalisms in the Balkans that have erupted in war throughout what was Yugoslavia and the rest of the Balkan peninsula. Whatever else Papandreou learned from his long years of exile in the United States, he saw that Greece could only fulfil its destiny in the light of its own history and traditions. A new Greece had to be built from the bottom up, in the countryside in particular, and the power of Athens was strictly limited. Unfortunately this fact does not always seem to be very well understood in Brussels, still less in Washington. Perhaps now that the Cold War has ended, and there is no need for Greece to be manipulated by bigger outside powers for their own ends in the superpower rivalries, Hellenism can develop in a way that is both European and universal. Perhaps, too, it may make possible better relations with Turkey, in that for so long this dispute has been symbolized at a certain level of the Greek political mentality as a contest between the civilized Christian West, represented by Greece, and the authoritarian, anti-democratic Turkish East with its Moslem religion and unhealthy political traditions – the modern equivalent of ancient Persia whose hordes threatened to over-run Greece before the battles of Marathon and Salamis.

4. The Advent of PASOK

But he who has achieved a new success
Basks in the light, soaring from hope to hope.
His deeds of prowess let him pace the air,
While he conceives plans sweeter to him than
     wealth.

                              – Pindar, *Pythian* 8

At certain times in the Eighties PASOK, its leader Andreas
Papandreou and Greece seemed virtually indistinguishable.
The strange, green rising-sun party logo was on every poster-
board and painted on concrete at the side of the motorways. The
face, manner and thoughts of Andreas Papandreou seemed to
be Greece; 'our Andreas' was both President and Prime
Minister and replacement for the not-long-deposed monarch.
Yet the party had been founded only in September 1974 and
had come to power in the autumn of 1981; it was a remarkable
achievement. Change was promised after the long years of
stagnation before the junta, then the traumatic years of
dictatorship and the struggle to restore democracy after the
colonels departed. No one doubted the great achievement of
Karamanlis in this last respect but remnants of the old world
still existed. To many Greeks, structural modernization of
their society was what was needed.

   Greek political parties have a habit of being one-man bands
and PASOK was no exception in its genesis. It is also true
that most do not survive the death or retirement of their
founder and leader. About sixty significant political parties

have contested Greek elections since the War, in one sense the same as saying sixty potential Prime Ministers wanted power.

At Athens University in the late Thirties Andreas Papandreou belonged to a small Trotskyist group and was imprisoned and tortured by the dictator Metaxas' secret police. Despite his long years in America he retained a solidly Marxist outlook, although he had no time for the KKE's Leninist, or many would say Stalinist, approach to party organization or discipline. In his book *Paternalist Capitalism* Papandreou sets out his analysis of the world and shows that he belongs to what, in crude terms, might be called the Third-Worldist school of Marxism, where the central feature of the modern class struggle is the contest between an exploiting metropolis, embodied primarily in the United States, and a poor, dependent periphery to which Greece certainly belonged. He rejects conventional roads to socialism and calls for a Third Way, emphasizing a potential alliance between Greece and other periphery countries in order to secure their national liberation.

PASOK won power in 1981 on a very radical platform: the long years of subservience to American policy dictates were to be finally ended, there was to be a major redistribution of wealth, a promise to withdraw from NATO and to remove US bases from Greek soil, and a referendum on whether Greece should remain a member of the European Common Market. The history of the PASOK years is by and large one of withdrawal from these commitments. In the process, Greek–US relations were severely strained, as the election of the party of change also coincided with that of the most conservative Republican US President of recent times, Ronald Reagan. The image of the party in the United States was not assisted by the presence in its leadership and parliamentary group of many people who had had leading roles in EAM and ELAS in the Civil War and were still seen as communists or fellow travellers by Washington.

PASOK sought to bring a new democracy to Greece but its vehicle, the PASOK party itself, was a far from democratic organization in many respects. Although espousing populist policies on most issues, the party had a strongly centralist pattern of internal life, and in the end few decisions of any importance were taken without reference to the leader himself. Although disagreeing with the Leninist democratic-centralist method of organization in the formal sense, opponents of PASOK claim that it sometimes had a little of the atmosphere of a Leninist party, with a considerable cult of personality growing up around its charismatic leader. Supporters would say that this is an inevitable feature of all Greek political parties.

But it was this atmosphere, as much as anything else, that was to lead to PASOK's demise. There have been a series of trials of major party figures including Papandreou himself, and although he was acquitted there is no doubt from what is already in the public domain about the Bank of Crete scandal in 1989, and other issues, that an atmosphere of sleaze and corruption had grown up around the PASOK government. This was also symbolized for conservative Greeks by the Prime Minister's estrangement from his wife and long public liaison, then eventual marriage to his mistress. Whatever the rights and wrongs of all the corruption issues and the personal life of the leader, Papandreou's personality cult took such an intense form that it blighted observers' perception of Greece and obscured the genuine achievements, despite problems, of the PASOK years.

Up until 1985 a pattern of moderately radical economic policies improved the position of low-paid workers and brought much-needed investment in education, health and social welfare provision. The trade unions established a pattern

of successful militancy and rich Greek and international investors moved as much money as they could out of the country.
As a result the normal balance of payments crisis became
utterly intractable and the drachma was subject to more
devaluation than usual and to an ever-rising inflation rate.
The country appeared to be heading for bankruptcy until the
Common Market intervened with loans to help stabilize the
currency – but at the price of a severe austerity programme
which cut living standards considerably. The sense of purpose
and optimism that marked the first years of PASOK disappeared. Disillusion set in among the rank and file of the party,
although Papandreou himself was as popular as ever. When
the scandals finally drew in upon him, many ordinary PASOK
voters regarded them as a set-up invented by the opposition.
Conventional figures were wheeled out with the CIA being
the most popular villain. But among all the accusations and
counter-accusations what should never be forgotten is that
PASOK was the first socialist government the Greeks ever
elected. For ordinary Greeks, like Maria Georgiou, a restaurant worker from a socialist background, there was something
unique about PASOK worth defending at any price: 'I believe
in the movement, of course. And in our Andreas. They would
do anything to bring him down.' These few words come from
a 1989 notebook, but no doubt if she were asked today she
would say exactly the same. Her use of the word 'movement'
is revealing. PASOK has always seen itself as more than just a
political party – as a fundamental impulse in Greek society.
When someone has a dispute with PASOK and leaves the
party, the person is said to 'have placed themselves outside the
movement'.

   To many observers, including those ideologically sympathetic to PASOK, it appears to be a peculiarly Greek mess,
but few can explain why events developed in the direction
they did. A key, or *the* key even, lies in the all-pervasive role

of the state in many areas of the Greek economy and society. On the surface the state's share in productive activity is not that much larger than in many other western countries, where services such as gas, electricity, water and railways are in the state sector. In other countries a state-owned airline such as Olympic is common. But the network of state control goes much further in Greece in that 80 per cent of the commercial banking system is state-controlled through majority shareholdings, petrol wholesaling is a state monopoly, the role of government in agriculture is great, and so on. The scope for patronage on a party political basis is enormous. PASOK inherited this framework and perhaps the central contradiction of all the early PASOK years was the short-term need to keep it all going, with reinforcement of the old élites and traditional ways of doing things. Meanwhile the rhetoric of the party was strongly populist, leading towards destruction of the old power structures – a socialist party where already very large areas of the economy were state-controlled. The scandals of the last years showed how little change there had actually been and how the rhetoric had foundered on reality, with leading figures in the party using the old state contacts and procedures for corrupt purposes. The party was elected to promote a non-statist type of socialism but found itself locked ever more firmly into existing state structures and procedures.

In the economic sphere PASOK was elected on a programme of decentralization. This was a policy widely supported outside the ranks of PASOK itself. The problem of bureaucracy in modern Greece is particularly acute, with its Ottoman administrative practices, the privileged position of bureaucrats with status, tenure and employment advantages quite absent in the private sector, and a population conditioned to a good deal of state regimentation for political reasons in the post-civil-war years. 'Socialization' was the PASOK answer to the problem, both in industry and in social projects.

In terms of industry it was an alternative to the socialist nationalization and the command economies of Eastern Europe, and it drew on leftist theories of workers' control current among post-1968 thinkers in Greece and elsewhere. The general framework, though, was of traditional planning, with a five-year plan for the country produced for the years 1983–7. Each *nomos* (prefecture) was asked to prepare a local plan to be included eventually in the national plan.

Another dimension of socialization, a cornerstone of the early PASOK years, was that involving the social accountability of public enterprises. Again, this was a sensible target, with much support for the original policy initiatives coming from outside PASOK. Like nationalized industries everywhere, the Greek public enterprises had been run more in their own interests than in those of their customers. Complex proposals for a three-tier system of management were evolved to bring elected workers' representatives into the management process along with external groups such as industrialists, farmers, shopkeepers, and so on. A second tier consisted of working directors and government appointees, with a third tier of a separate workers' council. The chief management role of general director was laid down by the guidelines of the three management tiers. Unsurprisingly, in view of the complexity of the arrangements, the loose drafting of the legislation and the unclear lines of management authority, the socialization principles as applied to industry proved to be a bureaucrat's paradise and a manager's nightmare. In the economic sphere they contributed to the collapse of the loss-making state enterprises that were to become such a millstone for PASOK after 1985. The private sector, on the whole, was spared this process, with the socialization legislation requiring the development of supervisory councils of the workforce on the West German model. The proposals were modest and went no further, in most respects, than the European Community policy but they

were fiercely resisted by Greek employers and to date very few
have been set up.

Apologists for PASOK, in this area, as in others, would
claim that when the party came to power in 1981, the Greek
economy had not begun to adjust to the oil crisis of 1979, and
that it was burdened with the unwise budgetary expansion
that the previous government had allowed in its efforts to win
the election. But the urgent social priorities of PASOK and
its promises, particularly towards the low-paid workers, were
expensive: the 94 per cent wage rise in 1982 was a decisive
factor in this respect, combined with the wage indexation
scheme that had serious long-term effects in the public sector.
There is, unfortunately, a widespread perception of the Greek
state as a tireless and generous father, always willing and able
to put a hand in his pocket at the time his children need
money. Although the Left was blamed for this philosophy by
market-oriented economists and their political opponents
during the Eighties, there was already a very long tradition of
it in Greek political life.

The main beneficiaries of the early years of PASOK were
the low-paid workers, especially in the cities, in the public
sector and the lower ranks of the bureaucracy. There is no
doubt that in a country where many public-sector jobs are
part of the political spoil system, rather than part of a
meritocratic civil service, there was a very considerable expansion of the state *apparat* under PASOK despite the anti-
statist intentions of their original project. The inbred dynamic
towards the growth of government regulation and the difficulty the government, like its predecessors, had in getting the
electorate to accept any of the disciplines of a market economy
– for that is what Greece was, and would have remained, even
if every last element in the original PASOK programme had
been implemented – meant that room for manoeuvre was
always very limited. In the early years the activities of the

PASOK government were strongly disapproved of by the international financial community but as long as the public-sector deficit could be financed there was little to be done about it. This situation changed radically in PASOK's latter years.

Another reason for this neglect was the almost exclusive international concentration on Athens foreign policy that marked these years. Papandreou's theories about the nature of Greek economic dependency and underdevelopment, and the practical policy response to this, led him to adopt positions strongly critical of the United States and NATO in the international arena. There were several main strands determining policy. One was the inheritance of the Cyprus problem after the Turkish invasion of 1974. As more became public about these events, it seemed not only to PASOK or to Communist voters but to the Greek public generally that the national interests of Greece and the United States were virtually irreconcilable in the eastern Mediterranean, and that Greece's security was threatened by its commitment to NATO, an organization in which Turkish interests always seemed paramount. Another strand was the problem of Middle East terrorism, a high-profile matter in the early 1980s, where the United States considered that Greece was a *de facto* base and refuge for anti-American terrorists, with the authorities turning a blind eye. A third important strand was the atmosphere of deterioration in East–West relations in the revival of the Cold War then, US and Soviet land-based missile deployments, what the United States saw as a fellow-travelling government in Athens at the time and what Athens saw as a revival of the type of US government that had treated Greece as a minor client state rather than as an independent country. Greece became a gadfly to the US giant, a very irritating one since there was really no answer to Greek allegations about CIA complicity in the colonels' coup and subsequent subversion of democracy. A major factor in this process was the opinion of the US State Department that in view of the regional 'policeman' dimension of Turkey's role, it should have priority in bilateral relations. Turkey's long land frontier with the Soviet Union, it being an Islamic but secular state, staunchly pro-western and anti-communist, in rhetoric at least, in a way that Greece was not, were contributory reasons. By and large, proponents of this view were dominant in Washington in the early PASOK years, mostly in the upper reaches of the State Department and among President Reagan's policy advisers. Papandreou was not slow to exploit the widespread Greek perception that the US did not fundamentally care about the future of democracy nor for prosperity in Greece and that it would end the traditional 7:10 military aid ratio with Turkey if it could do so.

The European Community took a somewhat sympathetic view of Greece's difficulties during this time, whereas NATO tended to follow the American line. But after the fall of the Shah of Iran the proponents of the regional policeman role for Turkey had had much more difficulty making their case. The enormous financial and military aid given to the Shah had clearly not advanced US interests in Iran, and the Greek lobby on Capitol Hill was quick to draw the analogy, as they saw it, with Turkey. The disputes now seem ancient history, with the end of Communism and the Cold War, but they were part of the process of emancipation from American influence and the integration of Greece within a fully European national security and economic framework. This process culminated recently, incidentally, in Greek admission to the Western European Union defence pact in which Turkey only has observer status. The days of American soft loans to Greece were over and Greece would look increasingly to Brussels for financial salvation in the following years. Economic emancipation from the post-war dollar-based regimes and the linking of the drachma to the dollar after Bretton Woods had come and gone; it was not surprising that the Greeks were also rejecting a policy of mechanical adherence to US interests in the national security field. But there were difficulties for both parties.

For all his anti-Americanism, Papandreou was a child of Uncle Sam. The United States had given him refuge from foreign invasion and civil war, and he had established his academic reputation there as an outstanding economist. He had many family and personal links with the United States and in the way some of the quarrels were conducted, mainly those with President Reagan, there is as much a sense of Freud as of Marx: the prodigal son rejecting the values of his adopted father. The bitter rows, recriminations and public slanging matches between Athens and Washington in the early Eighties also have something of the atmosphere of the end of an affair or of a difficult divorce. There was the feeling of a trust betrayed, a partnership lost.

It is an axiom of many Greeks that their country is at the centre of the political world, always subject to the threat of conspiracies, takeovers, invasions and general interference. The United States in the early Eighties provided the ideal demonic figure in this respect, but with the end of the Cold War this option closed. Some Greek commentators fear a consequent growth of internal conflict in Greece, along with a revival of nationalist sentiment, whose roots may well lie in the early Eighties.

The early PASOK years were seen by many Greeks as a time of great social optimism when it did seem as if the country was going to be modernized, when state institutions and large economic enterprises were going at last to be made more responsible to the population at large, and when some kind of national independence in foreign and defence policy was going to be attained. It was a time of great hopes, particularly for peace. The Greek people as a whole strongly supported the worldwide movements that developed for nuclear disarmament and the end of the Cold War. One of the major causes of popular resentment against the United States in Greece was the type of thinking exemplified by an unwise speech made by the American Ambassador in Athens in 1982 accusing peace activists of being Communist dupes. The Greek army had been fully mobilized as recently as 1976 because of the Cyprus crisis, and all Greeks of whatever political viewpoint had no illusions about the fragility of peace in the eastern Mediterranean as a whole. The prospect of an escalation of some regional crisis, over Israel or Turkey, into a major war or even a nuclear Armageddon was very real at that time and fully understood in Athens. Although Papandreou never succeeded in ejecting the US military bases from Greece, a climate of opinion developed across party lines that made a helpful contribution to the end of the Cold War and to the transformation in the international climate that has taken place recently.

The early Eighties was also a time of greater freedom in personal life. The patterns of social reform that had begun after the fall of the junta continued, broadly all following the same direction of secularization. The Church was one institution that did not really benefit from the PASOK years, and it was not surprising that it fought back strongly against plans to take over church-owned land which, after the degree of opposition made itself clear, were quietly dropped. The ethos was urban, hedonistic, perhaps a little flashy, a kind of Greek version of the Swinging Sixties after years of artificial restraint. Some of PASOK's more socially conservative critics would say that it was exactly these qualities, with the absence of traditional moral restraint on social behaviour, that later brought the party to its knees. But the view of political professionals was rather different and more practical. In 1981 PASOK had a large ragbag of policies difficult for a nonrevolutionary party to implement within a framework of parliamentary reformism; they were forced to change course and in the process ditched their rank and file support. Constantine Mitsotakis, the New Democracy leader and Papandreou's great rival, characterized the process in a speech in 1988: 'The government took to the road: Mr Papandreou began his course as a Third-Worlder, cursing the European Community and NATO to end up applying, badly, our own policy, in the name of reality and necessity.'

But to say this does not imply that by the mid Eighties PASOK had lost all the arguments, and the support for many policies concerning defence and national independence was as strong as ever. The Right had changed as well and had been forced finally to recognize that there was no future for Greece as an American client state in any shape or form. Necessity was the first god in the ancient pantheon according to some accounts of the theogony: it could not be avoided even by those who had been brought up in a political culture that owed almost everything to the United States and its allies.

5. The End of PASOK:
New Democracy without Karamanlis

But even wisdom feels the lure of gain,
Gold glittered in his hand, and he was hired.

– Pindar, *Pythian* 3

It was death by a thousand cuts. From the heroic anti-imperialist leader who had been the only politician in the EC to oppose the Thatcher–Reagan remaking of the world, someone who had opposed passionately the growing power of free market and pro-capitalist policies in the Eighties, Andreas Papandreou became ammunition for the tabloid gossip columns, a whisky-drinking old man who happened to have fallen in love with a woman a good deal younger, and who unbelievably, in terms of traditional Greek patron–mistress relations, wanted to marry her.

Greece rates few column inches in English-language newspapers. Long stories of politicians with incomprehensible names who try to defeat each other, the strange problems of many Greek businesses and the world of the ordinary person in Athens matter no more than the man in the moon, especially to tabloid readers for whom Greece is just a place to go on holiday. But although Greece as a country, in good times or bad, has appeared to be pretty un-newsworthy, Greek personalities have occupied a good many inches of English newsprint. In the Fifties and early Sixties, the doings of the Niarchos and Onassis clans were one of the mainstays of the gossip columns; later on their demise occupied almost as much space. The shipping dynasties faded; their world, as super-Greeks who actually had little contact with most aspects of Greece itself, was a limited phenomenon, a glamorous side of the great power of American business in the country then. It was, after all, in New York, not Athens or Piraeus, that the original Onassis fortune was made, when Greece was a bankrupt little state facing the Axis powers almost alone. Onassis had always been an outsider, the refugee from Smyrna who had had to fight to get himself accepted in mainland Greece – but who never really succeeded in doing so. More recently, and in quite a different context, contemporary equivalents have been neglected. One of the richest men in the world, John Latsis, lives in London, in the magnificent Bridgewater House in St James's. He is a colourful character, a lover of choice demotic bad language, a fanatical monarchist, perhaps the first shipping man really to understand computers and someone who has made not millions but billions out of moving Saudi oil. But there has been very little written about him in England. But with the Papandreou love affair, suddenly Greece was news. Photographs of Dimitra Liani, dressed in Parisian couture in the PASOK colours, waving to cheering crowds, were splashed in the papers. And, amidst the sexual scandal, news seeped through that all was not going well either for Papandreou's government.

But something fundamental was wrong with PASOK long before Andreas's love life began to dominate events. From the ordinary rank and file of the party who thought that PASOK would bring social justice and better hospitals to the analysts in the US State Department and the CIA who saw Papandreou to all intents and purposes as a Communist, someone hellbent on the destruction of the West, the PASOK government had spelled change. But, in many ways, so little change had taken place. The US bases were still in Greece although all opinion polls in the mid Eighties showed massive majorities for their closure, a feeling not confined to PASOK or KKE militants but shared by many right-wing voters. The main elements of social and economic structures were untouched as the government had been unable to collect more than a modest proportion of the taxes due to it. Tax evasion was endemic among the professional élite in Athens, those whose high standard of living was often viewed with envy by less fortunate Greeks, and also among farmers who, by and large, never fill in tax returns and are outside the state revenue system.

The 1986 Kalamata earthquake is a good example of how the relationship between the government and the governed had not really altered. Kalamata is a solid provincial town of about 45,000 people, capital of the rich agricultural area of Messenia in the south of the Peloponnese, land that had once been the breadbasket of the ancient Spartan military machine with helots sweating in the sun to grow food for members of the phalanx.

Kalamata is also the regional centre for the wild Mani peninsular. It was the scene of an early victory in the Greek War of Independence when Maniot chieftains, magnificently dressed, rallied their followers and rode into town to attack the Ottoman administration. Later in the nineteenth century, Kalamata was populated largely by people from the Mani villages and grew into an important port, exporting its famous olives, and with something of a reputation for sin and vice. Although the port has gone into decline, with improved road communications since the War, the town is still the vibrant centre of the southern Peloponnese where many Greeks go on holiday, the hub of an agricultural area of Greece that has benefited enormously from Common Market arrangements. Ancient Messene, fifteen miles inland, is one of the great unknown classical sites in Greece, the large, mostly unexcavated remains of a sprawling hellenistic city — first capital of Messenia after its emancipation from Sparta — a classical landscape with ruins that eighteenth-century painters, travellers and dilettanti loved. Today marble columns rise from the ground amidst fig and olive plantations. But Messenia is right on the fault line in the earth's crust that runs around much of the Greek coast from Corfu in the north, down the side of the Peloponnese, then southwards under the Bay of Messenia and Kalamata city itself. In antiquity earthquakes were thought to come from the sea, from the god Poseidon; the epicentre of the 1986 earthquake was about six miles out under the sea in the Bay of Messenia.

In September 1986, about midday, a new ferry to Crete was being launched and a large crowd of wellwishers had gathered on the Kalamata quay. Few people were inside their houses when two earth tremors suddenly hit, demolishing hundreds of buildings in the city and in the mountains behind it. Loss of life was heavy in the tiny mountain settlement of Eliochorion, nestling on the edge of the Tayetos, high above Kalamata. In the immediate aftermath, the emergency arrangements worked well. Greece is used to major earthquakes and the army is trained very professionally in disaster relief. Hundreds of tents were brought in for the homeless and emergency food and water supplies were efficiently organized. Worldwide support came from Greeks and friends of Greece, especially from Australia where many sons and daughters of Kalamata had gone to make their fortunes.

But later, after erecting hundreds of Portakabin-type homes, the army left. Winter was approaching and the flow of immediate humanitarian aid decreased as the city began its long task of reconstruction. As well as the government in Athens, both the nomarch (the regional prefect) and the local council were PASOK-controlled so, in the view of local people, there should have been no problems caused by political rivalry during the reconstruction period. But this was not the case. A substantial sum from European Community funds had been paid to the central government in Athens to help pay for the reconstruction but there were long delays in getting this money released and the earthquake victims continued to live in deteriorating conditions. They complained that after the earthquake the town had been full of high-level officials of every kind, but that after a few months they had felt abandoned. In particular the village people who had been moved down to temporary settlements in Kalamata felt no effort was being made to get them back to their homes. The villain of this story is centralization itself. Even in a major disaster that had no political dimensions, the old vices of the political system rapidly appeared – the main one being that without influence in Athens it was well-nigh impossible to get any large share of Greek resources as the intervening layers of government and bureaucracy seemed to have little or no power.

It need hardly be said that if PASOK's proposals for decentralization had had any substance most of the problems in Kalamata after the earthquake would not have arisen. But for the typical provincial city that had turned with the rest of the country towards PASOK in the early Eighties, the Papandreou rhetoric was all a sham and little or nothing had changed in the way Greece was governed. It was not surprising that Kalamata swung heavily back towards the Right in the late Eighties and has remained there since.

On a wider canvas, most commentators date the demise of PASOK to June 1985 when, soon after winning a decisive election victory, Papandreou introduced a radical two-year package of economic measures with the emphasis on austerity and restraint. It was a fundamental reorientation of economic policy from the first four years in office, followed in October 1985 by a 15 per cent devaluation of the drachma. The policy of the race for growth in the first four years had failed because of a lax monetary policy, with income redistribution achieved

only through government borrowing and an accelerating inflation rate. And, despite having more expansionist policies than
most western countries, output had actually stagnated. A
central part of the stabilization programme was an incomes
policy which effectively undermined the existing wages–prices
equalization scheme.

On the fiscal front government borrowing was to be reduced
by 4 per cent a year and domestic credit controls were
introduced, coupled with various restrictions on imports,
mainly consumer goods. But the most important dimension
was an application to the European Community for a loan of
1,750 million ECUs which would be raised in the financial
markets, with the release of funds conditional on the stabilization programme. The overall aim was a reduction in the
balance of payments deficit and a clamp-down on domestic
inflation. The programme also marked a major stage in the
process of readjustment in Greece between wages and profits,
which had been in relative decline soon after 1974 and the
introduction of democracy. The target was to bring inflation
down to single figures by the late Eighties and to reduce the
current account deficit of $3,300 million to $1,250 million in
time to allow a relaxation of policy before the next general
election. This timing reflected the fact that the policy would
have a potentially high political cost for the government,
mostly among its numerous supporters in the salaried public
sector.

The programme achieved some success in reaching its
targets in that as early as the end of 1986 the current account
deficit had been brought down to the projected target, inflation
was falling and the public sector borrowing requirement had
dropped from 18 per cent of GDP to 14 per cent. On this basis
the second half of the EC loan was released to Greece,
although not without misgivings among the Community
partners, especially Germany. But the good days did not last

long. Hardly had the loan been received than oil prices began to rise and the dollar began to depreciate. The current account deficit soared, the public borrowing target was abandoned and some of the worst fears of Greece's EC partners began to be borne out by events. The promise to raise larger sums through more vigorous efforts to collect taxes was never fulfilled and relations with the public sector workers continued to deteriorate as they felt, with some justification, that they were being asked to bear all the weight of the economic crisis. Although the state sector of the Greek economy can be regarded as a ball and chain that slows down and often completely stops any progress in modernizing the economy, the workers in it have been asked repeatedly to make considerable economic sacrifices for the public good although they are a far from well-off section of the population. Greek teachers, for instance, are notoriously poorly paid both in schools and universities.

Whatever the details in terms of high finance, the effect of the austerity programme on ordinary Greek families who supported PASOK was clear: the promise of better days to come that had sustained morale in the early years had gone for good and there was little to put in its place. What saved PASOK from total disintegration were the chronic problems in New Democracy and the inability of the Communist party to modernize itself. New Democracy was still in a mess after the 1985 defeat and in any case, privately, saw little alternative to the unpopular policies of PASOK. The KKE had one strong card insofar as the humiliating negotiations with Brussels had shown the Greek public how little effective national sovereignty remained in the sphere of economic policy. In every other respect the KKE belonged in a political museum, putting forward a vision of Greece in which a monolithic command economy helped by the Soviet Union might, in some unspecified way, restore the prosperity of the Greek working class. None of the main parties seemed to recognize the underlying problem that, in terms of consumption, the country was living well beyond its income and had been doing so for some time, and that the commercial and industrial world that had given rise to the high growth rates of the Fifties and Sixties had gone for ever.

So the scandals of the last years of PASOK took place against a very difficult background, where leading members of the party were lining their pockets while the general public was expected to make sacrifices. But Greece was far from convinced that the opposition had satisfactory alternative policies and it was not until two unstable coalition governments had been formed in 1989 and 1990 that New Democracy was eventually able to win a small but workable parliamentary majority. The new Prime Minister, Constantine Mitsotakis, had a distinguished record in the resistance and had been condemned to death by the Germans in the Second World War. The major events of his premiership mimic uncomfortably the early days of PASOK after 1985, with a humiliating recourse to the European Community for further loans to shore up the economy. When Mitsotakis took power the economic situation was as black as at any time in the last twenty years. Inflation had risen to nearly 20 per cent, the public sector borrowing requirement was rising inexorably and foreign capital investment in the country was steadily declining. But fellow EC leaders, mainly Margaret Thatcher and Helmut Kohl, were anxious to assist Mitsotakis now that the despised PASOK regime had at last gone and a government with a stable majority had been elected. A 2.2 billion ECU loan facility was made available with similar conditions as the last loan to PASOK. But in this case teams from Brussels and the IMF moved to Athens to supervise policy and the last vestiges of Greek economic sovereignty disappeared. The money is being disbursed in three tranches,

1 billion ECU in 1991 and 600 million ECU in 1992 and 1993, conditional on satisfactory performance in meeting targets. As well as the inevitable preoccupation with current account and government borrowing, there is also a strong emphasis on selling off unproductive state assets. It is difficult to generalize about the success or otherwise of the programme other than to say that apart from one or two relatively attractive companies, such as the state cement company Aget Heracles, the pace of privatization has been slow and notorious loss-makers, such as the state airline Olympic Airways, are still firmly in the public sector. Eastern as well as Western Europe is full of second-rate businesses in the state sector that are up for sale and it may be difficult for many Greek companies to find buyers, especially if their capital equipment is old or, as in the case of Olympic Airways, they are perceived to have expensive overmanning problems and a workforce used to considerable protection and privilege.

In other respects the pressures put on the government to achieve the international bankers' targets have resulted in almost identical policies to the PASOK austerity period with, for instance, a two-year wage agreement being reached with the public sector trade unions in exchange for an average wage rise of about 12 per cent. With inflation still running at nearly 20 per cent, although the rate is falling, the pressures on wage-earners are obvious and may prove to be the Achilles heel of the programme. Already in 1991 the strong banking trade union negotiated a considerably higher settlement and the available cake is getting smaller, with industrial production falling by 2.3 per cent in the first quarter of 1992 and unemployment rising by 40,000 to 170,000 in July 1992. The worldwide recession will not help Greek efforts to boost exports, nor will the war in former Yugoslavia.

The main burden in 1992 again fell on the public sector workers and the citizens of Athens were rewarded by a prolonged dustmen's strike. It was broken by the use of Albanian immigrants, a highly unpopular move reminiscent of their use to undercut Greek trade unionists before the First World War, and there are more strikes in the offing. Refuse collection in Athens has become a problem too, as the main municipal sites are becoming full and there are no obvious alternatives. It looks as though Greece could be settling in for a period of prolonged social unrest as the Mitsotakis government struggles to enforce economic reforms that most Greeks know in their hearts are necessary but which may damage their individual interests. Traditionally militant groups such as the Olympic Airways pilots are threatening strike action and it remains to be seen whether the government will be able to face the inevitable confrontations.

Many of the less privileged vote for New Democracy and during 1992 and 1993 they became progressively alienated from the government. The PASOK opposition swept to power in the important Athens electoral district in April 1992 which was to prefigure victory in the general election held in autumn 1993. The Mitsotakis government had lost its parliamentary majority after the formation of a breakaway party, Political Spring, formed by ex-New Democracy Foreign Minister Antonis Samaras, with a major issue in its genesis being the Macedonia problem. It is a strange irony that Andreas Papandreou has returned to govern Greece again, in these circumstances, after his previous sad and undignified recent exit from power. It is probable that neither party leader has managed to convey to his followers the full gravity of the economic crisis facing the country, but what may well be more important in the long term is that it was an issue arising from the Balkan crisis that led to the downfall of New Democracy, an ominous portent for the future.

Above: The bitter mountain war: Greek troops in the Devoli Valley in Albania in 1941

Below: Anti-fascist resistance: ELAS andartes. Their style draws on the klephtic tradition, the heroic bandits resisting foreign occupation

Wartime starvation in Athens: the famine claimed
over a hundred thousand victims

Above: For a while, national unity: right-wing EDES resistance leader Zervas with a young ELAS fighter

Below: Liberation: demonstration in Athens in October 1944

After years of resistance and civil war, fighting became a way of life: Democratic Army leader, Markos Vafiades

Above: The terrible price: relatives identify bodies after a massacre near Piraeus

Below: The British protectorate: Churchill and Eden with Archbishop Damaskinos, Regent of Greece, in February 1945

Above: The Civil War left much of the north ruined: a valley in Epirus

Below: The struggle of the peasants: subsistence agriculture in Crete

Above: Improved relations with Yugoslavia: Prime Minister Karamanlis with President Tito of Yugoslavia in 1960

Below: The victory of the Centre: George Papandreou in 1964

Above: Education was always central to Hellenism in the Diaspora: Russian playwright Chekhov attended this Greek school in Odessa

Below: The English intellectual in Greece: Sir Arthur Evans at Knossos, Crete

Part Two

CONTEMPORARY
PERCEPTIONS

6. Tourism: The Visit to Paradise

> Her [Virginia Woolf's] reaction to Greece was very
> much what might have been expected of any culti-
> vated young Englishwoman in the year 1906. She
> was wholly unaware of Byzantine art and uncritical
> of that of the fifth century; for the modern Greeks
> she did not care and she preferred the uncivilized
> Vlachs on the Noel's estate at Achmetaga . . . it was
> an odd unhappy view of Greece. Virginia spent
> much of her time in an Athens hotel bedroom read-
> ing Mérimée and heating saucepans of goats'
> milk . . .
>
> – Quentin Bell, *Virginia Woolf*

The tourist enters a world of political and economic stress, a
country in many ways profoundly at odds with itself. But this
is not usually apparent for Greece, like many other holiday
destinations, is sold as Utopia and most people visit it to
forget about the rain, vandalism on the council estate, or the
possibility that Mr John Major or Mr John Smith, or whoever,
might win the next general election – to forget their social and
political realities. The Greek people are small figures in the
landscape, necessary but minor and as decorative as the well-
dressed eighteenth-century peasants who appear in small
corners of antiquaries' drawings when the rediscovery of
Greece began in the eighteenth century.

The history of tourism in Greece can be seen in some ways
as the admirable attempt of people of each generation to

understand something of the roots of their civilization but in others as an endless catalogue of thefts of antiquities, looting of churches and the insensitivities and stupidities of eighteenth-century gentlemen wanting souvenirs from the Grand Tour. In this context the Arabic proverb that says to travel is to conquer seems apposite.

Greece represents something infinitely desirable to most visitors, a combination of unsurpassed natural beauty and antiquity and, perhaps most of all, warmth and sensuality – Byron's 'sweet south'. In tourist terms it has not suffered as badly as the coast of Spain, but there are parts, especially on Corfu and Rhodes, so popular with mass tourism that they have been taken over and despoiled as thoroughly as the pillage of Slavonic invaders in the seventh century when they swept down from the north into Greece. But even here the images and stereotypes can be deceptive: the hordes of backpackers who troop off boats are performing a rite of passage of a kind, now they are usually refugees more than conquerors.

The ancient Greeks were, to an extent, tourists themselves, with a special fascination for Egypt. The historian Herodotus from Halicarnassus, a city state on the south-west coast of Asia Minor, wandered extensively throughout the ancient world and was, in a real sense, the first travel writer. In Egypt, Asia and in Greece itself, he visited classical sites as people do today, noting the famous offerings from King Croesus at Delphi, the pyramids, the battlefields of Thermopylae and Marathon, the famous city of Thebes, and so on.

Very few people travelled out of curiosity or for pleasure. Most were the ubiquitous Greek traders who set up colonies throughout the Mediterranean, but kept scarcely any records. Later the Romans travelled widely, in a recognizably modern sense, throughout a country that had become a Roman province, starting the long process of looting Greek antiquities and writing down what they did and saw. The long afternoon of the Hellenistic world saw Greek culture spread to countries as far away as India and it came to be seen as a universal civilization. At certain times the Roman world was dominated by Greek teachers, doctors and administrators, and Greek was the language of the eastern part of the Empire and of nascent Christianity. Scions of leading Roman families were sent to Athens to study, the Emperor Hadrian attempted to renew the greatness of classical Athens with his own monuments and St Paul tried, notably unsuccessfully, to convert the questioning philosophers of the Athens *agora* to Christianity.

But in the long period of Athens' decline, its monuments fell into neglect or were damaged by earthquakes. The city became little more than a collection of villages and in Ottoman times Athens was seen as a rather mythical city by northern Europeans, a city with a fantastic past, an echo in medieval legend. Travel in the form of the Grand Tour became more or less impossible as Europe was permanently at loggerheads with the Turks, changes in the sea-level had transformed many coastal areas to malarial swamps, and road transport routes had broken down. This situation remained much the same until the end of the sixteenth century. Although occasional travellers went to Greece, much of what interests a contemporary tourist was either totally unknown such as the Minoan sites in Crete or the prehistoric monuments at Mycenae, or distant and inaccessible, such as the remote, great fifth-century temple at Bassae in the Peloponnese. The northern countries were preoccupied with national development and became excessively self-confident about their cultural identities and disparaging about the ancient world. The great Elizabethan writer Robert Burton wrote: 'Greeks have condemned all the world but themselves of barbarism, the world as much vilifies them now.' It was not surprising if in this climate educated people thought there was little worth visiting, even if it had been possible to do so.

Very slowly, the situation improved. After the battle of Lepanto in 1571 the Turks ceased to be a menace to Europe, and travel in the territories they controlled became more feasible. After their defeat at the battle of St Gotthard in 1664 their military power continued to decline, and after the Venetian invasion of the Peloponnese in 1685 it was possible for the traveller to visit substantial areas of the country. During the eighteenth century trade expanded and by the time Byron arrived in Athens in 1809, an English reading public was ready for his passionate philhellenism, already educated by the accounts of great antiquaries such as Stuart and Revett who had made the first systematic description of visible classical monuments in Athens in the 1770s.

But many practical difficulties remained to hinder the traveller. The fever that killed Byron was endemic throughout the lowland regions of the country, and although the defeat of the Turks in the Greek War of Independence in the 1820s brought many benefits, good roads were not one of them. There were conflicts, such as the Napoleonic wars, when any sort of European travel was more or less impossible, and it was not until the Pax Victoriana that a substantial number of foreigners was able to visit the country. But by now the spell of Greece was at its strongest in the educational world, and many nineteenth-century travellers were falling under the wider spell of philhellenism. The once remote and mysterious country of Italy had become more frequented and some of its cities were almost part of Victorian England – Florence, for example, with its English exiles. This world no longer had the freshness of the classical past and intellectuals turned to Greece as the original source of so much in the Italian Renaissance.

Travel was predominantly by boat, often the only practical method of transport as Greece had no connection with the European rail network until 1916. Apart from the pleasures of sailing in the Mediterranean sun, it avoided undue contact with the locals. The vision of Greece was still very much that of ancient Greece and modern Greek society was irrelevant. Today's holidaymaker on upmarket Swan Hellenic Cruises is in direct line of descent from these Victorian upper-middle-class journeyers. A glance back at the records of the Hellenic Travellers Club in the late 1920s also shows the same pattern. Travellers, predominantly academics and clerics, took the train from London to Venice and embarked there to sail down the Adriatic coast to Piraeus – after a brief call at Ithaca to satisfy Homeric curiosities.

In 1506 the Tudor traveller Sir Richard Guylforde, on his way to the Holy Land, had taken a ship at Trieste and sailed south via Corfu, where 'they all speak Greke, and be Grekes in dede', down to Modona (modern Methoni) with its great fortresses, which, perhaps wisely, Sir Richard sailed past 'for fere of the Turkes'. The successful new states of northern Europe had control of the sea of the eastern Mediterranean long before they had control of the land, mirrored later by the fact that Scobie's British troops in Athens could probably not have won the battle to liberate the city in 1944 without Royal Naval sea power and the influx of soldiers from Piraeus. Overall, the patterns of travel reflect underlying political and military realities.

So the intrepid traveller finally encountered Athens, then crossed to Constantinople, Kos, Rhodes and Delos. Then followed the Peloponnese for Nauplion, Tyrins and Mycenae, with a final visit to Olympia and then back on the boat to Venice. Although it was a fine itinerary, the travellers probably had next to no contact with Greek people of any kind and did not see large areas of the country or many major sites. The lectures and talks organized on these voyages during the inter-war years were very much designed to complement a classical education and did not normally touch on modern Greece.

A generation earlier, the traveller by land was seen as a

pioneer, with dress appearing to be a particular problem. Reuters war correspondent W. Kinnaird Rose, in the preface of his account of the war in Thessaly against the Turks in 1897, devotes many lines to the heavy tweeds protecting him against night chills and fever in the plains but, as he admitted, they were a little warm at midday. In 1906 Baedeker advised on clothing for a Greek holiday in the form of a moderately thick overcoat, puttees, a grey tweed suit and woollen underclothing. It seems as much a method to protect the traveller from self-exposure in Greece rather than anything to do with health or the weather – a way of keeping the Englishman or woman secure in their northern cultural values. The notion that modern Greek society might have anything of cultural interest to the visitor – or Byzantine or Ottoman Greece, for that matter – was not entertained.

By 1916 the railway took visitors to Athens. But then a dragoman, or courier, had to be engaged to organize the trip into the interior by horseback, and to make all practical arrangements on the route, but the impecunious traveller could settle for a mere horse-boy. Baedeker was even now warning travellers that 'pedestrian expeditions of a day or more are more or less impossible, owing to the climate, the difficulty of obtaining food and shelter and the badness of the roads, the savage dogs that will be encountered and the total absence of sign posts'. It was not altogether an enticing prospect and hardly improved by occasional brigandage in the north, although not confined there. The celebrated abduction and murder of Lord Muncaster's friends in 1870 had taken place in Attica within thirty miles of the city of Athens. In April of that year, while sightseeing, the English party had been ambushed by brigands. Four of them were abducted, but Lord Muncaster was released to raise a ransom for the captives. The Greek government feared that they would be taken over the border to Turkey and troops surrounded the bandits' camp, provoking a shootout that resulted in the murder of the hostages. The incident caused an uproar in Britain and Queen Victoria herself spoke out against the Greek government.

Just as shipping determined patterns of tourism in Greece in the nineteenth and early twentieth centuries, so a revolution has been wrought by cheap air travel starting in the 1960s. Although Athens was an important early stopover on the way to India for Imperial Airways, air tourist numbers were small until the Sixties. Characteristic accounts of Greek holidays by road in the Fifties – with the car to Athens – concentrate on the motoring side *en route* more than on what was to be seen in Greece. The advent of the charter flight and the example of Spain showed other Mediterranean countries that an untapped market existed for sunny holidays in the south. The younger generation was becoming more European-minded and less worried about the shibboleths of cleanliness and drains that seemed to restrict the travel of the wartime generation. Although these reservations influenced people long after they should, there had been a real basis for them in the years up until the Second World War. There was widespread malaria in the lowlands, tuberculosis in the cities and the mountains, and a wide variety of serious diseases associated with poverty and poor living conditions – such as rickets in children. Improvements in public health in Greece and the conquest of malaria after the War – one of the few absolutely genuine achievements of the American client era – did remove the worst problems.

The transformation that cheap air travel brought to Greece, especially the islands, cannot be underestimated. Before Heraklion airport was built in the early Sixties, Crete had changed little since the early years of the century. Patterns of agriculture were beginning to be affected by Common Market contacts but the traditional way of life continued in the mountains, with few people living on the coast as it was thought unsatisfactory, potentially dangerous and unCretan, with the land used only for summer grazing. In the War the coast-dwellers were known as 'long-trousered men' and resistance fighters told British liaison officers like Paddy Leigh Fermor that they didn't have souls and were not people to be trusted. A small community such as Kheronisos, a speck on the road along the north coast and a few miles from the important Minoan settlement at Mallia, had only a few hundred people living there. It had been a large Roman port, with bits of imperial masonry sticking out of the beach sand, and on a promontory there is a ruined Byzantine church with a fine floor mosaic. It was an ideal place for flower people to settle in the late Sixties and early Seventies, with beautiful girls in embroidered jeans pretending to be shepherds, but otherwise it had seen few foreigners since Australian and New Zealand troops put up their heroic fight against the Axis paratroops on the beaches there in the War.

In recent summers the population of Kheronisos has been about twenty thousand people. The hippies have long since gone, as have the shepherds, and the old summer grazing is covered with a monstrously ugly shanty town of wall-to-wall bars, discos and apartment blocks. There was a nasty riot a year or two ago when British lager louts fought their Dutch counterparts, a kind of hell on the beach. Most bars have a predominantly nationalistic clientele and getting tanked up and thumping someone who doesn't speak your language is a common event. Most of the newcomers are not Cretans but Athenians who move in for the summer, open a bar, make a great deal of money and then disappear back to Athens at the end of the season without paying any tax. When the construction boom slumps and the building jobs go, little of the tourist money comes back to Crete. And the next year the Athenians return, bars open under new names to confuse the taxman and the whole cycle starts again. It is, in its way, a crucifixion of the beauty of Greece, of the strong Cretan traditions of hospitality, of the dignity of the island and its rural culture. Or a rape, perhaps, where the island is subject to violent destruction of its innocence and beauty.

But all this did not happen at random. The road, on which everything depended, and the development permits were part of a plan drawn up under the junta. Although little had been done while the colonels were actually in power, the same Athens-appointed officials were in office after the junta fell and carried on as if nothing had happened. Local objections to the total loss of all the area's summer grazing meant nothing in the highly centralized bureaucracy. The development of nearly all the worst aspects of Greek tourism started in this era of authoritarian government.

Only in some areas of Crete and Rhodes and a large part of Corfu has this kind of mass tourism taken over. But it is a horrible warning, not least because such development is the goose that kills the golden egg. In Greece, as elsewhere, the package holiday industry is declining, as many tire of the beach, cheap drink and little else. And Greek tourism faces other, more immediate, problems. Numbers of visitors dropped to almost nil because of proximity to the Middle East during the Gulf War and the tally of rich Americans visiting dropped after the security scares and criticism of Athens airport during the Reagan years.

The events of 1985 are important in this context and illustrate how vulnerable the Greek tourist industry is to political pressures and diplomatic manipulation. After the hijacking of TWA flight 847 over Greece in June 1985 by Lebanese members of the Shiite Hezbollah group, President Reagan gave a national television broadcast about the hostage crisis it had precipitated, focusing on alleged security deficiencies at Athens airport where, it was claimed, the hijackers' weapons had been smuggled on to the plane. Reagan said that the US State Department would be issuing a travel advisory warning of the alleged careless security, even though the flight in question had been through Cairo, where the weapons could well have originated. The advisory hit the lucrative but vulnerable industry at the height of the season, with Pan Am cancelling all its Greek flights and many thousands of Americans their holidays. The Greek Tourist Organization estimated later that the advisory cost Greece $400 million.

So a new approach to tourism is needed. Whatever else happens in the next few years, Greece is going to get more expensive for the ordinary person as the single European Market begins to operate. In particular, alcohol taxes are likely to be harmonized, removing at a stroke the inexpensive drinks that are an attractive part of a Greek holiday. The Greek authorities have a number of worthy and imaginative approaches but it remains to be seen what will materialize from them.

The classic solution of most countries has been to specialize and go upmarket in the way that the Algarve, for instance, has established a near-monopoly on a special type of golfing holiday. But this sort of tourism means long-term planning, a strong partnership between the public and private sector and enlightened local planning policies which simply do not exist in many parts of Greece. And there is the problem of the relationship between Athens and the islands. Many islands had very depressed economies before the arrival of tourists and the temptation to make quick money and not worry too much about long-term problems has been strong. Many of the smaller islands have extremely weak local government structures and a large influx of outsiders during the tourist season who have no permanent stake in the local society, still less in the preservation of the environment. There is little trust in the Athenian bureaucrats and policy-makers, particularly if they stop local interests making investments that seem to be needed.

There are some success stories, though, and one is the planning and organization of the souvenir industry. Visitors can buy holiday mementoes of a higher standard in design and manufacture than those to be found in most European countries, and the mountains of ugly junk that dominate souvenir shops in Spain are not quite as evident in Greece. Traditional objects, especially statues, have been copied using modern high technology manufacturing methods, making the timeless images of ancient Greece available to visitors on a modest budget.

The challenge for Greek tourism in the 1990s is to find a partnership between private initiative and government coordination, especially in the environmental field. Many Greeks have become complacent about tourism, seeing it as an inevitable annual invasion that has many disadvantages but enables Greece to pay its bills. But a renewal of investment and the international promotion of Greece, better facilities and higher hotel standards for the more discriminating tourist, and more facilities for families, will be needed. However romantic it may have been in the Sixties and Seventies, if the single market means anything in Greece, it may well be that the days of the backpacker as the symbol of Greek tourism are numbered. But it is not easy to see what will replace them. The hedonistic gastronome middle classes are not going to give up their restaurants in the Dordogne for the fare of an average taverna; new destinations such as Florida have much more to offer small children; and places further afield, such as the new resorts of South-East Asia, cater for the energetic and trendy young. And although popular interest in the classical world is certainly great, as the response to translations of Homer and television series on archaeology show, those with a traditional classical education who provided a hard core of independent travellers are on the decline. Greek tourism is in danger of falling between the two stools of being too expensive for the mass market and not offering enough to the more specialized traveller.

7. Archaeology

> At this moment – January 3rd 1809 – besides what
> has already been deposited in London, an Hydriot
> vessel is in the Piraeus to receive every portable
> relic. Thus, as I heard a young Greek observe in
> common with many of his countrymen – for, lost as
> they are, they yet feel on this occasion – thus may
> Lord Elgin boast of having ruined Athens.
>
> – Byron, Notes to 'Childe Harold'

In his autobiographical memoir Heinrich Schliemann, the great
excavator of Troy and Mycenae, referred to his temperament,
his 'natural disposition for the mysterious and the marvellous',
as something that led him towards archaeology and his epoch-
making excavations in the nineteenth century. But for modern
archaeologists their habitat is as much the science laboratory
as the sunlit hillside smelling of pine and lemon blossom – and
heavy work with pickaxe and shovel.

How far digging up the past has really changed is a moot
point. It is a political question that goes to the heart of the
relationship between Greece and its northern neighbours.
Schliemann's obsessive rediscovery of the Mycenaean world is
inextricably linked to the enormous influence images of classical Greece had on nineteenth-century German intellectual life
as, for example, the power of the classical images in Hegel's
philosophy. In a less attractive context the excavations at
Olympia were a major influence on what was to become
fascist architecture in Italy and Germany. In many cases, not

only in Greece, the excavation process seems now to be an exact mirror of colonialism, with monuments removed lock, stock and barrel to museums in northern Europe. The Pergamon Altar in Berlin is perhaps a case in point and the Elgin Marbles are by no means a rare example.

In the United Kingdom controversy has centred on what should be done about these great statues. The sculptures from the Parthenon were removed from the Acropolis in 1817 by Lord Elgin under a permit granted by the Ottoman government and have always been seen by Greece as stolen property which ought to be returned. No one could regard Elgin as an archaeologist, he was merely the most prominent – his defenders would say the most influential and successful – of the long line of eighteenth-, nineteenth- and twentieth-century travellers who borrowed, bought, begged or stole statues from the ancient world. As early as 1623 Sir Thomas Roe, the British ambassador to the Sublime Porte in Constantinople, wrote to the Earl of Arundel that 'about Troy, Zizium, and all the way to Aleppo, are innumerable pillars, statues and tombstones of marbles, with inscriptions in Greek; these must be fetched at charge, and secretly; but if we ask leave, it cannot be obtained . . .' In the view of his defenders Elgin and his ilk may have had doubtful motives but they preserved statues that otherwise would have been lost – even if they are now in the wrong places. For example, the Aegina marbles, housed in the Munich museum, were rescued in 1811 from the Doric temple on the island of Aegina in the Saronic Gulf near Athens as the local peasants were breaking up the temple and selling the marble for the price of chalk to make cement. The Germans undoubtedly saved these marbles from oblivion – and at a very low cost. But the whole process reflects foreigners 'giving' the Greek people a past of which they were previously unaware.

This seems remote from the world of contemporary archaeology: the highly organized academic congresses, the tidy and self-confident worlds of the foreign schools, like the British School in Kolonaki, with its great library, beautiful gardens dense with acanthus and mimosa, and a tennis court that looks as if it should belong in Oxford or Cambridge. When PASOK came to power in 1981 part of its programme was to close down foreign archaeological schools as relics of foreign and imperialistic influence in Greece. That they were not shut down might at first sight not seem significant; after all, a great deal of PASOK's programme fell by the wayside. What is important is that the schools were threatened at all; a great many intelligent Greeks disliked their presence and agreed with the PASOK proposals. Ancient history is enormously important in Greece and the loss of the Elgin Marbles and similar treasures is bitterly felt. But northern Europeans may feel with some justice that the treasures have been well looked after in their museums. None the less, the modern archaeologist in the foreign schools in Athens is seen as Elgin's descendant by some Greeks.

Archaeological life in contemporary Greece has often little to do with dramatic finds of great treasures and this is one of the reasons why the foreign schools have survived. Considerable time and energy is applied to using modern scientific techniques to analyse objects excavated decades ago which now belong to Greek museums. Science has advanced dramatically in the last generation and archaeological investigations involve the use of high-tech equipment that Greece would find difficult to finance on its own. And as the country is still covered with thousands of unexcavated sites threatened by industrial or commercial development, changes in agricultural practices or just simply by general environmental degeneration, it is all hands on deck among archaeologists to try to save them – or at least to excavate them professionally and record their contents and location before the bulldozers move in. In these difficult circumstances to expel the foreign archaeological community would have deprived Greece of an invaluable corps of experts in the battle against development.

A vital but deeply unglamorous piece of work was undertaken by members of the British School in Athens at Tskona near Sparta in 1989. The history of this minor site is a paradigm for the threat to the past in Greece, although other countries too face similar problems with the destruction of valuable remains in Britain or the ruination of sites from different cultures in Turkey, caused by the flooding of the Tigris and Euphrates valleys for irrigation schemes. Tskona was one of several hundred unexcavated sites described by members of the British School in their survey of the southern Peloponnese area of Lakonia carried out between 1983 and 1988. In 1984 Tskona was examined by a team who noted that the small hilltop seemed to be suffering rapid erosion. The cause was almost certainly overgrazing that had destroyed the natural scrub cover and allowed winter torrents to wash away the thin layer of protective soil. This was hardly a new problem in Greece as much of the ancient forest had been lost by Plato's time.

But the site was also only a kilometre to the east of Sparta's main rubbish tip, a major fire hazard to the surrounding countryside in the bone-dry summer months. This was noted by surveyors in 1984 who found telltale traces of terracotta statuettes, indicating that Tskona was probably an ancient religious centre. In 1985 the threat to the site was increased when the local farmer with grazing rights over the land started to cultivate part of it with a heavy tractor-drawn plough, scraping off much of the surface soil in the process. In July 1988 the disastrous fire that archaeologists had long feared destroyed thousands of acres in the vicinity, fully exposing the top of the hill and accelerating the erosion rate.

The British School organized an emergency survey in the late summer of 1988; the necessary excavation permits were applied for and work started on site on 8 May 1989 and carried on until 9 June when all surviving ancient structures had been completely excavated. In England it is perhaps customary to think of rescue archaeology in terms of our cities, where developers of offices or factories have to be persuaded to delay their plans to allow Celtic or Roman remains to be recorded – while we peer through holes in hoardings at the archaeologists at work. In Greece the same activities take place on top of beautiful hills, miles from any city, but the ancient remains are no less threatened there than in Blackfriars or York.

Tskona duly turned out to be a prehistoric cult centre dating from the eighth century BC. Most of the tiny statuettes recovered were concerned with human reproduction: bulging little pregnant women and roughly carved ithyphallic men. The cult seemed to have continued on the site for several hundred years but the excavation report commented: 'the absolute chronology of Tskona is imprecise and incomplete' and 'there is little to say of the nature of the cult itself'.

Now the hilltop is left to goats and tractors, and the artefacts will go to museums, once the scientists at the British School laboratory have finished with them. Although it does add to knowledge, this type of excavation is pretty routine and the few weeks on site for archaeologists are preceded by a great deal of paperwork and difficult negotiation with local interests.

Others are active in the 'rescue' business but the ends of science and academic knowledge of the past are not theirs. The little terracottas at Tskona, discovered on or near the surface by the British School survey team, could as easily have been found by anybody in the right place on the hill looking down at the narrow, stony and eroded gullies. Although there are stringent laws against illegal excavation, it is quite easy in many parts of Greece to dig up artefacts without any chance of discovery. This is particularly so in the drier areas of the southern mainland and on the islands, more difficult in the wooded north. Crete is a special problem for the *ephors* (regional heads of the Greek Archaeological Service) as it is large, dry and rich in unexcavated sites of all periods, and farmers ploughing perfectly legally often turn up priceless ancient pottery.

There is a black market network in Athens where these finds can be sold. The peasant receives a tiny sum and the artefact is passed through numerous middlemen, frequently in Switzerland, before ending up with private collectors in the United States. In practice the laws against export of antiquities are very difficult to enforce, given the long land borders that Greece has and the countless small boats in island and mainland harbours which are rarely subject to customs checks in the summer season. Greek government officials try to hold the line as best they can and there have been notable successes in recent years, often at the point of sale in organizations like Christie's and Sotheby's, rather than in Greece itself.

Some of the greatest finds of the century, such as the classical bronze statues now exhibited in the Acropolis museum, were found in Aegean shipwrecks. Basic scuba-diving equipment has meant that almost anybody can, in theory, scour the seabed to find – and loot – ancient remains. But underwater archaeology is an extremely expensive and complex business done professionally, with detailed surveys of the seabed followed by meticulous description before anything is removed. The international experts, even those in the best-funded American universities, have long lists of potential sites to explore, delayed by lack of finance.

With the sea, as with the land, archaeology is a political minefield. The government can hardly discourage popular interest in the treasure-hunting side, not least because some of the greatest discoveries in archaeological history have been the work of obsessive amateurs rather than of trained and supervised professionals – or have happened by chance when fishermen dredged up significant objects in their nets which pointed to the existence of an ancient shipwreck. And archaeology has provided the Greek tourist industry with a potent lure for the visitor to enter the landscape of the ancient world.

A great deal depends ultimately on the art market and how it works. It will never be possible to stamp out the black market in antiquities in Athens as long as the peasants can make more money from selling one ancient wine bowl than they can earn by a year's hard work. But eventually almost all antiquities of any value must pass through one or other of the major salerooms. Even if the objects were originally sold directly to unscrupulous elderly private collectors, they are often put up for sale after their death by relatives or executors not too long after they were stolen or illegally exported. The salerooms have the most modern scientific techniques for identifying the origin of an antiquity; for instance, the type of clay used in a pot can be isolated so that it is possible to say exactly where it came from. There is consequently little excuse for buying objects which should not have been in the possession of their current owners. Unfortunately the record of some of the big international salerooms has not been very good and recently a prominent figure in one of the best-known and most prestigious companies was accused of handling stolen goods. Although employees of these organizations may have the highest moral standards, it seems that some in essence embody the mentality of an Elgin in modern form, for whom the physical preservation of the antiquity, even if it has to be removed from its Greek landscape, is all that matters. The unspoken implication is often that the precise legality does not necessarily matter much in these circumstances, specifically the Greek laws against illegal export of ancient finds. Many people might find this attitude a good deal more reprehensible than Elgin's, for whatever can be said against the Scottish lord he had a genuine wish to preserve ancient statuary for the public good. The modern dealer on the 'grey' market in antiquities almost always ensures that the statue or art work disappears from public view into a secretly held private collection.

But apart from this somewhat depressing aspect, there is much to hope for. Great discoveries are still being made by inspired individuals, transforming our understanding of the past and providing deeply evocative monuments for future generations of tourists who will generate large sums of money for Greece. Perhaps the best most recent example is the work of Professor Spyridon Marinatos on the volcanic island of Santorini, ancient Thira. The group of islands between Ios and Crete was the scene of one of the largest explosions known in the earth's history and has been considered by many ancient historians as the site of the mythical kingdom of Atlantis, described by Plato in his dialogues *Timaeus and Critias*, and destroyed by a huge tidal wave. Thira was probably the site of the city he calls Metropolis, taken up in the great black-and-white film of the same name by the German pioneer Fritz Lang.

After many years' study and work on Thira, Professor Marinatos came to the conclusion that Minoan Crete and Thira had been destroyed not by earthquakes but by the volcanic eruption of Thira itself, a theory he had formed as a young man on the island. His excavations at the coastal site of Akrotiri were rewarded by the discovery of a wonderful Minoan Pompeii, an extensive and well-preserved Bronze Age settlement dating from about 1500 BC. Although the site is only partially excavated, it is possible to see urban life virtually intact with houses and buildings, including their fine wall frescoes, and remains of food and possessions preserved under the pumice stone and ash. It seems that the inhabitants must have had some warning of the cataclysm as no human remains have been found and valuable objects seem to have been removed.

Whatever emerges, Akrotiri is a tribute to the vision and persistence of Professor Marinatos and to his tenacity in argument with critics in the archaeological establishment who did not believe that the Minoan world had been destroyed in this way – and also to his skill in excavation. The results can be seen at the site itself, an opportunity to venture into an ancient Minoan town among the lizards and bare rocks on Santorini. After bringing this relic of the Minoan world to life, Professor Marinatos was killed in a minor accident on the site. A touching small memorial stands inside the ancient house where he died.

Another great archaeologist who died recently was Professor Manolis Andronikos, excavator of the Vergina tombs of the royal family of Macedonia, probably including that of Philip II. Although excavations at Vergina had long been in hand, it was the combination of luck, inspired judgement and experience that brought the great gold wreaths of oak leaves, the silver ossuaries, the ivory reliefs and the marble statues to light in 1977. But, as always, politics and archaeology are not far apart. Professor Andronikos notes in his book on the excavations that the palace lay 'beyond the thick belt of leafy trees which mark clearly the course of the Aliakmon River where the entire Macedonian plain unfolds before the eye like an unending prairie'. This volume, and popular versions of it, are now prominently on sale at Greek airports because the discovery of the tombs shows conclusively the Greek nature of Macedonia in antiquity, an issue in the disputes over the future of the neighbouring southern part of former Yugoslavia. Andronikos, a man of great dignity, with the highest intellectual and personal qualities, came to Greece as a child refugee from Asia Minor, and it is very sad that his discoveries, which should illuminate humanity, are caught up in the growing Balkan controversies about identity and new nationalisms.

8. *Athens and the Urban Crisis*

> ANTIGONE: The city is Athens, that I know, but
> not this place.
> OEDIPUS: Of course it is Athens – the roads are
> crowded with people telling us of
> Athens.
>
> – Sophocles, *Oedipus at Colonus*

In many senses Athens is the Ideal City in our culture, somewhere to encounter the wisdom of antiquity physically and intellectually. Istanbul is more remote, no longer Constantinople, once *I Polis* itself, the queen of cities, but now a vast driving megalopolis nine million strong that has qualities of its own but is certainly not ideal. Istanbul is also foreign in a sense that Athens is not – eastern, Moslem, culturally different. Athens seems to be ours, touchable, with mimosa flowers in March breaking into yellow dust and the welcoming glow of its buildings in the heat of a summer night. Even Jerusalem has lost much of its cultural power in a secular age. Under illegal Israeli occupation for many years, it is a holy city that should belong to the world but has been partly taken over by zealots. Athens is holy ground, too, but open and accessible.

But Athens is also the city of the *nefos* – the cloud of air pollution that can bring normal life to a standstill – of awful traffic jams, of non-existent public transport in many areas and a housing shortage but, as yet, no homeless. On one

August day with the temperature over a hundred, feeling ill and with the doctors on strike, I could hardly see across Omonia Square past the glass statue because of the *nefos*, the car jammed solid in traffic. In the south-east corner of the city your ears are assaulted by deafening noise from planes landing at the airport. Athena, the ancient goddess of wisdom, may have lived here once but her knowledge seems to have escaped the urban planners. However, as Kevin Andrews pointed out, there *is* a Greek god involved, not one best known like Zeus or Hermes but the Goddess of Strife. Togetherness is part of being Greek, even if it means endless minor and sometimes major conflict, as Hesiod, one of the earliest of ancient Greek poets, pointed out centuries before Christ was born.

How far Athens is actually a western city at all is debatable. In one sense it certainly is in that its period of modern growth began with Greek Independence, but the old heart of Athens around the Acropolis is, to all intents and purposes, Turkish, particularly the souvenir quarter around Monastiraki. And the whole of Plaka itself was an Albanian quarter in the nineteenth century, with the Albanian language used in the law courts and in public business. *Plaka* in Greek means a slab or paving-stone, but it is also Albanian for old – the old quarter. It seems odd that the Plaka area, which contains the largest concentration of tourist shops in one place in the world and which sells Hellenism in the form of millions of statues, rugs or ashtrays shaped like the Parthenon, is not wholly Greek. Nineteenth-century Athens grew as a result of external events and this process has continued to the present day. Organic growth, even of the kind in nineteenth-century London, has not really happened in the capital, rather there have been a series of long periods of stagnation, even decline, interrupted by dramatic influxes of hundreds of thousands of people. Patterns of urban growth in Greece have less to do with gradualism than with the unpredictable political life within the country. This relates to the arbitrary way in which a city works, or doesn't, and to the many districts which look similar externally, in terms of the modern concrete buildings, but which are of completely different cultures.

Athens is a city of strangers with as many as 40 per cent of today's inhabitants born elsewhere. Greek loyalty is ultimately to the birthplace, even if this is an inhospitable rocky island in the Aegean or a poverty-stricken mountain village in Thessaly. Athens may be an irresistible magnet but for many Athenians it is not their home and never will be. Major exceptions are the intellectuals who tend to live, love and work in Athens, even if it means commuting each week to a university hundreds of miles away in Crete or Yannina. But for most Athenians there is always a home elsewhere and civic problems are complicated by this fact.

A generation or two earlier, there used to be a home that existed in reality elsewhere. After the disaster of the Greek army in Asia Minor in 1922 in the final apocalypse of the *Megali Idea* (Great Idea) that had dominated so much of Greek political life in the late nineteenth century – the scheme to recover lost Greek territories in Asia Minor – the Greek quarter of Smyrna (modern Izmir) was attacked, and the Greek and Armenian communities there, numerous and often wealthy, with a sophisticated, sensual, cosmopolitan culture, were destroyed. Hundreds of thousands of refugees fled into Greece – the Swarm of Wasps, as it was known – carrying little more than the family icons. The destruction of Smyrna was a terrible event which haunts the Greek imagination and it is still possible to come across destitute elderly refugees who are in that miserable state in Greece – without family. On Poros many years ago I remember a ragged old man who lived in little more than a shed and who spent his days sitting by the statue of Demosthenes, staring into space. Perhaps his mind was full of the images of 1922 – the fall of the city, the crackle of flames, the screams of women violated by troops from Anatolia, the butchery of the men – a vision that has echoed throughout Greek literature since the fall of Troy itself. Poros was very underpopulated in the early years of this century and many Asia Minor refugees were sent there to settle among the lemon groves and pine forests. The old man was a reminder of past turmoil, lost in a beautiful island landscape.

But many more refugees were settled in Athens itself. The area between Athens and Piraeus, hitherto open fields or factories, became a vast shanty town where over half a million people lived in squalid conditions. The best description of this grim *bidonville* world is to be found in Henry Miller's *Colossus of Maroussi*, an account of Greece in the late Thirties, with the houses of corrugated iron, Armenian soothsayers, and prostitutes making for the bars of Piraeus. It is a masterful evocation of the slums and it is significant that when Miller saw them, fifteen years after they had been built, they still flourished. The government did what it could and gradually better housing was provided and employment found. But this was before the days of United Nations refugee organizations and, with economic depression in Greece and actual bankruptcy in 1932, progress was inevitably slow. The suburbs around Nea Smyrni were inhabited almost exclusively by these refugees who brought the world of Asia Minor to Athens – the music of rembetika, hashish, new words to the language – and bitter competition for the available work and housing. They were a sub-culture both in social terms, in the resettlement districts, and in politics, where they provided several leaders and many members of the fledgling Communist party. One of the most accessible introductions to the world they left is to be found in the early chapters of Peter Evans's excellent biography of shipping magnate Aristotle Onassis, *Ari*. The billionaire's family came from Asia Minor and the devastating ruthlessness and driving energy that characterized

Onassis's *modus operandi* was born in what his father called the challenge of the Smyrna waterfront, the vibrant Levantine business culture.

An interesting sidelight on the Smyrna issue is provided in the rivalry between the Onassis and Niarchos shipping dynasties, the aristocratic Niarchoses regarding the Onassises as little more than Smyrna upstarts. But their attitude and that of old money Athens was far from universal and the people of Athens have a lot to be proud of during this period. There was hardly a family that did not make room for the refugees, a large proportion of whom were women, children or old people. Although they put an intolerable burden on the economy, the refugees provided an economic stimulus and some had valuable skills. Employing the women was a problem which was to some extent solved by setting up rug-weaving workshops whose products could be sold in the Athens markets or exported.

Hardly had the city begun to integrate these people, as best it could, than the grim years of starvation during the War began, followed afterwards by physical battles in the streets for the political destiny of Greece. The starvation of the winter of 1942 was terrible, with huge crowds wandering the streets in search of bread. Many did not survive the night and lorries picked up the dead early every morning and buried them in mass graves. Most families had a loss to mourn, whether from hunger, the occupying forces or the Civil War. The physical fabric of the city also suffered badly. The first stage was after the Occupation started, with the Axis troops trying to crush the resistance. A central objective was to find the EAM printing presses, hidden deep in the labyrinthine streets of working-class Peristeri, which poured forth a stream of anti-German pro-resistance propaganda. Some presses were successfully hidden throughout the Occupation, but when others were found the Axis forces dynamited whole streets and started fires in reprisal. Then also, after the liberation, the ELAS batteries were set up along, and above, Syngrou Street, linking Athens and Piraeus in an effort to prevent the British army being resupplied. In the chaos of the battle for Athens many old landmarks were destroyed.

The Civil War brought refugees, mostly from the north. Some were economic migrants, some fleeing political discrimination. Until a year or two ago there was an Epirot taverna in the heart of tourist Monastiraki serving bean soup and lentils to hard-up old men. On the wall was a large framed photograph of Aris Velouchiotis, founder of ELAS, black-bearded, black-bonneted, on his horse in a Roumeli forest. People from particular places stayed together, those from a single village congregated in one apartment block. Then the industrial boom of the early Fifties brought people from the country looking for work, believing all the village stories about dollars pouring into Athens that could find their way into the pockets of ordinary Greeks.

If this did happen, then the usual ambition was to own a house – and whole districts were taken over by illegal developments, spreading far north into Attica. Housing is a DIY process in Greece, as many Greeks, then and now, do not have access to much credit, let alone mortgage facilities, and in a society so often struck by disruption people have an understandable horror of long-term debt commitments. Greeks do not on the whole like or trust their banks very much and judging by the behaviour of many bank officials towards their customers, the feeling is mutual. Most of the new Athenians in the Fifties and early Sixties had very little capital and it is not unusual today to find a family living in an unfinished house who have been slogging away at it for twenty or thirty years.

So each suburb tends to reflect settlement patterns that go back a long time. Broadly speaking, the traditional east–west dimension of settlement in most western cities, with prosperous middle-class districts in the west and run-down and industrial areas in the east, is reversed in Athens, with eastern Athens desirable and the west verging on the industrial and commercial areas of Piraeus. Some of the approach roads to the west are a wilderness of scrapyards, derelict land and an unbelievable mess of signs, screaming traffic and general urban dereliction. The road to Eleusis is perhaps the most tragic of these urban nightmares; in antiquity it was one of the great processional roads along which people made their way to the home of the Eleusinian mysteries, to the secret world of ritual and initiation that dominated one aspect of ancient Greek religious life. But Eleusis now is the Eleusis of the cement factory and the ship repair yards, and the atmosphere, overlaid with fumes from the nearby petrochemical complexes, is about as far from the world of spiritual health that Eleusis represented as can be imagined. But the stones remain, bewildering ruins that need specialist interpretation; lizards run in and out of the cracks in the masonry as they have for thousands of years, oblivious of their surroundings.

Settlement to the north does, though, reflect other western cities, with the rich of Kifissia living uneasily adjacent to one of the main roads leading north to Thessaloniki. It is an empty, soulless place, where very large houses alternate with foreign-run schools and private clinics which specialize in every type of malady announced in detail on little brass plates. The area is obsessed by security, with electric gates and angry dogs a speciality, not surprisingly given that several of the November 17th terrorist groups' attacks on foreign diplomats and businessmen have taken place here. Kifissia is where the heads of American corporations in Greece tend to live, as well as embassy staff and some of the wealthiest people in Athens. The shops are a long row of foreign names, not only the predictable Benettons but French couturiers like Louis Feraud.

It is difficult to avoid the feeling, even in a friend's house, of being culturally separate from most of Greece and this feeling intensifies out on the streets. They are quiet, suburban and totally lacking in the vibrant popular life, the colour and sound and smells, that makes Athens. Kifissia does not have the style of the wealthy inner-city areas, like Kolonaki, where the same French shops are to be found but along with old tavernas, local wine cellars run by a man from Santorini and a good place to get your shoes repaired. But Kolonaki is not loved by all Athenians; one nickname is Kolograd (arsehole town).

Part of the problem for Kifissia is that many houses are not lived in for significant parts of the year. Many company houses are maintained as secure habitations for senior executives but in the nature of things they are often not in Greece, even if they are based there. Many foreigners' houses, especially the not-insignificant Arab element, have been bought as safe boltholes in the event of political turmoil at home. During the Gulf War I met a pleasant young Iraqi who had been stranded in Athens and was working in a souvenir shop, finding it exceptional to be in the city for more than his normal fortnight a year. And there are the wealthy Greeks who, if they do live in Athens all the time, officially, will almost certainly have other houses. An acquaintance of mine has, as well as a house in Athens, a summer refuge on an island, a house in London and an apartment in New York. Despite legislators' efforts, there has been no effective inheritance or capital taxation in Greece since the War and efforts to control hard currency leaving the country have been unsuccessful. Many of the types of business where real money can be made are involved with the entrepot role of Athens and Piraeus, shipping and transport most obviously, but there are others and many involve international banks and complex trading patterns, with different currencies employed. Even if the Greek tax authorities were efficient, it would be easy for people to exploit legitimate loopholes in the law to build up their personal wealth. Greeks, generally, do not trust paper investment media very much and have lived recently in a world of continual drachma devaluation. Property is a favoured solution to this problem, outside Greece if possible. If all this seems very considerable wealth, it omits the sure sign of the Greek super-rich, a Swiss base.

But eastern and western Athens are both on the margins of a culture in a city that otherwise is remarkably homogeneous in its external way of life. For nearly everybody there is the crush to get to work, whether on the bus or in the traffic jam (work starting early in the morning, especially in the summer), then the long slow lunch and siesta, and the reopening for business from teatime until late at night. It is a punishing routine which involves two forays into the rush hour if you go home for lunch, four journeys a day, in the summer at least. Some people who have their own business can avoid doing so, no doubt the source of an Athens catchphrase about hot summer afternoons being the time to start an affair. But more than in most European cities, there is a shared and democratic popular life, an enormous sense of genial humanity among the muddle and cheerful rivalry, the colour of the markets, the welcome of the tavernas and the never-ending fascination of the rough and tumble of political life matched by that of the streets.

But the city is in crisis none the less. Although, as European cities go, Athens is remarkably safe and happily free of the threat of violence so common elsewhere, there is a sense of social fabric in decline. The worst single problem is, of course, the *nefos*. For a period it seemed as if it could be tolerated by the inhabitants, even if it was very difficult for visitors, but during 1990 and 1991 several factors finally moved the city authorities and the government to action. The very hot spells in three summers resulted in many deaths from respiratory diseases that most Athens doctors ascribed to the *nefos*. Tourist numbers started to drop and the smog was cited by the Olympic authorities as one of the main reasons, along with security problems and facilities, for the failure of Athens to be selected as the site for the 1996 Olympic Games. This hurt. The government had put a great deal of effort into the bid for the Games and the penny seems finally to have dropped that something fundamental had to be done about the pollution problem. Significantly, a good part of the obloquy for the Olympic failure came to rest on Mr Miltiades Evert, the mayor of the city for some years and a leading pretender for the leadership of the New Democracy party, but his chances of succeeding Mr Mitsotakis for the party leadership were only marginally damaged. So a radical programme of measures has been adopted, all directed at the transport crisis, with the pedestrianization of large areas of the city centre, the removal from the roads of some of the oldest cars responsible for a high proportion of the pollution, a scheme of road sharing so that car owners are only allowed to use their vehicles on alternate days, and for the first time bus and taxi lanes to encourage people to use public transport. Although there will be a considerable delay before the problem is solved, it does appear that at last the political will is there to tackle it. The next step will be to try to see what can be done about the central-heating boilers and their fumes which often cause serious *nefos* problems on still winter days. The city is paying a high price, quite literally in terms of lost tourism, for the years of unplanned urban and industrial development in the Fifties, Sixties and Seventies. The Greeks, especially the younger Greek males, are profoundly attached to their cars, and driving in the city sometimes seems to be an alternative to combat. The death rate on Greek roads generally is very high, the highest in the European Community, and it may take more than the useful but modest programme of measures announced so far to bring the motor car in Athens properly under control.

In other respects the development of the city depends on the continuation of the programme of public investment in facilities that started in earnest under PASOK; previously derelict land sprouted basketball courts and small public gardens, and children's playgrounds appeared everywhere. In the public health field there is a large and ambitious sewerage scheme under construction that will drastically reduce pollution in the Saronic Gulf, a sign of the respect for the sea and a determination to avoid the looming environmental crisis beginning to affect Istanbul. Raw sewage will be pumped out to a little island off the coast of Piraeus and will be treated and dispersed there. It is a scheme far in advance of those in most Mediterranean littoral cities and something of which Athenians can justly be proud. There is perhaps some substance in the complaint of the city fathers that the foreign press has concentrated exclusively on the problems of the *nefos* and has failed to give praise where it is due in respect of the efforts to humanize the city and bring in modern concepts of urban planning. But they have a difficult task. Some first-time visitors come to Athens with an image of the society of a fifth-century city as a near-perfect world, and they expect to find a sense of it in the modern city. This is a tall order for even the richest and most tranquil city as, say, the drug problem in modern Zurich shows, and well nigh impossible for one that has a history of political and social upheaval. So perhaps the visitor should be sympathetic to the many problems in trying to civilize modern Athens. None the less the city authorities should have listened to foreign (and domestic) critics of the direction things were going.

But the magic of the city remains, although it is best not to try to look for it in a conscious way. Plenty of time is needed, a willingness to merge into the background, above all time to spend in the city in winter when visitors are few and Greeks are left more or less to themselves. It is a labyrinth of a city, just as much as one to be found in mythology, and perhaps the first essential to remember is the ability to get lost in both a physical and psychological sense. The physical is all too easy as so many streets and blocks of flats look the same. The second is more difficult but it is the same process as the one involved in learning the Greek language, a willingness to surrender a kind of northern European independence. Then the shadows in dark churches will reveal their mystery, stallholders in the markets will behave differently, a strange new sense of energy and lightness of step will become apparent. Athens is a great humane city with an almost infinite capacity to make the visitor feel at home and an equal facility to renew mind and spirit. Perhaps that is both its glory and its tragedy, for the same transparency and accessibility, its ability to assimilate the stranger into the conventions of metropolitan Greek life, also leads so many of its inhabitants to take it for granted, to neglect matters that need attention and so produce urban problems. But the energy remains, the popular indifference to the ancient past almost defying belief but founded on dedication to a fullness of life in the present, like Zorba on his journey to Crete. I remember a conversation on a bus many years ago with one of the first Athenians I met. When I asked the man what job he did, he replied, 'zo' (I exist in my way of life). It was partly a reply borne of defiance – he had done six months in gaol after the War for some offence he preferred not to disclose – but also a nod to eternity, meaning that he passed his short life in Athens, the greatest Greek city, and was determined to wring every drop from it.

9. Agriculture

Sweeter, shepherd, and more subtle is your song
Than the tuneful splashing of that waterfall
Among the rocks. If the Muses pick the ewe
As their reward, you'll win the hand-reared lamb;
If they prefer the lamb, the ewe is yours.

     – Theocritus, *The Idylls*

An influential study on the Greek economy, *A Political and Economic Survey 1939–53* by Bickham Sweet Escott, published in Britain in the 1950s, commented that in much of Greece agricultural techniques had changed little between Homer's time and the outbreak of the Second World War. Many people might feel that the judgement could be extended to the present day, the apparently timeless visual images are so strong: the olive groves with their annual rituals of pruning and harvesting, sheep and goats finding a meagre diet among the carob and thorn trees, elderly peasant ladies scrambling up fig trees to pick the crop in August, the ubiquitous vines. But a good deal has, and does, alter, even if the changes are not always obvious.

In the years since the Second World War crops that were once the mainstay of the economy in whole areas, such as tobacco in northern Greece, have declined in importance, while others have taken their place. In 1938, for instance, there was not a single peach exported from Thessaloniki and only 110 tons of grapes, whereas in 1959 over 23,000 tons of peaches and 4,000 tons of grapes left the port – and these kinds of exports have increased considerably since. Entry into the European Community and the development of better relations with the former Yugoslavia gave Greek farmers direct access to markets they could only have dreamt of in the past, coupled with a pattern of basic change in diet and cuisine in northern Europe that gave greater prominence to many Mediterranean products such as olive oil.

But within the general patterns there are considerable regional and local variations and generalizations are almost invariably incorrect. During the War, and the Civil War, many people abandoned their villages for a variety of reasons, starting with the traditional flight of refugees from danger, the wish to escape the extortions of various guerrilla groups, and as a result of the policies of right-wing governments in Athens who enforced population movements from villages in some areas to stop the Communist guerrillas receiving supplies. The damage to the traditional rural patterns of life was devastating and many people never went back to their villages, staying on in the cities or emigrating after the War ended. From this period dates that familiar and sad figure of most Greek villages, the widow seen against the landscape, looking after goats or a vegetable patch, with all her sons abroad, or seen in a queue at the bank, waiting to pay in the small cheque drawn in foreign currency that is all that stands between her and destitution.

But however devastating the Civil War was, its aftermath did in some respects bring a period of essential agricultural modernization that had been sought by all pre-war Greek governments but had never materialized. Up until the War, the pattern of land ownership had been based by and large on tiny peasant plots, just a few jealously guarded acres that were usually hopelessly uneconomic. The country was of necessity a heavy importer of wheat and cereals, and this vulnerability was seen tragically during the War with mass starvation in

Athens and the major cities when the supply of imports stopped. Over quarter of a million people died in the famine and there were terrible scenes of privation. These are not well known or remembered outside Greece, but they have coloured Greek attitudes to agriculture and land ownership, and much else. The editor of the Turkish newspaper *Vatan* who went to Greece on the first food ship sent there in 1942 described the situation in Piraeus:

What I saw in Greece exceeds a hundred times anything that has been written about her plight. It seemed to me as if I had entered Hell. When the ship's crew went ashore they were surrounded by hundreds of people crying, 'Give us a crumb of bread, we are dying of hunger.' And walking through the town, we were overcome with horror, the people we met looked like skeletons.

There was not a cat, dog or pet bird in Athens that had escaped being eaten. The suffering in the city was witnessed; the same mass starvation was not seen in the countryside but people lived in conditions of bitter hardship, often eating little but maize bread, beans and lentils, with many children dying of malnutrition and epidemic diseases. And the German and Italian troops had not been slow to help themselves to whatever food was available, with the villages powerless to resist. After the end of the conflict there was little to keep people in the villages and in the early Fifties peasants were drawn to the new factories in the burgeoning Athens basin. For some years there were high wages to be earned for the ex-villagers, particularly in the flourishing construction industry.

But like peasants everywhere, the Greek does not part with ancestral family land easily and the formation of larger agricultural units was slow in many areas. Most people during the wartime famine had kept alive only because the family had land and could grow crops. The memory of the horrors had not faded and there was no incentive to sell the family plot for probably a pathetically small sum. As the government found, it was one thing to get the peasant off his plot and into the urban labour market, but quite another to persuade the family to part with the land, especially as in many areas there was no regular or orderly method of transferring land and no figure more distrusted by the peasant than the Athens lawyer. Large proportions of the money available for agricultural investment had to be spent on restoring the livestock herds depleted by the Civil War. According to the official figures (not accurate but a guide to what was happening), the number of goats in the Evros prefecture area dropped from 92,000 in 1940 to 52,000 in 1947 and in 1957 it had still only risen to 82,000. Although this area of the north was severely affected by the War, and government policy had been to reduce flock levels, the same forces were at work elsewhere. Animal diseases had run rampant and by the end of the Civil War foot and mouth disease, anthrax, sheep pox and fowl cholera were prevalent. The decimation of the sheep and goat flocks had hit low-income families very severely as their main source of protein was home-produced cheese.

The policy response of the post-civil-war governments and their predominantly American agricultural advisers was a mixture of investment, restoring the shattered port and transport facilities, and a certain amount of adopting their left-wing opponents' policies in forming agricultural producers' cooperatives. Their main policy instrument was the Agricultural Bank, which offered preferential loans to farmers whose development plans were in line with government policy. At the same time a good deal of foreign livestock was imported, mainly American breeds of cows, to try to improve the national herd.

The American agricultural advisers spread their gospel with missionary zeal over rural Greece to wean peasants from traditional agriculture and towards what was called 'progressive',

that is, market agriculture. The main emphasis was to get
farmers to produce crops for sale rather than for subsistence.
How much was achieved is debatable and varied from place
to place. Where there was reasonable infrastructure and access
to large centres with new communities of urban customers, no
doubt substantial changes were realized but in the poorer
remote areas it was all rather a waste of time. The cooperatives
were a much more lasting achievement and one of the bases of
rural life in Greece.

Although accurate information is difficult to obtain, there is
no doubt that after the brief fillip provided by the post-civil-
war reconstruction period and accompanying foreign capital
inflows, stagnation returned in the 1950s. Although some
investments might have resulted in better products, the state
of rural transport was so bad that there was often no means
of getting these to market. Progress was made in opening up
the German market for wine and fruit, but the great step
forward for Greek agricultural production took place at the
same time, and for many of the same reasons, as the tourist
explosion in the Sixties. Both were entirely dependent on
revolutions in transport: air travel for tourists and the
motorway for goods. It was then possible, particularly when
allied to the development of the modern refrigerated lorry, to
get perishable agricultural products into west European and
Middle Eastern markets in first-class condition and on a
regular basis. The removal of tariff barriers and the deepening
association with the European Community were central to the
process and revolutionized some regions. The citrus growers
on the west coast of northern Greece, close to good land and
sea routes to northern Europe, became prosperous overnight.
But in other areas, perhaps as little as ten miles away, the old
way of life continued and subsistence farming did not totally
die out.

But all these changes of the Sixties and early Seventies,

however important, pale into insignificance beside the fact of full EC membership after 1981 and the Common Agricultural Policy. At a stroke a range of subsidies, grants, loans and new markets, never known to the Greek farmers, were open to them as well as membership of the most powerful agricultural lobby in the world. To say that agriculture was transformed is in some ways to say that Greece was transformed, at least by comparison with other Community members, as agriculture was a more important industry than in any other member state, making up 17 per cent of the economy compared with an EC average of 3.9 per cent. The country with the nearest comparable economy, Italy, showed a much faster drift from the land in the Seventies.

Even in 1981 land holdings were still dominated by the small peasant farm, with seven out of ten farms smaller than five hectares of usable agricultural land, and with very few large farms by Community standards. The main impact of membership has been in the form of production subsidies. In 1982 gross expenditure under the price guarantee system amounted to 685 million ECU out of a total community expenditure of 12,406 million ECU. The main crops to benefit in the first years of membership have been tobacco, fruit, cereals, vegetables and olive oil, although this has changed somewhat under the system of integrated Mediterranean programmes in more recent years. Tobacco has been a major beneficiary, taking up no less than 205 million ECU out of the 6,854 million ECU spent on Greek agriculture in a typical year in the early Eighties. But a major problem for Greek farmers has been the subsequent full accession to membership of Spain and Portugal. In the early years, traditional Greek products of say, oil and fruit, had not been very important to a Community dominated by northern dairy and cereal products, and Greek production had in many ways been complementary. The sums required from the EC for subsidy purposes were, in Brussels terms, small. But more recently there has been a tendency towards the development of mountains and lakes – of tomatoes, wine and fruit – and pressure has begun to build up to reform the Common Agricultural Policy to cut down on the direct price support system for Mediterranean farmers and to reduce overall production.

There is a clear political dimension to all this in Greece, as might be expected. One of the foundations of the PASOK government was its strength in rural areas and the success Papandreou was seen to have in dealing with the EC machine both in terms of the general price support system for Greek products and the particular achievements in the social and regional development programmes which meant, as only one example, that rural inhabitants had their old age pensions subsidized by the EC in the late Eighties. But the rural cooperative was one of the rocks on which the PASOK vote machine was built, and it would be an inauspicious development if subsidies and the number of small farmers were reduced. Many areas of rural Greece have a distinct thread of political radicalism, from the middle classes who suspect that the over-centralized bureaucracy in Athens knows little of their needs to the peasants who have the traditional country-dwellers' distrust of city-dwellers who ignorantly consume what they grow by the sweat of their brows.

The costs and benefits of EC membership in agriculture have been open to dispute. In the early Eighties it seemed as though a new vista was opening with booming exports of crops such as peaches and major investment in some regions that transformed local economies – such as the intensive vegetable-growing schemes in southern Crete. But, for most people, the miracle has faded. Messenia is as good a region to examine as anywhere. The basin of fertile land on the Messenian plain has been used for agriculture for millennia and it was in these fields that the helots toiled to maintain ancient

Sparta, with the power of the ancient city state in many ways linked to the fertility of Messenian agriculture.

In the nineteenth century long-neglected land had been brought back into cultivation, and the ports of Kalamata and Gythion grew on the basis of agricultural exports not only of olives, as might be expected, but of cotton from the important cotton-growing area in the Gythion hinterland. Road communications with Piraeus were bad or non-existent and shipping was an integral part of the agricultural economy. Until the time of the junta the means to get crops to market or, in the case of the olive oil industry, the presses were in the hands of a very small urban élite in the port towns. In Kalamata they were generally believed to operate as a cartel.

But Messenia, as elsewhere, has not been evenly developed. On the richer land, stretching from the western outskirts of Kalamata across the Parmisos river for about thirty kilometres and northwards towards the beginning of the central mountains, a great deal of money has been made with intensive use of irrigation and fertilizers, the drainage of previously swampy and unusable land, and investment in sales and marketing facilities so that the Kalamata olive is available in virtually every city in Europe. Yet twenty kilometres to the south of Kalamata, in the upper reaches of the Mani peninsular, Kalamata olives are growing that in many years are not picked at all, let alone sold or marketed. Another twenty or thirty kilometres to the south this is the norm, at least for olives growing on the hillier and less accessible land. An attempt to found a Mani olive-marketing organization along the lines of the Kalamata set up collapsed in the Seventies and has not been revived since. Rural depopulation affects many of these villages. Who owns these olives? Ironically many are owned by the same families to the north who are doing very nicely thank you out of the European Community and ultimately out of the pocket of the European taxpayer.

The reason for this state of affairs lies, like so much in Greece, both in the immediate and distant past. The immediate, or semi-immediate, reason is that the more remote areas of Messenia suffered the same sort of continuous depopulation as most other parts of mountainous Greece and there is a chronic labour shortage with nobody there to pick most of the olives. Local farmers who are struggling on would also say that olive oil prices are too low. The more historic reason is to do with the settlement pattern of the region after the Greek War of Independence. The town of Kalamata was very much a Turkish stronghold, as some features of its culture reflect today, and when the Turks left it was settled by Maniot peasants. But, as always in Greece, although the Maniots moved they did not part with the original family land, nor did those who settled on the better land on the Parmisos plain to the west of the city.

There is no incentive to sell the olive groves now as European Community producer subsidies are paid on what is grown rather than on what is marketed, so although growers may not bother to pick any of the Mani olives, they nevertheless obtain a certain amount of income from the groves. Nor is there a very efficient or functioning market in land, any more than there was after the end of the Civil War, especially in the more remote Mani regions, many areas of which are subject to long-running disputes between families that from time to time explode in bloody vendettas. There is also the problem, common all over Greece, especially in northern areas and in Crete where Turkish rule continued into this century, that many of the land deeds relating to particular holdings are written in Turkish and hardly anyone, even at the universities, and certainly not in provincial courts or lawyers' offices, is now capable of reading the language. So although one part of the plain of Messenia has fulfilled the hopes of the government, those of the agricultural experts in Brussels and of the peasant farmers themselves, another part of the same region preserves the past, as if in aspic or like the Maniot winter delicacy of thrush preserved in olive oil.

Just as many people do not now take to the subsistence life if it involves cultivation, others reject the traditional life of the shepherd. Flock numbers have decreased in many areas of Greece and this has undoubtedly benefited the general environment, so long a victim of overgrazing. But as with crops, generalizations are dangerous. In some parts of the north, and on some islands like Crete, the shepherd is still a common figure, paradoxically, often because of tourism and the supermarkets of northern Europe. A generation ago Greek yoghurt was almost unknown in northern Europe and pretty well unobtainable. Now almost every decent-sized supermarket in the EC sells one of the many brands, and sheep's yoghurt has become one of the great success stories of modern Greek business – demonstration of what a combination of EC producer subsidies, planning, and investment in modern production facilities and transport can achieve. But traditional patterns of migration have all but disappeared, at least in the archetypal forms of the north where whole communities of shepherds, especially the Vlachs and Sarakatsans, moved lock, stock and barrel between summer and winter habitation. In the Pindus, in particular, the black-caped Vlach is still a common sight but confined to the lowlands for a greater part of the year, his sheep likely to be eating 'improved' grass fed by EC fertilizers.

So although some of the timeless quality persists, there have been many changes in the Greek countryside and there are likely to be more as the politicians in Brussels endeavour to cut down on agricultural subsidies in the budget. But an overall impression of healthy development remains in all but the poorest and remotest areas, or those unlucky enough not to have a strong politician to put the local case for a share of

EC largesse in Athens. The grinding poverty of many areas really has gone and there is money for investment. On the whole it is used productively though many northern European taxpayers might raise their eyebrows if they knew the full extent to which loopholes in the Common Agricultural Policy were exploited. But these may well be the same taxpayers who come to Greece on holiday and bemoan the loss of agricultural land to tourist 'development' of the wrong kind. Many of them might, if they knew the whole picture, be prepared to forgive the Greek peasant if it keeps rural incomes up and an economically healthy agriculture in existence.

But there are clouds on the horizon although the Greek agricultural lobby seems largely unaware of them. Up until now, for instance, there has been little political opposition in most of Greece to the ever-increasing demands of agriculture on the water supply. Many rivers have been channelled and streams diverted to help the farmer boost production. But there is only a finite amount of water in Greece and if it is used on the farm it cannot be used in industry or by the tourist in the shower cubicle. There are disturbing signs in many parts of the country of recurrent serious water shortages, as over the last five years the Balkans, generally, have suffered a drought. Water rationing is expected to be introduced in Athens itself in the summer. The fact that the EC structural investment programmes are designed to help the farmer does not mean that they are necessarily environmentally sound, and it seems as if the major problems and challenges facing the farmer in Greece in the next generation will be connected to the harmonization of his activities with the environment, as much as anything else. In this respect, despite its unique character and history, Greek agriculture will face the same environmental crisis as elsewhere in Europe.

10. Religion: Oppression and Freedom

And there is another hill that is cleped Athos that is
so high that the shadow of him reacheth to Lemnos
that is an isle, and it is seventy-six mile between.

– Sir John Mandeville, *Travels*

The last paragraph of the Patriarch's obituary was brief: 'The election of the new Head of world Orthodoxy will take place in Constantinople according to the tradition of the Greek Orthodox Patriarchate and also according to Turkish law, which limits the candidacy for the position to those of Turkish nationality.' Patriarch Demetrios the First, a wizened old man born Demetrios Papadopoulos in a suburb of Istanbul in 1914, was head of world Orthodoxy for nineteen years before he died in October 1991. He succeeded the great Patriarch Athenagoras, a legendary figure who had led the Greek community in Turkey through some of the darkest years of persecution and religious intolerance and was thought irreplaceable. But Demetrios was beloved by his flock and respected by the Turks, not least for his charming personality.

The obituary sentence expresses the central dilemma of Orthodoxy today: the head of the Greek Church is not in Greece, and the succession is a matter of intense political importance for both Turkey and Greece. Although the Church is strong in Greece in a cultural sense (to be Greek is to be Christian is to be Orthodox), in other respects it is a church without a centre in the country. Although holy sites like Mount Athos and the rock monasteries of Meteora have great spiritual importance for Greeks, they play only a modest part in the administrative life of the Church.

The new Patriarch, previously Metropolitan Bartholomeos of Chalcedon, exemplifies the decline in numbers of the Greek community in Turkey in that he was born on the island of Imbros which now has virtually no Greeks left. A brilliant academic theologian, who speaks Italian, Latin, French, English and German, apart from Greek and Turkish, he travelled and taught widely before he became spiritual leader of more than 300 million Eastern Orthodox Christians. He is in his early fifties and should be able to give a degree of continuity to the patriarchiate, but he will need his formidable intellect and force of character to do so, surrounded as it is by so many palpable dangers.

The tragedy at the heart of the Greek Church can be experienced by a walk through the Fener quarter of Istanbul, a small, very old part of the city on the east side of the Golden Horn. The houses of the Greek merchants who controlled large sections of the trade of the Ottoman Empire are now derelict, rat-infested ruins inhabited by Kurdish refugees from the war zone in far south-east Turkey. At nearly every corner there are beautiful old churches built during the Byzantine period; many are blackened ruins with trees growing up through fallen roofs, victims of the anti-Greek riots that swept the city in 1956. Thousands of Greeks left as a result of these pogroms: the Greek population of the city has fallen from over 75,000 in the mid Fifties to only 3,000 today. Although it is possible to find Greek gold traders in the central bazaars in Istanbul, who make a living in exactly the same way in exactly the same place as their fellow Greeks have done for two thousand years, there is an unmistakable impression of a church and culture being slowly strangled by Turkish bureaucracy and cultural repression. It will be very difficult for such a small community to continue to produce men of the calibre and stature needed to give Orthodoxy leadership in the future, and many feel that in the long run the Church may not survive.

On the hill above Fener is the dark red-brick structure of the famous theological college of Megali tou Genous Skholi, closed for many years on the orders of the Turkish government, where, ironically enough, the deceased Patriarch studied. It is a long way from the pleasant, secure existence of a village priest in Arcadia or the more stressful life of a parish in Athens. It is further still from the Utopian beauty of many mountain monasteries, or Athos itself, where the divine appears to permeate the landscape to give even the most hardened atheist a glimpse of what Paradise might be like. Orthodoxy in Istanbul, for so long capital of the Christian world but now a brutally tough city, is fighting for its life. In 1992 there were over three hundred mosques under construction and Islamic fundamentalism is steadily gaining more adherents, as indicated by the results of the spring 1991 election in Turkey.

The Greek Orthodox Church is heir to a cultural tradition of vast antiquity and strength, ultimately that of the Roman Empire itself and of the long twilight of Byzantium. When the Empire was divided, the eastern half with its capital at Constantinople survived for hundreds of years under the Byzantines, finally succumbing to the Ottomans in 1453. The Church today has inherited much of the psychology and the attitudes of the theocratic Byzantine world, down to the explicitness involved in one of the Patriarch's many titles, that of archbishop of the 'New Rome'.

In the last years of the nineteenth and the beginning of the twentieth century there was a strong link at a practical political level between the Church and the policies of Greek irredentists (the word means unredeemed in Greek) who were trying to recover Greek territory, such as large areas of northern Greece that were not free of Turkish domination until 1913 and the end of the Second Balkan War, from the Ottomans. Generally speaking, even today, it is the bishops from these regions, like Metropolitan Sevastianos, who are the most ardent defenders of the interests of militant Greek nationalism against neighbouring states. In the past irredentism meant the disastrous expansion into Turkey of 1919–22 when, under the protection of the Entente powers of Britain and France, the Greek army sought to invade much of the country and re-establish Greek rule over the coastal cities of Asia Minor – a strange parallel to the Trojan War. The attempt ended with the catastrophe of Smyrna in 1922 and the beginning of a long process of Greek cultural decline in the region which has still probably not run its full course. Just as the Church was intimately involved in Greek expansion at Turkish expense during the nineteenth century, so it has been hostage to the decline in Greek culture in Turkey itself in the twentieth.

In other parts of the world the picture is very different. Millions of Greek Orthodox Christians live in Europe, the United States, Canada, New Zealand and Australia. There, churches flourish without fear of persecution or oppression and, as in nearly all émigré communities, the Church takes on an importance as a focus for cultural identity and numerous social and welfare organizations. The use of the Greek language does provide some historic links, just as under the long centuries of Ottoman rule one of the mainstays of Greekness was the use of the language in church services. Today the little Greek-American boys and girls who struggle through Saturday morning language classes in New York or Boston do so to understand something of the language of their church.

In these disparate communities something of the ancient pattern of life in Greece itself is preserved. The Church is the guardian of social tradition, expressed through numerous rituals appropriate for different social circumstances from a wedding to the blessing of a new office block. As Greek life is dominated by many small rituals and customs, the Church pervades every aspect of daily life. In rural Greece the job of priest is in one sense nothing special, little different from that of plumber or taxi-driver in terms of practical influence.

But in many parts of Greece secularism is growing and the numbers seeking admission to the priesthood are declining. Last year a village near Kastoria in Macedonia needed both a priest and a fireman. There were over five hundred applications for the latter job and none for the former. One Athens newspaper commented, understandably enough, that young men in Greece seemed to be more attracted to putting out flames on earth rather than in Hell. Some of the decline can probably be traced to the aggressive promotion of 'Christianity' in Greek life during the junta period. Although many prominent figures in the Church fought for the return of democracy some did not and some, like ex-King Constantine's chaplain Archimandrite Ieronymos, were prominent collaborators and supported the colonels through thick and thin, paralleling the colonels' purges in state institutions with others in the Church. The PASOK government in the mid Eighties tried to exploit this situation by attacking church lands but without much practical effect and in the face of opposition from unexpected quarters. The same divisions had occurred in the Civil War when some priests, mainly in the left-wing areas of northern Greece, took up arms and fought for the socialist revolution alongside the Communists in EAM, while the majority of bishops backed the right-wing forces. Generally speaking, many priests have turned to the Left in recent years. For instance, during the great peace movement demonstrations of the 1980s against the siting of American missiles in Europe, priests were prominent not only as marchers and protestors but as platform speakers as well.

In the last analysis, many of the problems of the contemporary church in Greece centre around the future of monasticism. There are also problems of a fundamental nature appearing in Athos that may in the long run shake the Greek Church to its foundations. Athos has always had many different monasteries, three of which were run by, and for, monks from other churches in the Orthodox world, from Serbia, Russia and Romania. For many years these monasteries were in decline as the Communist regimes in those countries prevented novices from travelling to Greece and in some cases the national churches seemed to be in decline themselves. The overwhelming majority of monks on Athos were Greek or foreigners who were in the process of being admitted to the Greek Church. Now all this has changed. With the collapse of Communism there is a major religious revival in Eastern Europe, in Russia especially, and young men are queuing to come to Athos. Monasteries, where the number of monks had dwindled, are coming alive. But although there has been a revival in the life of Athos, and in other centres of monasticism in Greece, the number of young Greek men and women coming forward to join the ascetic communities has been limited. If present trends continue during the next generation, the Greekness of Athos will be threatened.

At the turn of the century there were perhaps about 7,500 monks on Athos, divided into those living in the idiorhythmic system – where a monk lives in a cell by himself, has his own possessions and a private kitchen – and those living in communities on the wild, rocky peninsula, forty kilometres long, its stony paths thick with heather and wild flowers, the whole area forbidden to women and female grazing animals. There are now about 1,500 monks on the mountain but there are more young monks among this number than there were. Some of the Greeks are elderly, strange old men, who clearly have come to escape the world, a family tragedy perhaps. It is the same all over Greece. The monastery at the northern end of Poros is inhabited by a solitary monk who sits most of the day in the courtyard, chain-smoking under the lemon trees. To their secularist opponents among the Athens intelligentsia, the monasteries are a refuge for the idle and little else. To their defenders, they are strongholds of Greek spirituality, places of hard toil and prayer in the cold, early hours of the morning, which can act as essential reservoirs of Greek values, irrespective of individual beliefs. These are often more than a nod at what are essentially pagan rather than Christian beliefs, a way of recapturing something of the atmosphere and *frisson* of a visit to the ancient holy place, often on the same site, where the combination of great natural beauty and remoteness brings the worshipper near to God – or the gods. Theology is less important, in some senses, in Orthodoxy than in other Christian denominations and the monastery is a good place to understand this.

Underlying the various disputes between the Athos monks about numbers and organization, and the difficulties non-Greek novices have in getting admitted, is a deeper issue, that of relations with the Roman Catholic Church. Ever since the Latin Crusaders and the Venetians, the western expansionists of their day, sacked Constantinople on 12 April 1204, and in many ways began the process of weakening Byzantium that culminated in its capitulation to the Ottoman Turks in 1453, relations between the Orthodox Patriarchate and the Vatican have often been poor. At the heart of it lies the notion of papal authority. For all its addiction to hierarchy and colourful ceremony, and its mystical understanding of the nature of God, the Greek Orthodox Church is not inherently undemocratic and has a long tradition of local Orthodox congregations exercising a reasonable degree of autonomy from the mother Church. This was essential for practical reasons, apart from anything else, during the days of the far-flung diaspora of Greek Christians. It has put the Orthodox Church at loggerheads with the notion of papal authority, with the Roman Church seen as a great undemocratic pyramid with its apex in the Vatican in the person of the Pope. There has been a split in the Greek Church since the Sixties between those who want to move closer to Rome and those who resist it. With the development of the world ecumenical movement, there is little doubt that many Istanbul officials would like to move closer to the Vatican, whereas the monks in Athos and elsewhere in Greece generally disagree. The apologists for this move see it almost in terms of self-preservation, with the future of the Patriarchate threatened by the Turks. The monks believe that in exchange for better relations, the Vatican would force doctrinal compromises on the Greeks and eventually try to take over the Church.

The new situation in Eastern Europe and the war in former Yugoslavia have accentuated these fears. The Vatican has shown what many Orthodox Christians consider to be an aggressive attitude in establishing new bishoprics in ex-Communist countries which historically have been predominantly Orthodox; and the fact that in the conflict between Serbs and Croats in ex-Yugoslavia one side is Orthodox and the other Catholic has not helped the Greeks lose their fears. His Holiness the Patriarch said in April 1992 that he was concerned that the years of improved relations, exemplified by the Dialogue of Truth that was initiated at Patmos and Rhodes in 1980, had all but collapsed, and many unbiased observers feel that relations between the two churches are as poor as they have been in living memory. Particular difficulties have arisen with the situation in countries where the Uniate churches exist, such as the Ukraine and Czechoslovakia. The Vatican has been seen as wanting a Catholic Croatia established at the expense of Orthodox Serbia, and it has been noticeable in Athens that, whoever else has disagreed with the Greek policy of a close and uncritical alliance with Serbia, the Orthodox Church has been a firm supporter. The hidden agenda on the Catholic side is often put in terms of the need for a united front to contain fundamentalist, potentially expansionist Islam, whereas the counter-argument is of the importance of coexistence with the Moslem world, something that with its long history of heroic survival under Ottoman domination the Greek Church claims to understand as well as anybody. In response to the main international problems that confront his Patriarchate, His Holiness Bartholomeos called a Holy Assembly of all the Orthodox Churches in the spring of 1993, to be attended by the Patriarchs of Russia, Jerusalem and Serbia, among others. Although many different matters will be discussed, the need to work out a united front to cope with what many Orthodox see as unwarranted Vatican expansionism will be prominent in the minds of many attending the Assembly.

But Athos itself has managed to move forward recently, despite these conflicts, especially in the area of the physical restoration of its buildings. Although these were not damaged in the Civil War, many of the extraordinarily beautiful but chaotically built monasteries were in danger of complete collapse about forty years ago. Investment in forestry and a discreet encouragement of tourism has brought more money into the monastic republic and much of it has been very wisely spent on long-term building restoration projects. But the medieval peace of the monasteries has been seriously compromised by road-building and construction vehicles. Some monks think that it is now too easy to visit Athos and that the kind of spiritual tourism which has become increasingly popular should be gently discouraged. It is perhaps appropriate that a monk from Athos has composed a hymnography for the protection of the environment which will be chanted in Orthodox churches on the first of September each year, a way to express the Church's understanding of the sacredness of creation.

In other places where peace and quiet is in short supply, such as the streets of Greek cities, the priest is a ubiquitous figure, black robes blowing in a winter wind or unruffled in the summer calm. Although priestly vocations are falling, the Church at a local level within Greece trundles on in a way strangely reminiscent of the cultural position of the Church of England, where its role as preserver of the national identity is paramount. One great advantage of both these churches, compared with the Roman Catholic Church, is that priestly celibacy is not an issue and is only required of Orthodox bishops. As a result, the catastrophic decline in Catholic priests that has affected many parts of rural France, say, has been avoided in these churches. The Church in Greece also offers secure employment and social position. The critical state of the economy over the last few years has meant that the priestly vocation has appeared more attractive to the Christian Greek who is not too ambitious and does not mind the routine of clerical life. Another factor which is beginning to assist the Church is the reaction against the axioms of the technological society and western materialism that is becoming noticeable in Greece, as elsewhere. Orthodoxy is quite a 'green' church, with a love of remote and naturally unspoilt places for its monasteries. There is also the educational aspect of church life to consider. There is a parallel concern in Greece and England about the decline in educational standards, and many Orthodox monasteries run classes for children that are open to the local community. Some people are drawn to the Church as a repository of traditional values in education and spiritual knowledge.

A man like Alexander Kostas combines these qualities. A priest near Nauplion, he was an engineer for some years but his company went bankrupt. He tried working in Nigeria but found the climate unbearable and trained for the priesthood on his return to Greece. Like many of his generation who grew up in a village, he feels profoundly alienated from the superficial materialism of Athens life and has no interest in living or working there. Nauplion is busy in summer but quiet in winter, and Alexander has time for his painting. He has become something of a father figure to local artists who are rediscovering old techniques and developing a neo-Byzantinist style.

At the opposite end of the spectrum is Father Ambrose in the monastery at Fili, about twenty kilometres outside Athens. Profoundly English under his priestly garb, he is a convert to Orthodoxy and has risen to a high position in the Church in Greece. He is in effect responsible for relationships with the newly free Orthodox Church in Romania, a country whose language he speaks fluently. After eighteen years at Fili, he now speaks English with something of an accent and with the occasional Greek construction. The monastery, in existence for only twenty-five years or so, occupies a stunningly beautiful position high above the ancient road between Athens and Thebes. It shows the modern face of the Church: the buildings are freshly painted and there is a large car park and prosperous shop. Inside, although the monks work at traditional occupations like tailoring, there is also a computer and a fax machine. The monastery, along with a nearby Orthodox nunnery, is also deeply involved in the local community. Apart from its educational work, it also runs an old people's home in Fili village, with an ambitious building programme. Ironically, like many other villages in rural Attica, Fili is predominantly Albanian and there is a large colony of gypsies living outside it. It is difficult to avoid the impression that the Fili monastery is altogether a community of outsiders in terms of the materialism that dominates the capital and that the dignified black-garbed monks are as much on the fringe of mainstream Greek society as the brilliantly dressed gypsy women with their swirling skirts or the old men in the kafenion who speak a rough dialect of Tosk Albanian. The Church in Greece now has its security but perhaps it is the security of the outsider. It is a long time since the priest stood alongside the klepht in the fight for a new Greece, a unity embodied in the statue in the middle of Kalamata, commemorating the beginning of the national uprising against the Turks.

11. Food, Drink and Material Life

> In the islands, the poorest peasant will ask you into
> his clean and tidy cottage, give you cognac, coffee
> and a glass of water, after the invariable Greek
> fashion, and offer you walnuts – which he will
> crack for you – or whatever else may be in season.

> – William Miller, *Greek Life in Town and Country*

The great French historian Braudel has taught us how much
can be learned about a people and their history from the study
of their material and domestic life and with regard to the
Greeks his theories certainly seem convincing. And perhaps
some of the uncomfortable social and cultural tensions that
affect the northern European visitor to Greece can be looked
at in this light too. The old Virgilian tag that Greeks bear gifts
which we should fear seems to acquire bizarre force if the gift
is a very ethnic retsina in some remote Attica taverna, taken
straight from the barrel and accompanied, say, by stewed
goat.

When a small number of tourists started visiting the country
in the Fifties and Sixties, Greek food was a major subject of
concern and guidebooks of the period are full of health
warnings on the topic. At that time in England olive oil was a
rare commodity, bought from the chemist in tiny bottles
rather than at the grocers and used only very occasionally. Its
liberal use in Greek cooking was something quite different.
And Greek wine was described as turpentine, usually by some

hardened ex-soldier who had been in Greece in the army in the 1940s or, if he was a very old man indeed, with the Allied army in Macedonia in the First World War campaign. But although the description can apply to some bad retsina now, few of the listeners then would have had an opportunity to find out for themselves as Greek wine and food was all but unobtainable outside London, and not widely available within it. It was not really until the post-war influx of a quarter of a million predominantly Greek refugees from Cyprus that this situation began to change, allied to the growing interest in European cuisine and to the efforts of a handful of pioneer cookery writers who knew there was a lot more to Greek food than a tomato drowned in olive oil.

But Greek fruit and wine had once been available in England. The windswept outcrop of Monemvasia (the name meaning single entrance), deep in the Peloponnese, gives us the word Malmsey, the staple tipple of the late Middle Ages. Ships would also bring Greek currants and dried figs, an expensive luxury for the rich in the seventeenth century. The word currant is believed to be a corruption of 'Corinth'. After the Venetians established control over parts of Greece in the late seventeenth and early eighteenth century, trade with northern European countries expanded considerably but it was a one-way traffic. As far as is known, the Greek peasant's diet has changed little from antiquity, with its staples of beans, lentils and maize bread, cheese as the main protein source, plenty of fruit and vegetables in season, fish for coast and island-dwellers, and meat for special occasions, usually festivals in the Orthodox Church calendar. Within the country there are regional variations, with game featuring in the northern forests and quail-trapping in the Mani during their migration. The British liaison officers who were dropped into occupied Greece and lived with partisan resistance groups survived on this diet which, although monotonous, is what health campaigners argue we should eat, one with a high ratio of pulses and little or no animal fat.

Processed products were all but unknown and the only important commodities that could not be produced locally were usually salt and sugar. The olive provided all vegetable fats and butter was unknown to many. Until very recently a kind of soap was made from olives by old people in the Peloponnese. The gap between the world of the Mountain and the City can be seen clearly here. By the end of the nineteenth century, the diet of the upper middle classes in Athens was based on imitations of French cuisine, echoes of which can still be found in some of its expensive restaurants. Today Athens also has a fair number of fast food restaurants and burger bars, scarce in rural areas and smaller towns except for the ubiquitous pizza parlour. Pizza, the predominantly vegetarian dish invented by southern Italians, is eaten by most Greeks and pasticcio, too, is an integral part of the diet – another Italian influence that resulted in the pasta dish with a cheese topping.

Local food traditions keep Greek heart-attack and cancer rates way below those of northern Europe. The further south you go, with progressively less animal fats in the diet, the more this is the case, so that although the Cretans drink and smoke very enthusiastically their healthy diet compensates. On the other hand the big food companies have their oar in Greece and, with the rapid pace of life and changes in traditional work patterns, convenience foods are becoming more common. But there are also Greek convenience foods that do not involve multinational companies. Very popular are the little filo pastry pies made with cheese and spinach that Greeks nibble on the street and the delicious products of the local *zaharoplasteion*, the corner pastry shop found throughout the old Middle East, which gave the distinguished cookery writer Claudia Roden happy memories of her Egyptian childhood.

Economics matter a good deal. Greeks love to eat out and do so more than most Europeans, as far as can be measured. It goes with the sociable, public nature of Greek life, the dedication to *I Polis*, rather than the more internal domestic life of northern Europe. But to afford to do so, a certain amount of simplicity is important, for the labour involved in some French cuisine would make prices prohibitive. Climate is important too. Until the present generation, refrigeration was far from universal in Greece and so whatever was made had to be eaten within twenty-four hours or so. In their attitude to food there is also the Hellenes love of plainness, a psychology that led to the Greek Orthodox Church being founded upon the asceticism and self-denial of monasticism, or on ancient Spartan virtues. Although many Greeks know about *haute cuisine*, there is an inborn tendency to prepare their food in a few straightforward, well-known ways.

Greeks understand that there are no short cuts with food, especially as far as freshness is concerned. This means that there is an enormous emphasis on food being eaten in season. This can involve a degree of monotony as those who have tired of Greek salad in the summer months well appreciate. But it does mean that the cuisine of winter is quite different from that of summer. The foundation of health in the Greek diet is the large amount of fresh fruit and vegetables that are eaten, a proportion well over treble the average in the United States, for instance. Greeks are eager visitors to the local market and good vegetable gardeners themselves. Anyone who has watched a vine being lovingly tended in some rundown Athens suburb or a row of *horta*, the popular green vegetable, growing in a plot the size of a postage stamp by the main road will know this. So, in some ways, Greek tradition anticipated aspects of the *nouvelle cuisine*, where the chef does not decide what to cook before going to market that morning.

There is, of course, a substantial Turkish influence on Greek food. After so long an occupation it would be surprising if this were not so, although the subject should be approached with circumspection in the company of nationalist Greeks. Many Greek dishes still have Turkish names, such as *tzatsiki*, the delicious mixture of yoghurt, garlic and cucumber, that is part of many *mezes*, another Turkish word. Some cooking methods are also inherited from the old occupiers, just as in other spheres, such as in the names of flowers, Turkish influence is also evident. Generally speaking, the words for luxuries are Turkish, whereas the simple necessities have Greek root words.

The Greek love of water, immortalized in Pindar's phrase from the first Olympian ode 'Ariston Men Udor', 'water is the best of all', persists. It is still possible to hear peasants discussing the merits – or otherwise – of different waters in a kafenion, just as their French counterparts might debate those of local wines. To Greeks the water supply in much of northern Europe, where people drink recycled water from the kitchen tap, leaves much to be desired. The overwhelming majority of the water in Greece is from fresh natural sources.

But if water is the best of all, wine runs a close second. By international standards, as a wine-producing country, the Greeks are not great wine drinkers. But the country has a continuous history of production, probably longer than almost anywhere in the world. The technique of adding resin to wine to preserve it was invented in the ancient world and has carried on in Greece ever since. The area of wine production in Attica, near Athens, is the retsina heartland, although it is made in many other places. Production for home consumption has been falling somewhat, although there are still many tavernas, mostly in Athens, where retsina drawn from the wood is the staple drink. Strengths and styles vary a good deal, but on the whole the trend since the War has been towards a wine that lasts longer and is more suitable for bottling – and, most important of all, for export. For with yoghurt, retsina has been a great export success for Greece. From being more or less unobtainable abroad, outside very specialized shops in the Greek quarters of one or two capital cities, the wine some of the older generation of visitors loved to malign has now become available to millions of German, French and British wine drinkers, happy to recall the taste of summer holidays and the atmosphere of the islands. Investment in modern production and vinification facilities, and despite transport costs somewhat higher than other competitors, has meant that retsina has found a niche in the northern European supermarket, although connoisseurs may feel that the lightly resinated product from a big firm like Kourtaki or Metaxas has little in common with the fierce potions of Attica villages. The economy of some islands is heavily influenced by retsina production and whole stretches of pine forest on Lesbos or Poros exist because of the demand for fresh resin for each year's vintage. This has been very beneficial environmentally in providing an economic base for the continuation of traditional forest cover as elsewhere it has often been cut down in tourist or urban development.

The story of Greek wine since the War has been less happy in other respects. Most production of table wine has been of very moderate quality, and a system of Appellation Controlé is only just coming into use in line with European Community directives. The table wines distributed nationally would not be able to compete on equal terms with international wines if they were not *de facto* protected, particularly in price. But there has been a sign of improvement in some areas. Major investment in Macedonia has resulted in the revival of an area capable of producing high quality white wines which have begun to be exported, as well as drunk in Greece. The Tsantali label has won some international prizes. There are also a few good red wines, like the famous vintages from the volcanic rocks of Santorini, but the quantity produced is too small for expensive promotion internationally. A wealthy shipowner has invested a good deal near the Athos peninsula to produce a 'château-bottled' burgundy-type wine based on the Cabernet grape, but with only limited success to date. The overall picture remains the same: general mediocrity in the mass market but careful local research can often be rewarding for the visitor. Greece should produce as good wines as, for example, Bulgaria; what was more or less a cottage industry there has been transformed within a few years into the highly successful hard currency earner of wines of very good quality. Some Greeks blame the European Community for stagnation in the industry as little or no investment money is available for a revival of the wine industry in Greece because the wine lake in Europe is growing and every effort is being made in Brussels to reduce it. Wine is overwhelmingly market-led in Europe and this means a poor future for the average Greek table wine at the moment.

Some of the same problems of bad organization and marketing have affected the Greek spirits industry. Although brands of Greek brandy and ouzo are sold internationally, these spirits are mostly on the margins of the international drinks industry. The exception is Metaxas brandy, known more or less all over the world. But in EC terms it has to compete with Spanish brandy at the bottom of what is not a very large market and it faces intense competition. Given this background perhaps it has not done too badly. But the marketing of the product is frequently unprofessional: to find evidence one needs go no further than the duty free shop at Athens airport, where it is often difficult to find Greek brandy in litre bottles despite it being the standard size for the duty-free spirit allowance. The case of ouzo is more puzzling. It is a unique Greek product, often of the highest quality, which commands considerable customer loyalty from those who have acquired a taste for it on holiday. It is also cheap to make and, by spirit standards, potentially extremely profitable in the export market. But, outside the Greek context, it has not taken off. Given that people drink what is most heavily advertised, the cause must lie in the variety of ouzo producers and the lack of a single large company with marketing muscle to launch ouzo in the way it deserves. It is a bizarre state of affairs that the big drinks companies are spending large sums on the promotion of spirits like Mexican tequila in the EC but neglecting a very strong homegrown product. Ouzo varies of course and some of the best brands, like Barbayannis on Lesbos, are small family-owned concerns.

What will happen if the Single European Market comes in its predicted form after 1992 is difficult to say. Some imported spirits like whisky are doing very well in the Greek market but many Greeks would probably not know what gin was if they tasted it. Aristotle Onassis played a small part in whisky promotion by a daily intake of Johnny Walker Black Label and whisky-drinking in Greece now is the sign of a successful cosmopolitan. But it remains to be seen whether the current fragmentation of the industry will continue after 1992 or whether there will be a series of takeovers to form one major combine capable of promoting Greek wines and spirits in a European-wide setting. If it does not, the future may be dark, and for wine-makers especially, as there is an awful lot of wine in the European lake and some of it is of a much better quality than Greek table wine. Without some degree of protection from imports, the weaker Greek producers may be unable to compete.

Tobacco-growers and manufacturers face a similar challenge, although from a more advantageous starting point. Greek cigarettes are in great demand in the newly free countries of Eastern Europe, and the Greek market itself has not been affected by the restrictive legislation and high cigarette prices in Britain. But there are EC pressures on the government to restrict consumption, which has been growing by an average of about 6 per cent a year for some years, the fastest rate in Europe. In poverty-stricken Albania a single Greek importer was bringing in twelve million cigarettes of one brand each month this year and he claimed that despite the difficulties of lek convertibility, crime and distribution problems, he was still making a good profit. And Greek cigarettes are a traditional smoke in many parts of the Middle East as well, going back to the nineteenth century when Greek traders were important in many local economies.

Smoking is enjoyed by most Greeks, possibly because there are so many minor, and sometimes major, delays in Greek daily life that can be filled by a cigarette. The kafenion is still very tobacco-oriented and in the last days of Turkish rule in the north a man would go to the café to smoke a *narghile*, the water-pipe of the Ottoman world. Refugees from Smyrna practised this custom in Greek cities for many years. Both private and state tobacco factories exist, the northern factories based near the main growing areas, while much the biggest privately owned company, Karelia, manufactures in Messenia and has a strong export presence in the Middle East market. This trade pattern is strongly reminiscent of Ottoman times when Greek-manufactured exports were important in countries like Egypt.

The soft drinks market is one area of material life totally dominated by the multinationals and the traditional lemonade and rosewater drinks are made only at home. Companies like Pepsi Cola invented their 'culture' in the post-war years, and their economic power is a lasting monument to that era now that there is not an American car to be seen in Athens and where the political profile of the United States is so diminished. The growth in soft drinks has in many ways been linked to that of tourism, with demand at its height during the summer months. Greek businessmen have attempted to get involved in the growing international market in fruit juice, but on the whole production is not large enough to allow the kind of major investment needed to make an impact on the export market. The citrus industry in Greece, with the exception of Crete, is rather fragmented and there has not so far been the concerted effort that put Cyprus products on the international map – even if this did involve the agency of the Polly Peck company on the Turkish side. There are certainly large potential markets developing in the newly free countries of central Europe. Greece gave Bulgaria 18,000 tons of oranges last winter as part of a food aid programme, but no doubt the orange-growers would have been happier if they had been able to sell direct to shops or wholesalers in Bulgaria instead of selling at intervention prices.

In the end the destiny of the food industry will be decided by the reform of the Common Agricultural Policy, as much as anything else. Perhaps some sectors of the industry will get a better deal over time, while others may lose their relatively privileged position. What will not change is the Greek sense of food and drink as part of the sacred process of hospitality, ultimately a religious obligation, and the charm and dignity of that ritual.

There are so many local specialities that never appear on menus in restaurants – and often not in cookery books either. Even the recent rediscovery of Greek food by writers in northern Europe has only begun to touch the variety and interest of local food. There are, for example, the different regional varieties of wild greens, with snails cooked in dandelions and several uses of dill. Then there are the less appetizing specialities such as lumps of hot mutton fat with herbs that British officers in the War were given as a luxury, and the boiled rabbit of the Cretan mountains that historian

Miranda Vickers describes. Many varieties of grilled fish, whose names never appear in guides to fish cookery, are available, with the thrushes and tiny hams pickled in olive oil of Kardamyli. Like the Greek nation, in Greek food and drink there are the familiar stereotypes, but also endless diversity and complexity.

In Greek food, as in their religion, there is the sense of understanding a relationship with nature mediated through ritual, whether it is the visit to a taverna cold counter to view what is available, the tiny dishes of *mezes* served in every home, or the great ceremony of spring: the roasting of the Easter lamb or kid. The fire is started early in the morning, so the old olive logs are gently smouldering cylinders covered in hot white ash while the meat cooks. Fat spurts into the fire and smoke drifts between the branches of the olive trees near by. The food is excellent as, indeed, is the company, and a great deal of wine can be drunk. But it is, above all, a ritual where consumption is a means not an end, as when the Homeric heroes stripped fat off the thighs of animals to sacrifice on the beach at Pylos in *The Odyssey*:

Here the townsfolk on the shore of the sea were offering sacrifice of black bulls to the dark-haired Earth-shaker. Nine companies there were, and five hundred men sat in each, and in each they held nine bulls ready for sacrifice. Now when they had tasted the inner parts and were burning the thigh-pieces to the god, the others put straight in to the shore, and hauled up and furled the sail of the stately ship.

In just the same way, in every Greek home today, at midnight on Easter Saturday, when Orthodox believers break the Lenten fast, it is with *mayeiritsa*, made with the intestines of the milk-fed lamb that the family will roast the following morning.

12. Language: Words, Music

There lay his book open, just as he had left it, and the capital letters on the title-page regarded him with fixed reproach in the grey starlight, like the unclosed eyes of a dead man: Η ΚΑΙΝΗ ΔΙΑΘΗΚΗ.

– Thomas Hardy, *Jude the Obscure*

In the car park in northern Athens a refugee from the Soviet Union is spreading out a modest collection of wares, all Russian: the ubiquitous little dolls that fit inside each other, ornate meat-tenderizers, boxes of spanners, tablecloths in garish colours. He speaks a guttural Greek to his wife, who brings goods from the car boot to set out on the stall. A customer approaches and buys something. The refugee's Greek is more or less understood, although until the end of the Soviet Union there had been no cultural contact between Athens and Baku on the Caspian Sea for many years. But Baku, like many places in the southern part of the Soviet Union, has had a Greek minority population for a very long time. This seems at first sight to be a testament to the lasting qualities of the Greek language as a means of communication: supple, beautiful, ever-changing, with the longest and most distinguished literary tradition in the western world. For some Christians, Greek is the language of God himself, the speech of dusty hot streets in Judea and Galilee, of educated people there. The strange patterns marching across the page are seen as signs of knowledge and wisdom, and to be the possessor, the user, of such a language is to be very privileged. It is said that the novelist Virginia Woolf once lay in bed and heard the birds talking Greek in Edwardian England and dreamed of becoming a writer.

Greeks are not always happy at the state of their language. George Seferis, Nobel Prize winner and the most distinguished Greek poet this century, lamented in one essay the 'anarchy' of the modern language and his feelings are widely shared. Language has become a major political issue in Greece and the reforms introduced by the last PASOK government have been bitterly resented and fought by the Church and other bodies representing linguistic conservatism.

To most foreigners, Greek is a language of fabled difficulty, one that in most northern European countries has traditionally been the preserve of a small number of clever people who went to expensive schools. But, in fact, Greek is spoken every day, in the sense of hundreds of words like philosophy and history that have not really changed in meaning or spelling. There are many words where it is necessary only to know the Greek alphabet to understand them easily.

The history of the Greek language is itself a subject of enormous complexity, and discoveries like the Linear B decipherment in the Fifties by the British scholars Chadwick and Ventris have revolutionized our understanding of the subject. As a result of their work on the tablets found in Mycenaean excavations just before the War, but deciphered only later, it is now known that the language is much older than previously believed.

The discoveries point not only towards the antiquity of Greek but to an extensive vocabulary running to over a million words. No scholar, however learned, however assiduous, can possibly 'know' such a language or have an immediate active comprehension of all the vocabulary. And new words and phrases are still being discovered, mainly from pieces of ancient papyrus preserved in the desert sands of Egypt. The past, therefore, can be a burden as well as a great heritage for modern Greek intellectuals. This can also be so for foreigners trying to learn the language, whether as tourists struggling to master enough of the alphabet to read street signs or as university students of modern or ancient Greek. Many Greek writers and academics, from disparate backgrounds, would share Seferis's view, although for very different reasons which lie in the politics of the national movement before and after the War of Independence in the early part of the nineteenth century.

At that time, with Greek emerging from its suppression under the Turkish occupation, the spoken language had a written history with its emergence in the Byzantine Empire in the twelfth and thirteenth centuries. When the modern Greek state was established after 1830, the spoken language of the people seems to have changed little from that of the Byzantine world, which in turn was remarkably similar to ancient Greek. It had successfully resisted the Slav incursions and the conquests of the Crusaders, the Venetians and the Turks. It was an axiom of the Greek nationalists of the nineteenth century that there should be a standard national language, essentially that of the Peloponnese, cradle of the Greek Independence movement and birthplace of many of the new citizens of Athens when it became the capital in 1834.

But there had been a marked divergence between the written and the spoken language for a long time and in the Byzantine period the spoken language was not used for writing. As Greek Independence burgeoned, it was inevitable that there would be a controversy about the correct written form to be adopted and the question has not been solved satisfactorily to this day. An acquaintance in London, an elderly Greek lady who has not lived in Greece itself for more than three months in her whole life, felt so strongly against the PASOK language reforms that on the first day after the New Democracy government was elected in 1990, she wrote to the new Prime Minister Constantine Mitsotakis asking him to restore breathing marks to the written language. Her passion may appear slightly eccentric in English eyes, but is far from exceptional in Greek terms. By and large, right-wing and religious Greeks, who are often but by no means always the same people, wish to see a return to formality in the language and the use of what has become known as *Katharevousa*, the purifying language, whereas the secular movements and the political Left have been champions of the Demotic, the people's language. *Katharevousa* itself was developed in response to the polemics of eighteenth-century theorists who wanted a complete return to ancient Greek, to a degree that would lead to the abolition of Demotic. Demotic contains a significant number of words of foreign origin – Italian, Latin, Turkish and, now, English and French – as a result of long assimilation of neighbours' words.

Whatever the details of these arcane disputes, *Katharevousa* was established for generations, with its odd mixture of ancient and modern elements, as the official language of government, the law, most spheres of education and the Church. It has never really been spoken by anybody, although there have been individuals who are said to have mastered it. In the nineteenth century there was continual pressure for further 'purification' to take place which, on the whole, was resisted. The modern struggle began in the latter part of the nineteenth century, where the proponents of Demotic and campaigners for the abolition of *Katharevousa* were often poets and writers who wished to use Demotic in their work. Behind them there is more than an echo of Plato and the ancient disputes about the relative values of poetry and philosophy, insofar as the poets were trying to appropriate the inherently democratic nature of a spoken language, whereas the theorists were concerned with reinforcing the power of an élite which had the necessary skills to write works based on ancient Greek. This was the subject of intense political controversy in 1901 in Athens when the publication of a Demotic version of the New Testament was allowed, and in 1903 when the National Theatre performed ancient tragedy in Demotic. One of the leading actors had his jaw broken by an enraged member of the audience who stormed the stage. But the people's language was seeping into the educational system, at the lower levels at any rate, even though the universities by and large remained wedded to *Katharevousa* until the Axis Occupation. The victory of the Right in the Civil War was also a victory for *Katharevousa*, which ruled unchallenged until the swing to the Left in the early Sixties allowed George Papandreou's Centre Union to put Demotic on an equal footing. But then the colonels' junta restricted its use, Canute-like, to the primary schools. It was not until the advent of PASOK in the early Eighties that Demotic was finally seen to have won its battles, in particular in terms of the formal education system. As a result of the same reforms, the amount of ancient Greek language and literature studied has been drastically reduced. This change was in turn reversed by the New Democracy government in the summer of 1992 with a decision for a major restoration of ancient Greek to the curriculum for pupils.

Perhaps the most important aspect for foreigners of all these developments is that they should help dispel the resistance to learning Greek, at any level, based on fear of transgressing linguistic correctness. Greeks make hundreds of 'mistakes' every day when they speak or write the language – at least in each other's eyes – and unlike the French, say, they are not at all censorious when the struggling visitor tries to get started in the language, knowing only too well what a labyrinth it is and how easy, like Theseus, it is to get lost. But it is a beautiful and unique labyrinth well worth entering, even if you stay near the entrance within sight, or rather sound, of the familiar consonants and vowels of English. Plato's famous myth of the Cave in *The Republic* seems so applicable to the process of learning Greek, an education in itself, an ascent towards the light, compared with the insubstantial world of fictions and shadows in the Cave itself caused by the limitations of other languages. In this context it is worth remembering that some historians of Christianity believe that the theological disputes and conflicts in its past have in part been caused by Greek as it was not possible to express some subtle theological distinctions in Latin but only in Greek.

The arts in Greece have always had a long history of popular creativity and commitment, and a relationship with the people that is one of the miracles of modern Greek culture and an important element in the struggle for democracy, whether in the songs of the Klephts, who fought the Turks from their mountain fastnesses, or in the improvised songs of the andartes in the Civil War. The arts have been a unifying, inspiring language when the formal language of written words so often seemed to produce only conflict and division. The songs of Theodorakis and contemporary composers fed the struggle against the junta and landed the composers in gaol or exile. The colonels banned performances of certain ancient plays because of their political content. Greeks really know about their contemporary artists and their work, and there is a sense of a living oral contact with them. Part of the writers' power is not unrelated to that of poets in the old Soviet Union, where censorship of the media and lack of democratic freedoms meant that writers and artists took on tasks that in other countries were left to the newspapers: reportage, communication, social and political criticism. Greek newspapers are not very widely read, for a highly literate and educated nation, and their contents are not always trusted by those who do not follow the paper's political line. Journalists do not have a particularly high or respected status, especially with politicans who tend to expect newspapers which support them to toe party lines, even by covering up information embarrassing to them. Television is mediocre and often subject to political influence, even control, although the situation has improved in recent years. But the respected figure of the crusading or investigative journalist in America, or elsewhere, does not really exist in Greece. It is artists who have this role, sometimes approaching that of the Shelleyian ideal of legislators or, at least, one of reminding the Greek people of values which their political leaders might wish them to forget.

Some art is very much a personal statement of the underdog, especially popular music. The sub-culture music of the interwar years, rembetika, is at the heart of this: the words and tunes of the *mangas*, men in sharp, broad-brimmed hats who often had come to Athens and Piraeus from Asia Minor as refugees. In the absence of anything better they became active in the underworld, smoking hashish and accompanying their songs on strange new instruments. *Mangas* would sing the blues, confronting the pain, misery and loss of shanty-town life, using music with Byzantine roots played by smart-dressing wideboys. Rembetika had not long established itself before Greece was occupied by the Germans and Italians, and the music of the slums quickly became that of political protest and comment. The Metaxas dictatorship in the late Thirties had already banned many singers and lyrics, and war or exile was all that was left for many – although it might be said that nothing was more damaging to the music and its performers than the suffocating embrace of commercialism that followed after 1949.

Now the tradition is flourishing after a period of revival that began in the movement for a popular music of protest under the junta. A traditional venue is near Panormou Street in northern Athens: the Maribou, a small restaurant with a stage, hidden away in a side street. The star attraction is the lanterna, a beautifully restored version of the old hurdy-gurdy on wheels that was part of café life in the old Greek cities of Asia Minor. Painted maroon, it stands about four feet high. It is played by turning a brass handle at the side which strikes a series of levers within, making the notes. If the handle is turned slowly, it is sad, elegiac, romantic; if rotated fast, then the sound is rough, urban, and it is possible to imagine an old *mangas* approaching. In the centre of the lanterna is a painting of a woman and each side is hung with red velvet and chains of beads – a secular icon. Theodore, who plays the instrument, has a day job repairing Athens's streets; a wise-looking sixty-year-old with a white moustache, he looks as if he could be a retired bank manager from Purley or Cheam in his woolly beige cardigan.

He begins to turn the handle and evokes a vanished world, cranking faster and faster, as the audience prods octopus and spreads dill butter on bread – an Athenian winter speciality. With the tone of an old mechanical piano, the Turkish music wafts around the room and silence falls on even the most animated company. Theodore's sense of rhythm is exquisite as he coaxes a shaking, trembling sound out of the clumsy old instrument designed, after all, to be played in crowded streets, perhaps with a monkey sitting on top.

But then Theodore pauses, hands over the handle to a friend and picks up his tambourine. He begins to shake and rattle it in time with the lanterna, then flexes his roadman's brown elbow and takes a steel peg which he begins to work inside the rim making a kind of drum, one that the troops of Sultan Mehmet the Conqueror would have known, marching behind drums, tambourines and zurnas as they swept across Turkey to extinguish the light of Byzantium, *I Polis*. The tambourine throbs, the tight goatskin sounding very different from the *amane* – the opening of the silky, sophisticated music of Smyrna. It is the primitive sound of Anatolia, that of a desolate village near Lake Van, from where Ari Onassis's grandfather escaped Turkish oppression. Here in Panormou it is raining hard, an evening during the Gulf War when Athens is deserted. The hotel over the road has CNN but the Maribou has the sound of stones, of conquest, of blood. Outside an old man in a herringbone overcoat picks his way past the scurrying cats to a cheap restaurant – John's Place – just past the parking lot where a sign for Hotel Cleo is painted on the wall. At John's taverna they will be eating a soup of bright green lentils every day this winter.

Elsewhere in the city is the language of violence. The November 17th terrorist group claim responsibility for a gaping black hole in one of the American Express offices where aluminium heating ducts hang out of the window at a crazy angle. This Athens is not a city of harmony and classical learning but somewhere close to Middle East turmoil.

A couple of hours away from this urban world is Epidauros, a drive along the motorway towards Corinth, a left turn into the Argolid. As rembetika and winter in Athens reflect the contemporary, drama in Epidauros on a warm summer evening is what is timeless and pure in Greek art: the combination of an exquisite natural setting, a great play and a sense of involvement that links the performance with the religious origin of drama and the ancient religious festival. But although the walk through the heavily scented pinewoods from the entrance up to the theatre takes on the quality of a pilgrimage, with a Jungian sense of the numinous, of what is very special and touched with a genuine sense of the Divine, it is not perhaps the best place to understand the origin of ancient drama. To find this, a walk to the side reveals ancient remains, open to visitors early on in the day. Flanking the theatre and museum is a widespread, low jumble of collapsed ancient buildings, at first sight seemingly of interest only to specialists. In one sense the remains have little majesty or grandeur compared with the theatre. But among them is the *tholos*, the home of the sacred snake, the link with medicine and healing, and the floor of the temple, where the sick slept, hoping to cure themselves by incubation.

Epidauros may be one of the great experiences a visit to Greece can now offer, where to see the sun set over the mountainside and the entry of the actors in procession to the stage evokes our deepest feelings of awe. But for the ancient visitor, a visit there had the underlying practical purpose to restore health in a very direct way. Our visit to see a play at the theatre today is only one aspect of what was then of more complex significance. And at a mundane level, then and now, Epidauros has an importance for the local economy: the Argolid has always been a poor, remote area of Greece, despite its proximity to major cities, and the stream of visitors meant prosperity.

Even here, in what seems the most unchanged and distant of centres, the language question intrudes. By and large, ancient drama is kept alive in modern translation, for a Greek audience today would not understand much of Sophocles – a problem which has worsened with the decline of ancient Greek taught in Greek schools in the last fifteen years. So, although in one sense a visitor to the theatre experiences drama as it was *seen* in the fifth century BC, that is as far as it goes and what is *heard* is different. It is a pity, in my opinion, that it is difficult to find performances in exactly the original language. In the plays ancient Greek is at its most beautiful, musical and accessible. Even if a crib or an aural simultaneous translation is used, the majesty of the language justifies the inconvenience. There is something almost hypnotic about the tight patterns of rhythm and the mixture of soft vowel sounds with the crisp hardness of the ancient Greek n word-endings that is quite lost in the modern quest for accessibility. Given the simplicity of most of the dramatic plots, many of them are very much alive in the culture of even the least-educated Greek peasant. It is an irony that Greek intellectuals, especially the middle-class savants of Athens, are not great devotees of ancient drama. The Greek audience for these plays is popular and in the junta period people would walk miles through the hills to see an illegal performance of a play such as Aristophanes' *Peace*. This relates to the fact that ancient drama is not seen as compatible with modernism and its ideological ramifications, perhaps echoing problems of the Platonic heritage, where philosophy has a role denied to poetic imitation and the much despised actor.

But theatre in Greece is not all Epidauros, any more than English theatre is confined to what happens at Stratford-upon-Avon. There are performances of the ancient plays in other restored theatres, large and small, around the country in summer, with the usual mixture of venues in Athens and major cities. On the whole, the latter have many of the same problems as the West End in London, or Broadway, with spiralling costs, static or declining audiences, and a diet of musicals or downmarket comedies about domestic problems with very small casts. There are a number of small fringe-type venues that do interesting work, but it is a matter of chance whether the visitor can find anything to suit – or even find the theatre in many cases.

Television has another language and there is the usual debate in Greece, as elsewhere, about its influence. Politics are not far away, of course. For most of its history television has been state controlled and during the junta period it was a conduit for propaganda. Its opponents would say that little has changed except that the propaganda is different. There was certainly a period under PASOK when the views of the government and the political outlook of most television executives had to coincide. Although matters have improved since, the idea of objectivity, in BBC terms, is a difficult one to take root, however hard its proponents try. Some think that one of the underlying reasons why the junta was able to hold on to power for so long was because the regime coincided with a great spread of television ownership in Greece and so it was able to influence people at home for longer than it might have done otherwise. As a result of this widespread and entrenched distrust of the medium across the political spectrum, 'alternative' television is proving popular. Blocks of apartments in many Greek cities take cable, and CNN and Rupert Murdoch's SKY channel are becoming much more common, particularly in Athens. Videos are also in great demand.

But Greek television and radio are short of money and foreign news is expensive. If there is a major international crisis, such as the Gulf War, it is difficult to fund coverage that can compete with what the multinational-owned networks can offer via satellite. On the other hand, Greeks are as addicted to soaps as any other nation and demand their own. But the general television diet available to the viewer is poor, with a mixture of old American films with sub-titles, soaps and lengthy 'talking head' discussion programmes that give intellectuals a platform for a length of time inconceivable in the United States or Britain – and which does not make very good television. But Greeks seem happy with the fairly low level of entertainment. Perhaps this may have something to do with being a visual people: the screen becomes a moving icon on the living-room wall and, like the religious object, something that shows a glimpse of another world – even if the world of Greek soap opera is as far from Heaven as that of *Brookside* or *EastEnders*. It could even be construed as a sign of a healthy culture to have plenty of junk television rather than follow the British pattern where relatively good television stifles other ways people could spend their free time. It is difficult to see many Greek men giving up their long, winding and fascinating discussions in the kafenion or town square under the plane tree to watch television. And, again, seasonality plays its part. In the summer the television often becomes a box collecting dust in the corner of a little-used room: in the winter, viewing figures can rise dramatically.

But in the end television is not taken very seriously. Greeks are not really at their best with machines that rely on a mechanical language. The cinema is a similar case although there are very gifted contemporary Greek directors such as Angelopoulos whose *The Travelling Players* is one of the few modern Greek films to have found an international audience. The heart of Greek art is the experience of language used between individuals. Where Greeks in this century have reached the highest levels are, predictably, in poetry, with the direct encounter of poet, Greek language and audience, and in the theatre where every performance is unique, and where each spectator has a separate, personal, specific and hence inherently democratic viewpoint.

13. The Family: The Domestic Fortress

> MENELAUS: It is your duty to obey, my lady. You must accept the husband who stands before you, and forget the one whose claim has ended. In your present position this will be best for you. And if I come home safely to Hellas, I will put an end to evil tales about you; only be the wife you should be to your husband.
>
> – Euripides, *Helen*

In societies where the state and government are weak or hostile, or seen as alien and oppressive, the family or clan tends to be strong. Whether it is in Sicily, faced with a distant and indifferent Rome, or the *fis* of the Albanian northern highlands, headed by the *Kryetar*, a patriarchal figure, or the inhabitants of a remote northern Greek village in the Meglen, bordering former Yugoslavia – the background is the same. Where you have little control over an external authority, or where it does little for you, the family tends to become the be-all and end-all of social organization, the only reliable source of fundamental security against an inimical world. To be alone is to be weak and threatened. The word in Greek is *monos* – as important a reality to the hapless traveller lost in winter in the mountains, as to the eye and ear of the city-dwelling waiter who uses the word with compassion as he sees a lone customer come into his taverna and shows him carefully to some corner so he does not risk depressing the other customers in their cheerful social and family groups.

Although in a superficial sense Greek society has become European – whatever that really means – the family has continued with many dimensions of its traditional role. It evolved as a response to the recurrent cycles of disaster and prosperity that have made up Greek history, ancient and modern. In the ancient world, the best place to see this is in the many tragedies, particularly those of Aeschylus, where the characters are torn over competing claims of family, the individual and the nascent state. In many ways little has changed since then. The play that the composer Mikos Theodorakis wrote about the Civil War was about a divided family, and in almost any Greek village living examples can be found of the same sort of conflicts and bitter quarrels, with the emotional basis that inspired characters like Orestes and Antigone. It is worth bearing in mind that many Greeks see their whole recent history – from the disaster at Smyrna in 1922, the political chaos of the inter-war period, the depression, the rise of Metaxas and the end of democracy, the Axis Occupation and Civil War to the post-war junta – as one series of catastrophes after another and, for many, the family is all there is left to cling to. And, also, it should not be forgotten that Greece was occupied by the Turks for hundreds of years with government altogether in the hands of a foreign, alien power.

But the family does change even if the basic sense of loyalties are pretty immutable. If times of serious political and social stress return to Greece, after the relatively calm period since the fall of the dictatorship in 1974, one certainty is that many people will turn to the family to help them through. But they may be turning to something different. Ties have loosened somewhat in recent years and feminism has begun to have some influence in Greece, although by no means as much as in northern European countries. But in many respects little has changed in terms of basic psychology.

Perhaps the first point to register when thinking about the survival of the traditional structure and division of labour in the family is that many tasks performed by state employees in northern Europe are simply not organized that way in Greek society, particularly those involving elements of the welfare state. There is some basic recognition, for instance, in the provision of old people's homes, say, but these are only for the really destitute. In most instances, the family – its female members – are expected to care for the old and declining members. The overwhelming majority of Greeks, of both sexes, would be very shocked if this was not so. The same sort of limitations appear in the field of childcare and nursery provision, although this area is more controversial with many young women wishing to return to work and finding it difficult to do so because of the lack of suitable assistance and facilities.

Where this is the case, the central figure on whom the freedoms, or relative freedoms, depend is *yiayia* (granny), the apparently timeless archetypal figure clad in black, with a paisley print overall tied around her waist. In a typical three-generation Greek family, especially in rural areas, the grandmother has a whole series of responsibilities to do with childcare and the bringing up of the next generation that in many instances act as a very satisfactory substitute for state provision. Where it all works, when a grandmother is available, it is an enormous source of strength and emotional security for the younger generation with small children – the boys mostly – being rather spoilt but also given healthy attention and care. The result seems to be children and adolescents free of many of the contemporary social problems of northern Europe, much better adjusted and behaved. It also means that mothers have time to help out on the family farm or in a small family business, with freedom from the guilt career women often feel about handing over their children to the care of strangers.

For despite the stereotype that everyone knows so well – of Greek women who do all the work and crowded ranks of men sitting doing very little in the kafenion, idling the day away playing *tavli* – family relations in Greece, as elsewhere, embody complex patterns of dependence and power. In one sense Greece is a typical Mediterranean macho society where the street is not merely somewhere to walk down but a theatre for male display, whether of the humble revving small motor cycle or the parade of rich sports cars in the Athens suburbs. It is possible to argue, though, that Greece is in some senses a matriarchal society where men have little real power. This is a highly controversial subject and, even more than politics, almost any opinion is bound to provoke violent disagreement. But the fact remains that Greek women *do* have a good deal of effective power. The kafenion denizens may have the pleasures of male society but in some respects they are powerless refugees from the family, the hearth, the centre of existence.

The life of the streets is a relatively gentle phenomenon and involves everybody, including women of all ages. At two o'clock in the morning the streets of Greek cities are perhaps safer than most in Europe. In a society where Greek men have been coddled by their mothers from an early age, violence against women, especially in a sexual context, is unthinkable and repellent. But, that said, Greece has not really been affected by modern changes in sexual behaviour in quite the same way as many other countries. The Orthodox Church, while maintaining traditional Christian precepts, has never held the extreme judgemental attitude to sexual behaviour espoused by the Catholic Church at an institutional level – apart from what is expected from its own members as priests and as monks. A degree of tolerance has existed towards married men, particularly in the cities, having lovers as part of the normal run of things. The double standard is in full operation with young men expected to visit prostitutes for their first sexual experiences, and female virginity still prized on marriage – mostly in rural areas. It should be emphasized, though, that despite the freedoms of ancient Greek society, homosexuality has never been tolerated by the Church. Today it is in the forefront of a fundamentalist campaign against homosexuality in respect of the risks of AIDS and HIV transmission, although this modern scourge has not, so far, appeared in Greece on a very large scale.

Greek pornography reflects their conception of sexuality. Although imported versions of American magazines like *Playboy* and *Penthouse* are popular, most original Greek pornography seems to emanate from Thessaloniki. It usually concentrates on straightforward genital sex in action, and there is a noticeable absence of the objectification of women's genitals that dominates magazines in Anglo-Saxon culture. Blue videos show every kind of sexual variation – but here the material is nearly all foreign and generally imported from Denmark.

As in other matters, the Greeks are a culturally conservative people who distrust excessive hedonism and there are long memories of their old oppressors, the Turks, who used to carry off young girls for humiliation in the harems and brothels of Constantinople. The prostitute is heavily protected, legally, from pimps and brothel owners, and the legal system makes a serious effort to separate sex from crime and exploitation. Prostitutes, themselves, in Athens at any rate, seem to come to the job by way of the traditional route of a poor rural background, or perhaps a deprived and unhappy childhood in some regional town, then ambition to be a singer in Athens, then failure. A club such as one of those found on the fringes of the Plaka district becomes a place to meet prospective clients; one, like the old, now defunct, Lady Bar in Apollonos Street, whose overweight Palestinian proprietor was usually to be found out on the pavement, talking to his friend the chemist from the small shop on the opposite corner, and failing to tempt customers to drink his overpriced ouzo.

But whereas, say, at certain times in nineteenth-century France, prostitution was a mirror for the way a whole society worked, as Balzac wrote, in Greece it shows nothing – or very little. The family is built on social and economic, not sexual, realities. In this context, the biggest change in living memory has been the end of the dowry system and of arranged marriages based on land and property criteria. That said, in many country places there are often considerable pressures on girls to marry from one particular family into another, and many do as they are told. The dowry has not completely disappeared either in rural areas, despite the legal prohibition. The family in remote and mountainous areas is far from the nuclear ideal of the northern European or American city with its two parents and 2.2 children. It is much closer to the old clan, where blood ties extend through a whole community like blood vessels through a body, with long chains of connection and obligation. In a village with a population of a thousand people, say, it would not be uncommon for someone to be related to perhaps two hundred people or more. These relationships have been exhaustively studied by anthropologists and are often shown to have a continuous life, going back hundreds of years.

The basis for this lies in the nature of Greek geography and society as much as anything else, a country with limited fertile land surrounded by high mountains and with difficult terrain in many areas. In the ancient period small city states started to develop which dominated specific areas and were more or less at war with their neighbours most of the time. The best example of this is the way that ancient Sparta developed, a city with an army so feared that there was no need to build a wall around it – in legend at least. Sparta preserved many features of Dorian social organization – the patterns of life of the original invaders from the north – with the *gerousia*, the assembly of elders who were politically dominant, its unusual monarchy and, best known of all, its fearsome education system that was designed to produce the ruling élite of a military superstate. Although the prosperity and security of the Spartan city was the central motive force of life, the government was in many ways only the expression of the different families within it. This is a very complex question and over-simplification is dangerous but it is possible to trace a continuous thread of the family in Greek politics with definite patterns of kin allegiances. At an obvious level there is the continued existence of well-known political families, like the Papandreou clan nowadays. The same dynamic operates at local level and produces the endless intractable conflicts that rack most small communities in Greece, but also generate the same great loyalties and allegiances crossing generations. To the outsider, it often seems as if there are really two systems of morality and ethics that coexist in the minds of many Greeks: those that apply within the family and those that apply outside it.

The question then arises, of course, of where the family stops and where society generally starts. Again it cannot be emphasized too much that the main reason for the abiding influence of ancient drama is because these dilemmas are so thoroughly explored there. Greek peasants, even those who still cannot read and write very well, really do know the stories of their classics.

There are also many notional families outside the formal pattern of blood relationships. The Orthodox Church is perhaps the largest and most comprehensive of all, being in some senses the expression, in spiritual terms, of the single family of the Greek nation – with the political party and business enterprise running a close second and third. Here, what can easily seem the most unrestrained and ruthless egotism can be justified by the potential to advance the corporate interest, untrammelled by considerations of morality. Perhaps the most colourful instances have been the various scandals and corruption allegations that have involved the PASOK leadership, with leading party members convicted of corruption charges of various kinds. Many PASOK members and supporters have found great difficulty in condemning them, or even believing that anyone might have transgressed, as in their eyes the progress of PASOK is synonymous with the good of the Greek nation. Therefore, in a certain subliminal sense, normal moral or ethical criteria somehow do not fully apply. The mentality can rub off on people in the business world to the great benefit of the business involved; Greek-run concerns can follow their aims through to a conclusion with the most single-minded dedication to the success of the enterprise.

So the terrain of argument about the Greek family is very different from the sort of conceptual framework developed by North American and West European writers to explore sexual politics, particularly those dominated by the Protestant individualist ethic and values. A minority of Greek women, among them those who have lived in the United States or Canada, have attempted to put some of these questions on the agenda, but on the whole they have not got very far. The Personal is the Political has not been a very effective phrase when, for so many people of each succeeding generation this century, the political has meant clear oppression from an external source, whether from the Nazi Occupation, the other side in the Civil War, foreign factory-owners, junta colonels or Australian slum landlords.

It is difficult to say whether the situation will continue as there are many conflicting pressures on Greek women. In Athens and the larger cities there is a large and growing number of educated women workers who can, in theory, become financially independent of their families (or, at least, to a greater degree than before), and they are finding it increasingly difficult to take on the dual responsibilities of motherhood and a demanding job, with all the domestic organization that goes with marriage. Without a drastic expansion of state provision, in terms of the welfare state or something similar, it is difficult to see how things are going to change for the better. Medical care is still a major problem with public hospitals, especially in Athens, overstretched and with doctors and medicines being very expensive. For something to be *farmacia* is a slang way of saying that it is expensive, even if it is a car or a fishing rod. Facilities for the care of the mentally ill are also very limited and in every respect this lack adds to the burden of work on women. And there is little sign of a basic change of outlook among Greek men; even if some are becoming 'new' in some senses, the process often does not go very far. The end of the routine of endless work necessary until very recent years to sustain peasant life has not been replaced by a more active male commitment to help in the house in the newly available spare time. An interesting literary outcome of these tensions has been a spate of autobiographies by foreign women who have married Greek men, or by Greek women who have emigrated with their husbands and then returned to Greece. Some of the earlier ones concentrate, understandably enough, on what it is like to enter a society dominated by an elderly matriarchy and with limited household appliances, whereas more contemporary studies focus on the culture clashes of emigration, where *exo* in many Greek villages still means an undifferentiated and hostile world compared with the safety and security of Greece.

Society has become more secular since the early Eighties and the behaviour of older generations – closely tied in with priestly conceptions of the good life and priestly sanction for many events – has provided less compelling models for the young recently, although there is a school of thought in Greece that foresees a return to more conservative patterns of behaviour, in line with developments in Europe. During the Seventies and the PASOK years there was a considerable liberalization of the social legislation that affected women in their personal relationships with, for example, secular marriage being allowed. Perhaps the most dramatic decision was the end of gaol sentences for adultery and a whole series of laws was changed that in effect tended to undermine the traditional family structure. But the economic framework has not really altered. Men still expect, and get, a more or less total realm of freedom outside the home, and 'business' is the main focus of existence, even if, in fact, what is involved means all sorts of social activities that in northern countries a wife might participate in. In traditional areas of the economy, apart from retailing, women usually play a very subsidiary part. They would not expect to be involved in major family business decisions, except perhaps the younger and more sophisticated sections of the Athens élite. Ownership of business assets tends to be a male preserve and the sons of any family have an immediate advantage in inheritance terms relative to the daughters. One of the ironies of the end of the dowry system is that in its original form it did at least fit in with the old patterns of peasant agricultural work. Although deeply partiarchal, and often involving splitting up family farms into ever smaller and less economic plots, it did in a certain sense reflect the economic value of a good wife to a husband, something that modern conventions neglect. In contemporary Greece the son of a family will all too often inherit the family assets *in toto*, whether or not he is capable of running the business, and the daughter will be encouraged to take a job that can be dropped easily after marriage or motherhood. Depending on education levels, white-collar jobs in banking and state employment are popular.

In the world of the smallest Greeks, little changes. To be a child in Greece is to be very fortunate. Most Greeks have an instinctive empathy and love of small children, and a recognition of their needs. The toddler is fêted like a king or queen. But in terms of the relationship of the family to the education system, it is perhaps a good thing that the early years are enjoyed as they are, and the emotional foundations of life are so strong, because there is less and less security as the child grows up. Greek education has many problems, with teachers complaining of poor pay and underfunding in much the same way as their European counterparts. But, considering the modest level of resources available, much is achieved, often in spite of the way things are done. Greek schools are honourable but rather austere places and facilities for drama, art and sport are usually poor or absent. Although the children are well treated and in most schools, at whatever level, there is a sense of order and discipline sometimes missing in Britain, standards are not always very high and there are frequent shortages of staff and equipment, mostly in scientific education. Perhaps it is to Greece's advantage that there is no problem of multiculturalism in the curriculum and that all children study the same programme of subjects within a clearly defined national culture. But, once again, the family has to come to the rescue and make up for what the state does not provide. Extra tuition is a common feature of Greek school life, particularly with languages, and the élite in Athens tend to send their children to expensive foreign-run language schools as a preparation for the international business life ahead of them. But this option is obviously only open to a very small minority and most of middle- and lower-income Greece has to help its children struggle on as best they can.

As elsewhere, Greek women will determine the pace of change, as they have in the recent past. In a family I know, the men of each generation have played typical roles and suffered typical Greek fates with the great-grandfather dying of a septic wound from an agricultural accident in the days before antibiotics. But the lives of the women in it have changed dramatically. The granny, actually a great-granny, is a very old lady indeed and more or less illiterate. She brought up her daughter on her own, cultivating vegetables in the mountains and living the life of a subsistence peasant. In the old days she virtually fed herself, as well as making soap and many of her clothes. She wove rugs on a loom Penelope in the *Odyssey* would have recognized and lived in a predominantly oral society with a rich range of songs and expressions. Now she lives with her family in their city flat.

Her daughter grew up in a different world. She was good at school and became one of the first qualified women teachers in the region. She, in turn, had a daughter, whom she took on the back of her donkey to the village school in the hills behind the city, when the only way of getting there was a precipitous track made by the Ottomans. This was in the early Fifties when many villages in Greece were isolated and self-contained communities lived without electricity. But education was spreading in Greece and women were among the prime beneficiaries. The family structure, like the Greek language, strong but infinitely elastic, had to change a little to fit it all in and there was no more making bread at home, to mention just one change.

In turn, the granddaughter was good at school and won a place at Athens University. She has since become a leading university teacher of philosophy. So there has been a radical shift in the transition from peasant woman to independent intellectual in three generations. But the great-granny, *yiayia*, is helping to bring up her great-granddaughter, who is being taught the traditional songs of the Tayetos villages at her knee. So although, in one sense, there has been a revolution in the family, in another little or nothing has changed.

Above: April 1967: the King with leaders of the dictatorship

Below: Manipulation of public opinion: a pro-junta demonstration at Patras

Above: King Constantine flees after a failed coup attempt, December 1967

Below: Syntagma Square in Athens: a battlefield after tanks attacked protesting students

Above: Nationalist imagery: junta Prime Minister Papadopoulos dancing with evzones

Below: 1974, the final crisis of the dictatorship over Cyprus: Archbishop Makarios with Papadopoulos

Above: The Katakouzinos family home in Bucharest: serious wealth abroad

Below: Tobacco workers near Kavala: low wages encouraged emigration

PASOK leader Andreas Papandreou: addressing a meeting in 1974 after seven years' exile

Above: Papandreou in London in 1988 with Dimitra Liani

Below: The tourist invasion: a waiting hall at Athens airport

Above: The strength of popular tradition: fire-walking by Orthodox believers in Macedonia on Saint Athanasios's feast day

Below: The profound humanity of the people: a village couple in the Peloponnese. Their tableau celebrates the unity of Epirus and Macedonia with Greece

ism and rebellion throughout its history. Petra is in the middle of its north coast, a small coastal village with winding Ottoman alleyways and fine merchants' houses along the seafront, a few miles from the famous fortress town of Molivos. Petra means rock and a delightful church stands on a solid block two hundred feet high that rises from the middle of the small town. It invites wordplay: St Peter was the rock on which Christ would build his church. Petra, rock, my strong St Peter – one of those small buildings in the Greek landscape that reverberate with layers of meaning and symbolic significance. Below it stand the crumbling Ottoman warehouses and customs post, a reminder of the commercial boom in this island at the end of the last century when it was a centre of trade, something that today's tourism and forestry have not replaced. Lesbos is just too close to Turkey now; across the sea on a winter afternoon the landmass looks grey and forbidding. The patrol boats of the Greek navy are a familiar sight off the coast.

The beach at Petra is not an attractive sight with rotting debris of unmistakable origin and cold unfriendly water. The latter gives a clue to the origin of the former. There is nothing wrong with waste-disposal arrangements on Lesbos but the north coast of the island faces the channel that flows south out of the Black Sea, the Bosporus and the Sea of Marmara into the Aegean. It brings with it waste from the ten million inhabitants of Greater Istanbul and the numerous factories in the satellite towns around the Sea of Marmara – as well as colder water. Contact with Turkey once brought wealth, now it brings sewage. But that is not all. Some of these wastes are more unpleasant than ordinary human detritus. For instance, the leather industry is a mainstay of the Turkish economy in the Marmara region and chromium chemicals are used in tanning. There is no regular system for the safe disposal of dangerous waste in Istanbul and no doubt most of it ends up in the sea and some on Petra beach. The whole problem is, of course, an aspect of the wider crisis of the Black Sea which is in a much worse condition than the Aegean, primarily as a result of pollution from the Danube. Fish stocks are declining rapidly, famous wildlife, such as the dolphins that the ancient Greeks regarded as the patrons of Trebizond, is dying out and remedial action is urgently needed.

Ios and Petra are the two extremes perhaps, but there is no doubt that the Greek environment is under threat from numerous quarters. Some are external. The citizens of Petra blame the Turks for their problems in a situation where traditional nationalist prejudice fits environmental reality. But foreign scapegoats are only part of the story, whether they are tanneries on the south side of the Golden Horn, Panamanian tankers washing out their tanks in the Gulf of Corinth or the British-registered tanker, belonging to one of the world's largest oil companies, I once watched trail a stinking line of diesel oil a mile long across the Saronic Gulf that was bound to end up on the Aegina beaches, a refuge for many British holiday-makers.

In between, are all the common threats, with many of them directly or indirectly connected with tourism. In most areas of Greece water is becoming increasingly short, making rivers carry more and more concentrated effluent. Farmers' demands for the supply of water seem to be insatiable as their profits depend considerably on irrigation schemes. The value of these schemes, if they destroy wetlands and change the height of the water table, is at last coming into question. As the waters feeding wetlands are removed, either by diverting source waters or pumping out the ground water, the land near the sea grows saltier. And water that is trapped behind dams no longer floods and restores plains each year. Lake Carla, in eastern Greece, was drained in the 1960s and now people want it reflooded to replenish local watercourses.

The villains behind these schemes are often in control of European Community structural investment funds, usually engineers or agricultural lobbyists with no ecological awareness. The schemes are designed to channel EC aid to the poorer members of the Community. The wrecked state of the Greek economy and the huge amounts of hard currency involved have an undue influence on political decision-making. Between 1989 and 1993 the structural funds made over 7.2 billion ECUs ($9 billion) to Greece, a sum which greatly exceeds the entire EC overseas aid budget. It has financed what many see as a series of environmental disasters in Greece and there is a substantial lobby for what may well be the largest yet.

The hot plains of Thessaly have always been short of water in summer and agricultural productivity could no doubt be boosted by irrigation. Ever since the mid-1920s engineers have wanted to blast a tunnel through the Pindus mountains to divert water from the Akhelóös river which flows into the sea near Ithaca in western Greece and use it to irrigate these thirsty lands. The plan has the atmosphere of some of the early Soviet schemes to make poor land bloom by megaprojects such as the project that has turned the Aral Sea into an environmental catastrophe thanks to irrigation for intensive cotton cultivation. The Akhelóös scheme would have similar effects, particularly damaging the marshlands of Missolonghi with their fish farms and delicate ecology. In the past, the scheme has always been stopped from getting off the ground because of the immense cost involved, but there now appears to be a real prospect of EC finance to make it a reality.

Compounding the problems caused by these grandiose, ill-thought-out schemes is the insidious effect of population growth around the Mediterranean generally. Greece is not badly off in this respect, with a population density of about eighty people per square kilometre of coastal area. Countries such as Syria and Israel have far higher figures of above two hundred people. But Greece receives a very large share of the eastern Mediterranean's tourists, and the Mediterranean Sea does not naturally cope well with pollution. Tides are low and it takes a long time for water to circulate. The Mediterranean basin generally accounts for a third of the entire world tourist market. The already vast number of 54 million foreign visitors in the mid Eighties is expected to rise to 170 million by the year 2025. And tourists tend to come in the summer months when water is scarce. At the moment the government in Athens seems to have little or no grasp of the scale of difficulties that are likely to be involved in managing Greece's share of this vast influx of people – no more than most other Mediterranean littoral governments to be fair.

It is not impossible to make progress. A few years ago it was very unwise to swim off Nice or near Barcelona, although many risked it. But there have been improvements, especially in the south of France, and Athens is doing all the right things with its new sewerage schemes. But the Mediterranean is a small sea and it can easily be damaged. Near a crossroads, in terms of marine communications, between the Middle East and Europe, Greece is very vulnerable to outside and international factors over which it has no control. Thankfully, there has not yet been a major tanker oil spill in the eastern Mediterranean or Black Sea, along the lines of the Amoco Cadiz disaster in Brittany. But with the intensity of shipping in the area, and the high proportion of oil vessels, many experts feel it is only a matter of time. The emergency services, compared with some countries, are not well equipped and, depending on where a major incident took place, a degree of international coordination would be needed that might be difficult to attain, given the uncertain political relationships between Greece and some of her neighbours.

Fishing is another problem area. Greeks love fish and in a country where meat has often been expensive and scarce, and with consumption restricted by Orthodox tradition, there is a great demand for whatever fish can be caught. But a walk around that mecca of demotic language, the Piraeus fishmarket, will quickly show at most times of year how much is expensive or imported – or both. Although Greece has inshore fishing limits, like most maritime countries, they are difficult to enforce, given the length and complexity of the coastline. That might not matter so much if there were equal developments as far as technology goes, but a major problem in recent years has been the incursion of huge Japanese, Russian and Korean fish-factory ships into the Mediterranean. They may not be fishing within illegal perimeters, but they are able to vacuum up whole shoals of fish with devastating effect on fish stocks. This particularly applies to what were popular treats like swordfish and tuna, leaving the Greek housewife with humble creatures like the *gopa* as substitutes.

The Greek forests present a different environmental case. There is little acid rain in Greece and the deciduous forests on mountain ranges like the Tayetos are reservoirs of health and beauty in the landscape. The pine forests near cities, in Attica mainly, are vulnerable, principally to forest fires. In the last few years summer temperatures in the Balkans have been abnormally high and any minor fire can, and does, easily turn into a major conflagration. Then there are the fires started intentionally. Near Athens there is intense pressure on land for new housing and although many forests are in theory preserved from development, the law can only be enforced when the land is actually forested. If trees are burnt and the land turns into scrub, in practice there is often little to prevent the developers moving in. Shepherds can also take part in the destructive process, setting fire to trees to produce grassland for their animals. This may happen because they, in turn, have been displaced from their traditional realms by housing or industrial development. The demographic nature of Athens is a root cause of the problem with so many of its citizens coming from the countryside or from the islands, seeing the metropolis as somewhere to be exploited for quick money rather than sharing in its long-term environmental considerations. Greece has invested heavily in aircraft that can scoop up large quantities of water from the sea or lakes to drop on to fires. In coastal regions they are very effective against small fires, but there have been some tragic losses of major forest expanses in the mountains and in Attica in recent years.

When this happens, the resident animals and birds are among the first victims and in many cases they do not re-establish themselves once the tree cover begins to grow again. Greece is home to some remarkable birds and mammals, to fish, flowers and reptiles. The tourist notices the brilliant displays of wild flowers on a spring visit to an island like Crete, the fast-travelling lizards or, later, the summer but-terflies. But the sea contains lesser-known rarities like the monk seal, now subject to a World Wide Fund for Nature rescue programme on its last island redoubts, and the moun-tains some of the last vultures in Europe and a marvellous range of eagles and other birds of prey. In nearly all cases their existence is under threat, except for that of the Golden eagle, which is still relatively common, and some of the smaller predators. Crete is a stronghold of the great birds and on the whole they have been treated well, with the Cretans having a natural respect for them. That unpleasant institution, the taxidermist's shop, still exists in many Greek cities and visitors should not under any circumstances buy what may well have been shot or trapped illegally.

Tourism itself, with its pressure on what can sometimes be a fragile environment, produces its own problems. The best example is the Mediterranean turtle on Zakynthos. The Ionian island has some of the last beaches where this creature nests regularly. It arrives on the beach to do so on spring evenings at the same time that tourists start to visit, and the baby turtles hatch out as the season gets to its height. The islanders want to build more hotels and encourage tourism – a response to the overcrowding on nearby Corfu. Although international wildlife organizations are active in the campaign to save the turtles, and some package holiday companies have cooperated by giving out information on the need to behave sensitively near the nesting beaches, their fate is still very much in the balance. The islanders resent outsiders telling them to do things which would involve a loss of money and relations between them and environmentalists active there are very bad. The German wildlife conservation agency has agreed, in principle, to organize a boycott of Zakynthos which may have a more powerful effect on the short-sighted inhabitants than anything else. The penny, or the drachma, does not seem to have dropped in Greece that environmentally oriented tourism can be exceedingly profitable, as say, the Everglades national park in Florida has found.

And the tourist is now more at risk personally from the environment than before. With the depletion of the ozone layer, it is possible that doctors may well actively discourage the kind of beach holiday spent baking in the August sun, previously associated with health. Already skin cancer cases are rising among Greeks, although they generally stay more covered up in summer than foreigners do. It is unusual in Athens, for instance, to see anyone other than very young men wearing shorts – outside the hottest weather. Cases of serious sunburn, even sunstroke, are admitted to Greek hospitals every summer and these people considerably increase their cancer risks.

The new awareness points up the basic fragility of some parts of the mass tourist industry in Greece. Profit margins of many hotels and restaurants are already very low and a small decline in numbers would produce bankruptcies on a scale similar to those in the Spanish industry where many hotels are unsaleable at any price. There is some evidence that health concerns are already beginning to influence the type of holiday taken in hot countries and Greece may be badly affected.

A neglected aspect of the environmental crisis in Greece is the threat to the over six thousand species of plants, of which one tenth are unique to the country. Some are valuable medicinal plants, the basis for many widely used drugs such as *Atropa belladonna* used for Parkinson's Disease and *Veratum album* for hypertension. As a result of over collection some, such as *Gentiana lutea*, have become virtually extinct. A possible reason is the old tradition of the quack doctor – the Vikos doctor of northern Greece, named after the great gorge in the Pindus, famous for its variety of medicinal plants. These 'doctors' toured the villages until recently, selling what were in many cases quack remedies, playing on the superstition of the people and on the expense of prescription drugs.

The most interesting animals in the country are not, on the whole, threatened in the same way as marine life and some birds. This is because they are mostly natives of the northern forests, or of remote mountain areas, where few tourists – or anyone else for that matter – go. In the mountains adjoining Bulgaria and Albania wolves and lynx, and the occasional brown bear, are still to be found – although the latter is commoner in nature reserves on the Bulgarian side of the border in the Rhodope mountains. General depopulation and changes in agricultural practices are thought to be behind an increase in wolf numbers on the border with Albania, east of Konitsa. These ranging pack animals, full of mythological and psychological associations, carefully make their homes in the high mountains, in the dark and deserted pine forests, then descend to lower areas, even to the outskirts of villages, in the winter. It is nearly always possible to tell when you are in a wolf area by the size of the shepherds' dogs which, even by the fearsome standards of Greek shepherd dogs, are particularly large and evil-looking. Wolves are also becoming commoner in the central Pindus mountains. The decline of traditional pastoralism and the consequent reduction in the supply of lambs has also meant fewer shepherds' guns to shoot predators. In southern Albania it used to be a pastime for the élite politburo members and friends to go on organized shoots, but these have happily ceased with the advent of democracy and pluralism. And so, among all the other unwanted border-crossers from Albania, there is some interesting wildlife as well – night-time voyagers from the hungry mountains heading towards richer pickings.

There are also many interesting small mammals in Greece such as the wild cat and the pine martin. The latter can be a domestic visitor at times, even in urban areas, venturing into people's gardens to rob birds' nests of their eggs on spring evenings. The wild cat is pretty well confined to the great northern forests and is in no way the same creature as the feral cat that lives a semi-wild existence everywhere in Greece, hopefully picking up scraps for its thin frame and making an atmospheric subject for the professional postcard photographer as it winds around café chairs.

Greek reptiles also thrive, subject to the decline in the number and size of wetlands that sustain many of them. The croak of frogs can be heard in parts of central Athens in just the same way as the sound must have inspired the ancient dramatist Aristophanes two thousand years ago. And the immense variety of rocky and scrubby hillsides are home to countless snakes such as the Balkan adder whose poison can kill. These are sometimes caught by eagles and carried long distances through the air. It is one of the great sights of rural Greece, high in the Tayetos perhaps, to see a Golden or

Booted eagle with a writhing reptile in its claws, something for the young in the far nest, something to evoke images of classical mythology for the visitor, something to conjure up danger and drama in the natural world.

Danger has always been in the environment. The demotic saying that the more beautiful the Aegean looks, the more likely it is to kill you alludes, perhaps, to the lethal storms that can blow up out of nowhere, those that Odysseus encountered on his wanderings. There is a belief in Crete about the dangers of living on the coast, with earthquakes usually coming from the sea, sent by the angry god Poseidon. But to the visitor, the environment is something to immerse oneself in, to find rest, renewal and inspiration. To the Greek it presents a different picture. Only recently have serious diseases like coastal malaria been eradicated and once every few years there is a serious earthquake – apart from the almost monotonous monthly reports of tremors. There has been no real industrial revolution in Greece and consequently no Romantic movement in literature to see nature threatened by man's activities. Greek poets and writers have tended to see nature as something to take for granted. Many outside observers have been astonished at the slowness of the ecological movement to get going in Greece and the absence of any powerful organized conservation and environment lobby along the lines of those found in most European countries. Political experts with inborn respect for Greek political awareness are surprised at the weakness of the green political movement, considering that the Greek system of proportional representation gives a very fair deal to small parties.

Government action has been confined to rather minor and marginal initiatives, welcome in themselves, such as the PASOK anti-litter campaign of the mid Eighties. Unfortunately, Greeks are cynical about the activities of their governments if they are involved with abstract invocations to the public good. They tend to think that if the government does anything it will be done badly – or that possibly it should not be done at all. This is a healthy scepticism in many respects, given what so many Greek governments have been like, but applied to environmental matters it is very unhelpful as many of the environmental threats need countering by long-term policies that often demand the sacrifice of short-term private interests. But it has been one of the very positive dimensions of the European Community in Greek life that many of its environment directives have been far in advance of what could have been achieved if matters had been left to the government or public opinion – with the neglect of the Athens environmental crisis as a cardinal example. But a good deal remains to be done. Perhaps public awareness will grow, beginning with the younger urban generation who are strangers to the normal peasant response to kill or drive wildlife away. Many years ago on a small island I remember looking down at a brightly coloured toad crossing the road. My pleasant, cheerful landlady was trimming her *bouzi* like any suburban housewife in England might clip her privet. I asked her the Greek word for toad and she answered '*vatraxos*', picking it up carefully. 'Shall I kill it for you?' she inquired solicitously. I said not and it was duly placed in the long grass by the side of the road to make its escape. But for how long? Maria came from a large peasant family and killing that creature would have been a natural expression of a little power over nature. How long a change of attitude will take is a rather depressing question. Nearly all the most threatened wildlife in Greece is protected with international help, without which local conservationists would not achieve much. Enforcement of environmental law, even if it reaches the statute book, can be problematic at the best of times, and the visitor can contribute towards a better climate by respecting the environment, arguing in favour of controls and avoiding involvement with environment-threatening businesses.

Part Three

NEIGHBOURS AND MINORITIES

15. The Hidden Patchwork:
Albanians, Vlachs and Sarakatsans

> No nation are so detested and dreaded by their
> neighbours as the Albanese: the Greeks hardly
> regard them as Christians, or the Turks as Moslems;
> and in fact they are a mixture of both and sometimes
> neither.
>
> – Byron, Notes to 'Childe Harold'

Historically, relations between Greece and Albania, and
between Greeks and individual Albanians, have been anything
from poor to very bad indeed. Among the seventy-one volumes
of the works of the Albanian dictator Enver Hoxha is *Two
Friendly Peoples*, his account of Greek–Albanian relations. It
would do well in a competition to find the world's most
misleading title.

The reasons for these problems go back in history but are
also contemporary. In December 1990 the police-state apparatus on the border between Albania and Greece was
abolished, and most of the Albanian armed guards were
withdrawn from the border area around Kakavia, high in the
Epirus mountains. Until then, any Albanian trying to leave the
country since 1945 had been shot on sight and the border was
protected by a high electric fence.

The immediate result was an influx of penniless, destitute
Albanian refugees into Greece. Thousands struggled through
deep snow and icy rivers to reach freedom and a better
economic life. At first they were welcomed by the local Greeks

who provided food for hungry mouths and shoes for the unshod. But as the influx continued intermittently over the next few months, tolerance and generosity began to run out, particularly in the regional capital of Yannina, where Albanians stealing garden vegetables or simply taking food from shops became a common problem. This state of affairs worsened, with armed gangs of Albanians robbing isolated houses, terrifying villagers and contributing to a general Wild West atmosphere around the border. Greek police action has been firm, not to say brutal on some occasions, with deaths of Albanian refugees and there have been numerous accusations of human rights violations.

The irony of the collapse of Communism in Albania has been that for fifty years Albania was protected by a wall of steel of the Albanians' making. People were not allowed passports and foreign travel or work abroad was almost impossible. This situation was replaced in 1991 by a very high security operation on the Greek side of the border, with crack units of the Greek army attempting to prevent illegal immigrants fleeing through the forests towards Yannina, Parga, Igoumenitsa and, ultimately, Athens. It was a very strange experience to witness the original influx in December and January 1991, lost souls arriving to wander the Greek streets. Small, dark people from mountain fastnesses, they were dressed in clothes thirty years or more out of fashion and appeared to come from another world. To the Albanians emerging from fifty years of poverty and isolation, the small shops of Greek provincial towns seemed like Ali Baba's cave, treasures beyond the ordinary imagination.

But this exodus had happened before. It is only necessary to travel about ten miles outside Athens into rural Attica to find villages like Aspropirgos or Fili where most of the inhabitants are Albanians and where many of the older generation prefer to speak their own language. Many of these Albanians were refugees from religious persecution under the Ottomans, Christian believers, and the extent of their settlement is not widely appreciated. The 1906 edition of the Baedeker guide gives the population of the island of Salamis, on Athens' very doorstep, at about six thousand people, of whom all but ninety were Albanian. The picture is endlessly complex as many of these were not refugees but part of the large Ottoman garrison and administrative apparatus based in Greece. Albanians held many responsible positions under the Turks throughout the nineteenth century in Greece. They were, at best, unloved by most Greeks then and viewed as part of the machinery of Turkish oppression and as Moslem collaborators. Elsewhere in the Ottoman Empire Albanians became rulers of Egypt and of what is now Syria. The great founder of Egyptian national consciousness, Muhammed Ali, was an Albanian.

A generation or two further back, relations had also been bad – but for different reasons. The first stirrings of revolt by Greek nationalists against the Turks took place in the late eighteenth century. After these failed, hordes of marauding Albanian irregulars were sent in by the Sublime Porte to 'pacify' the country. This pacification took the form of a notorious campaign of rapine and terror against the Greek population at large, particularly in the Peloponnese, then and later fountainhead of the independence movement.

Some of these Albanians stayed behind and many people with immaculate Greek credentials now are of Albanian descent. But the recent history after the War has been the most difficult. Albania became Communist through a genuine indigenous revolution in which the Red Army played no part. Albania tried to assist the Greek Communist army during the latter stages of the Civil War, both by providing supplies, as Yugoslavia did, and by acting as a base for the Greeks to regroup. Within Albania, many important leaders of the national liberation movement were from the 100,000-strong

Greek minority and Communism in Albania was always strongest in the southern regions where most of the Greek minority
lived. Enver Hoxha's partisans were able to win their first
important victories against the Axis Occupation forces in
these regions. The defeat of the Left in the Civil War meant
that Albania was kept in almost hermetic isolation from
Greece and shooting incidents on the border were a regular
event for many years. The important Albanian modernist
painter Zois Shuttie escaped from Albania in the 1960s by
dodging bullets from the Greek as well as the Albanian side –
and his experience was far from unique. Whatever the rhetoric
about Albanian freedom that issued from Athens during the
Cold War years, the uncomfortable reality was that Hoxha's
policy of isolation, rhetorical aggression and intense border
security suited Greek strategic interests down to the ground,
even to bizarre benefits such as the large amount of money the
colonels' junta was able to extract from NATO towards
improving the Epirus roads in response to a non-existent
security 'threat' from Albania. As a result, the two countries
were technically at war for many years and diplomatic relations were not restored until the 1970s. It was not until the
advent of the PASOK government in 1981 that trade and
economic links started to develop normally. It is perhaps
significant that the Albanian Deputy Foreign Minister then,
Mr Socrates Plaka, was, as his name so graphically indicates,
of ethnic Greek origin.

Underlying many problems is the fact that Greece has
historically laid claim to large areas of Albanian territory,
stretching as far as the Shkumbi river valley in central Albania.
What is now southern Albania is called Vorio Epirus (northern
Epirus) by many Greeks and was given to Greece in 1914
when the Great Powers were trying to sort out the results of
the Second Balkan War. About 200,000 Greeks live in Albania
and form the majority of the population in many southern

areas, mainly in the Dropull river valley. Although the 1914 decision was revoked by the Ambassadors Conference of Paris in 1921, when the Powers felt the only way to end the anarchy in Albania was to set up a centralized state based on Tirana, many Greeks, not all of the extreme Right, hanker after the return of these territories and their incorporation into Greece. This prospect has been viewed with understandable horror by all Albanian governments in Tirana – Communist and post-Communist.

The question of the numbers and origins of the Greeks in Albania is itself very controversial. Albanians claim that Greeks were brought in as indentured labourers by the Turkish beys in the days of Ottoman rule. Greeks claim that there has always been Greek settlement in the region since the original movements of prehistoric tribes. Professor Sederholm of Finland, in charge of the League of Nations inquiry into the problem in 1921–3, estimated the total number of Greek speakers as only 35,000 to 40,000 but his definition of Greek may have been unduly narrow. At the time of the invasion of Albania by Italy in April 1939, the Albanians only recognized a Greek minority of some 20,000, but by then the Greeks did at least have their own schools, separate representation on local councils and their own members in the parliament – however empty a body that was under King Zog.

Greeks also point to the use of the Greek language under Ali Pasha as an example of their right to this region. Not only Ali Pasha but even the Turkish beys would use Greek for business and official purposes as the Albanian language was seldom written. After Ali Pasha's overthrow in 1822 the Turks tended to encourage the use of Greek and, to discourage nascent Albanian national feeling, they banned the production of newspapers in Albanian and closed down Albanian schools. As a result of this repression many Albanians consider that Greek has had an artificial status and that Greek government actions and statistics are usually untrustworthy. They cite many examples in recent history of Greek disregard for international decisions taken in the region. One was the celebrated problem of 1924 when the Greek government refused to give up control of the 'fourteen villages' near Korca that the Delimitation Commission of the Ambassadors Conference in 1921 had decided were Albanian. So with these, and similar, memories, Enver Hoxha's cultural repression of the Greeks was not really unpopular with most Albanians, especially the southern Tosk Albanians who had a long history of contact with Greece.

Of concern too have been the activities of the Greek Orthodox Church in Tirana. There is a large minority of Orthodox Christians in Albania who became autocephalous in the 1920s under the great leader Fan Noli, but the northern Greek bishops are seen as having ill-concealed designs on the Albanian believers, an impression reinforced by the campaigns of the Church against the appalling persecution of believers in Albania under Hoxha in the 1970s.

A recent controversy involved the attempt by the Ecumenical Patriarchate in Istanbul to appoint a Greek Metropolitan, Anastasios Yanulatos, head of the Orthodox Church in Albania, as a 'missionary bishop' with the task of re-establishing the Orthodox Church. But the appointment set off a storm of protest in Albania in August 1992. It was seen by most Albanians as a Greek attempt to seize control of the reviving Church, especially as three other Greek nationals were named at the same time as bishops to other Albanian districts.

After Communism began to disintegrate in Albania the Greeks, in common with many other groups and currents of opinion, formed their own political party, Omonia. It succeeded in electing five MPs to the first democratic parliament in 1991, but since then it has been dogged by controversy and was banned from the March 1992 elections. Relations between

Greeks and Albanians have deteriorated within the country, with attacks on Greek-owned shops in Sarande and Gjirokastra. Greeks have been prominent in opposition to the last vestiges of Communism in the regional capital of Gjirokastra, both birthplace of Enver Hoxha and home of a large Greek minority. In a remarkable series of events in August 1991 the colossal marble statue of Hoxha overlooking the Dropull valley was demolished by a rioting crowd. Whatever the course of events, there seems to be one certainty in the turmoil that the increasingly unstable position of Greeks in southern Albania will lead to more applications to emigrate to Greece – something the Athens government will find hard to resist. It will add to their refugee problem, with so many ethnic Greeks to absorb from the Soviet Union and the other newly free countries of Eastern Europe who wish to return to the motherland. Some Albanian Greeks have family connections and can be expected to settle down quickly and play a useful part in the economy, but others do not and may find the process difficult. An unfortunate aspect of 'Albanian' violence and crime in Greece is that some of it is committed by ethnic Greeks as well as by the ubiquitous Albanians. Popular attention is diverted from the fact that most Albanian immigrant workers are not criminals and do not cause trouble. They often do hard-slog jobs, such as seasonal agriculture, which benefit the general Greek economy. A new tabloid demonology is emerging with undertones of racism.

At the other end of the minority spectrum in Greece are the Vlachs who have been in Greece since the fall of the Roman Empire. Most explanations of the origin of this community of pastoralists suggest that they are descended from the remains of the Roman legions based in the Balkans. They are a very well-assimilated people but there are emerging problems, although of a less serious kind than those with the Albanians or the Moslem Turks in Thrace.

Metsovo. The famous village is about twenty miles east of Yannina, towards the towering peaks of the Pindus mountains. It is in a valley, reasonably prosperous, with pretty wooden-faced houses with overhanging tiled roofs for the winter snow. There is a strange physical division among the male inhabitants. Some are very tall, by Greek standards, and often blond, while others are very short and dark. They are, respectively, Sarakatsans and Vlachs. The days of wearing ethnic costume are more or less over, unfortunately, except for weddings or high days and holidays. But there is still an unmistakable cohesion and shared indentity among the old men sitting on the bench by the bus stop: all in dark suits, with weatherbeaten faces and identical hand-carved walking-sticks. They are all Vlachs, as is the man by the side of the road who needs a lift. He sits silently in the back, staring out of the window into a landscape so like the Cotswolds: little beech coppices, rushing streams, a kingfisher in front of the car. We reach his destination, a small church on the outskirts of the next village. He points at the assembling wedding party, '*Numta*.' He coughs and climbs out of the car.

To say 'wedding' in Vlach is to speak the language of the Roman legions abandoned to the north of Metsovo. *Measa* (table), from the Latin *mensa*, is perhaps an easier word to pick up. But even this origin is not absolutely certain, although it is the most likely on linguistic grounds in that Vlach has some affinities with Romanian and the Latin basis of the Romanian language is generally accepted.

Vlachs live in Greece, Bulgaria, Macedonia and Albania, although there are also numerous communities in exile in the United States, Canada, Germany and Australia. The Vlachs were originally nearly all wandering shepherds and a basic cause of their conflict with the tall, unGreek blond men in Metsovo, the Sarakatsans, is because of the bitter and intractable rows over grazing rights, particularly summer grazing, that permeate life in northern Greece.

Vlachos is a slang phrase of disapproval in Greek. To be *vlachos* is to be thought low, dishonest and untrustworthy, but it goes without saying that there have been some very distinguished Vlachs in Greek life. The battleship moored in Piraeus harbour as a national monument, the great ancient grey warhorse of the Hellenic navy, so unfortunately moved from its old mooring point on Poros, the *Evangelos Averof*, was a gift to the nation in its hour of need from a Vlach, one of the richest Greeks of his day, and named after him. It was for a long time used as a training ship by the Greek navy in the Saronic Gulf and then retired. So the standard Vlach images do need to be treated with great caution. The strange little men in the northern mountains, wearing long black capes, are the greatest pastoralists of all, expert at running herds of three or four thousand sheep, surrounded by dogs so large and fierce that they inspire more fear among unwary walkers than the occasional wolf they are designed to deter.

The heartland of the Vlachs is the central Pindus. Here the language has still a reasonably strong foothold, with Vlach publications and cultural festivals. But it is not so flourishing elsewhere. The scattered herdsmen suffered dreadfully during the Second Balkan War in 1911–12 when they and their animals were massacred by armed bands of Bulgarians, Greeks and Serbs in the bloody conflict over Macedonia. Then there was scarcely time to recover before the horrors of the Axis Occupation, where to begin with the Bulgarians again played a nefarious role, followed by the extortions of the anti-Communist forces. Many of the naturally anti-authoritarian Vlachs tended to support the Left – although a few were lured into a 'Roman legion' by Italian fascists – and they all suffered in the Greek equivalent of the Highland Clearances organized from Athens. As a result, many northern cities have a substantial Vlach element in the population, as Athens does itself, and towns in Thessaly too. There were many Vlachs among the refugees in Tashkent in the Soviet Union, most of whom only began to return to Greece in the early 1980s. But the Vlach attachment to the land is surprisingly strong and many all-but-deserted villages were brought to life again, mostly in the northern redoubt of the Meglen area, next to former Yugoslavia. Here, a slightly different version of the language is spoken and many old traditions are alive and well. Another remote and beautiful region where many Vlachs are to be found is around Lakes Prespa and Ochrid. One of the great ethnic crossroads of the Balkans, I have found four languages – Greek, Vlach, Albanian and Bulgarian – spoken in a village of only three hundred families who fled from Macedonia during the Balkan wars. The main centre of the approximately forty thousand remaining Slav-speaking Greeks is in the north Vardar valley adjoining the former Yugoslav border. Vlachs are famous metal workers and carpenters and in Yannina and other northern regional centres a walk through the bazaar or street market is a sure way to find them at work.

There is a central ambiguity in Greece about Vlach culture now. Officially, as there are no recognized ethnic minorities in Greece, Vlach is not used in schools, whereas before the War there were many Romanian-sponsored schools in the Pindus villages. Vlachs now tend to be as patriotic as anyone else in Greece and there is no separatist or nationalist movement. The language is being quietly neglected by the inherently universalist nature of Greek language and culture. Some scholars might say this is not much loss. The Vlach language is ugly on the ear and there is little in the way of a literary tradition apart from a few songs and some interesting dances. There are no great primitive epic cycles as in Greece, Albania and the former Yugoslavia. But this is not a result of industrial society and mass market culture driving out the old traditions. German folklorists who studied the Vlachs in the nineteenth century were unable to find much to record, even though the societies they studied were to all intents and purposes little changed from medieval times. Increasing intermarriage has led to more and more Greek idioms introduced into Vlach to the chagrin of Vlach cultural activists.

There is a sense of unease when talking to Vlachs about their efforts to preserve their culture and traditions in the face of official indifference verging on hostility. Most Vlachs feel that as they have never done anything to rock the Greek political boat, in terms of separatist or nationalist ambitions, they should get a better deal. But in Athens there is little response and many independent observers feel that the whole issue shows the over-centralized and inherently authoritarian Greek education and cultural establishment at its worst. It would cost very little to satisfy the extremely modest ambitions of most Vlachs which, in terms of the formal educational system, extend only to the introduction of a certain amount of Vlach language-teaching for small children and some help with cultural publications. The Athens establishment will only have itself to blame if, in a time of increasing demands for cultural autonomy in the Balkans, the present very moderate and responsible leaders of Vlach opinion are replaced by more militant and difficult figures.

Their fellow villagers in Metsovo, the Sarakatsans, present no such problems. The evidence, magisterially summarized by the English scholar John Campbell in his seminal work on the subject, is that they are Greek, very Greek indeed, and there is support for the view some hold that they may have been in Greece since the ancient world. Campbell's work, *Honour, Family and Patronage*, is absorbing reading not simply because of its fieldwork and scholarship but because a comparison with the present day shows how the Sarakatsans appear to have lost more of their original pastoral culture more quickly and thoroughly than any other similar Greek community. The

Turks of Thrace, for example, or many Vlachs, live much as they always have, but the world Campbell investigated in the 1950s (which was also described by Paddy Leigh Fermor in *Roumeli*) has pretty completely disappeared. The Sarakatsans have suffered like other groups from the general decline of pastoralism and changes in land settlement patterns and agricultural practices, but there is a sense of a fractured culture and of a complete collapse before urban pressures that is very sad and also difficult to explain. It is significant, perhaps, that virtually every souvenir shop in Metsovo and the surrounding tourist area in the Pindus is run by Sarakatsans. The tall, immensely dignified men look uncomfortable and out of place behind the nick-nack shop counters, but there is also a sense of acceptance of their fate.

It is an irony that despite official policy in Athens it is the more openly non-Greek cultures, like the Vlachs, that seem to be surviving best and it must be a cause of great sadness to everybody who loves Greece that defined minority cultures of great richness and interest such as the Sarakatsans' appear to be the most vulnerable to technocratic standardization and cheap conformity. There is a problem though for any government in Athens, however well intentioned towards all these groups, that many of the communities are living in remote mountain places precisely because they wanted to get away from state power in the past and, to an appreciable degree, in the present. It is not easy to postulate how government action of any kind can help them and so preserve Greek cultural diversity and richness. But it would not be too controversial, say, for a Greek government to change aspects of its education policy to improve the status of the Vlach language. There are only perhaps forty or fifty thousand Vlachs and despite their general unpopularity their patriotism is not, nor has ever been, in question. However, the Albanians are quite a different matter. It would be unthinkable for any Greek government to try to put the Albanian language, beautiful and complex and of equal antiquity, with its descent from ancient Illyrian, on the same pedestal educationally. The dilemma is how far the perceived cultural superiority of Greek to all other languages necessitates its formal institutionalization in the education system in a way some have argued is quite contrary to modern, liberal educational precepts.

The re-emergence of the Macedonian question to the north will be likely to bring alive again the problem of the cultural repression of the Slav-speaking Greeks as a political issue. Concentrated in and around the city of Florina, but also found in many other parts of northern and central Greece, the Slavophones have been tarred with the Communist brush for forty-odd years and have endured several kinds of discrimination, from education and language restrictions common to all minorities to the more fundamental problems stemming from government decree no. 2536, enacted in 1953, which was designed to colonize the Slav-speaking areas of northern Greece with 'new colonists with healthy national consciousness'. In 1954 the Papagos government resolved to remove all Slav-speakers from official posts in the region regarded as 'Aegean Macedonia' and in 1959, in places such as Florina (Lerin) and Kajlari near the Yugoslav border, the inhabitants were asked to confirm publicly in front of central government officials that they did not speak Macedonian. As a result of these and other human rights violations, large numbers of people emigrated to Australia and Canada where they made up hard-core centres of anti-Greek agitation. The junta period saw many Slav-speakers interned or exiled and little has been done since for their communities. The property of Slavophones who went into exile in Yugoslavia after the Civil War was confiscated by decree 2536/53, which also deprived them of Greek citizenship. The PASOK government of Andreas Papandreou was particularly active in the anti-Slav cause. The then Prime Minister stated that no Macedonian minority existed in Greece and refused to enter into any public discussion of the matter.

In the last two years small numbers of Slavophones have begun to take their grievances on to the international agendas, with delegations to human rights conferences and the UN in Geneva, which have been met with a fierce response from official Greece. Towards the end of 1992 a group of people from the Florina area were to be put on trial in Athens for attempting to form a 'Macedonian Cultural Association'. Whatever the outcome – and there are numerous laws in Greece on the statute book as relics from the Greek Civil War that may well result in convictions – the very fact of such a trial taking place at all is bound to reflect badly on Greece. Many people may hope that the ethnic minority policy of the country will be reconsidered. In the current climate of concern about events in Skopje, and the spreading turmoil to the north, that may be a little much to hope for. The memories of Slav-speakers dancing the *horo*, that most warlike of Balkan dances, to celebrate victories over Athens government troops in the Civil War will take a long time to fade.

16. Thrace and Cyprus

The Turk represents force, as opposed to the law, yet not even a government of force can be maintained without an intellectual element, such as he did not possess.

– Rt Hon. W. E. Gladstone, *Bulgarian Horrors and the Question of the East, 1876*

The relationship between Greece and Turkey comes down to us through historic images of overpowering strength, whether in the Homeric material of Greek forces leaving home to fight at Troy or in the bitter and entrenched anti-Ottoman prejudice of most of British opinion in the nineteenth century. Operation Attila in Cyprus in 1974, when the Turkish army invaded the island and murdered and dispossessed thousands of Greek Cypriots, seems to many as just the latest in a long tradition of outrages.

The Cyprus issue is perhaps the most tired and flyblown on the international agenda, one that appears set in concrete with its entrenched parties, a UN peacekeeping force doing exactly the same job for decades, and a leader like Dr Rauf Denktash, who has been in his position for nearly forty years, making the same pronouncements, many would argue, with no apparent progress towards a political settlement. But the issue is only the most recent of the intractable disputes involving Greece and Turkey, and the Cypriots are not the sole victims of history in this respect.

A colleague once started his newspaper story with the sentence: 'When the Turkish Consulate at Komotini becomes a factor in international politics, we can be sure the Balkans are the Balkans again' – and he was right. Komotini is a one-horse town in Thrace that might make a good setting for a dark deed in an early Eric Ambler thriller, but it is also home to the Turkish diplomatic official whose job it is to look after the interests of the Turkish-speaking Moslem minority, some 104,000 people, who live thereabouts. In the exchange of populations that followed the Treaty of Lausanne in 1922, it was decided to exempt these people, along with the Greeks of Istanbul, and the largely Greek-inhabited islands of Imbros and Tenedos, from the imperative to move national borders. In some people's view in Greece this was an example of the tolerance the modern Greek state has shown towards minorities, while others would probably go along with the English Victorian Prime Minister Gladstone in seeing the Moslems as a relic from 'the black day when they first entered Europe, the one great anti-human specimen of humanity'. He was writing about the Ottoman Turks, of course, and without the Ottomans there would certainly not be a Turkish-speaking minority in Thrace. Gladstone went on to call the Turks 'a tremendous incarnation of military power, an advancing curse that menaced the whole of Europe, leaving a broad line of blood marking the track behind them', representing government by force as opposed to the Hellenic concept of government by law.

These sentiments show as well as anything how, behind all Greek–Turkish disputes, there is a ball and chain of old symbolism and iconography in which Greece is seen to represent law, decency, rationalism, Christianity and European civilization, while Turkey represents anti-democratic principles, Islam, totalitarianism, and so on.

In the down-at-heel world of rural Thrace, all universalist

political rhetoric seems remote. Contrary to Gladstone's view, the Moslems of Thrace are not a homogeneous mass. About half are fully Turkish, about 35,000 are Pomaks of Thracian origin (Bulgarian Moslems who speak their own language, which has never had a written form), and there are about 14,000 Athingani, descendants of Christian heretics who were expelled from Asia Minor during Byzantine times and later converted to Islam. There are also several thousand gypsies who have their own quarters in the larger towns, and who also speak their own language. Thrace is the most deeply Balkan part of Greece in the sense that here several ethnic groups compete for cultural precedence and authority, with an intertwined pattern of different religious and political identities, apart from the very proximate Bulgarians, Macedonians and Turks within their nation states.

The Thracian villages where this minority live look like any other Greek villages except that they have minarets on the horizon. But some villages have church domes too, and storks have been known to nest indiscriminately on either. Most of the time life goes in slow motion in this economically depressed area which borders Turkey and Bulgaria, with poor agriculture, the main product, tobacco, in decline and substantial areas of the countryside still taken over by the Greek military.

But Thrace is none the less a very important place. Before the First World War the territory was Turkish in culture and it was known as Turkey in Europe. Poor as it was, it has always been of considerable strategic importance – the doorstep of the great neighbour on the other side of the Bosporus, far into Asia. In the turmoil in the region after the collapse of Greek power in Asia Minor, the rise of Kemal Atatürk as founder of the new Turkey, and the victory of Turkish arms against the Greeks and Entente Powers after the Smyrna disaster in 1922, there were considerable exchanges of population between Greece and Turkey. Over a million Greek refugees left their old homes in Asia Minor, some of them Turkish-speaking and barely able to understand their mother tongue but regarded as 'Greeks' because they were Christians. But the Moslems of Thrace were allowed to stay on as Greek citizens. They numbered about 86,000, according to the 1924 census figures. Similarly, Greek communities remained in Turkey, principally the Greek Orthodox community of Istanbul, then about 65,000 people but now reduced to a pitiful remnant of about 5,000. This is at the heart of a long-lasting and bitter contention between Greece and Turkey, for the Greeks claim that the Moslem minority in Thrace has been well treated and has maintained itself, whereas the few thousand Greeks in Turkey have been a continually persecuted minority.

Whatever might be said about the Greek treatment of minorities generally, on this issue the demographic and other important material facts support the Greek case. Although Thrace has been starved of public investment and the economy is primitive – acutely so in the remote mountain villages – the numbers of the Turkish minority have increased and there are no restrictions against the Turkish language in schools or mosques, or in any sphere of social life, except those relating to government employment. But Turkish militancy is growing, although most Greeks claim that this is because of manipulation from Turkey rather than because of any problems emanating from the minority itself. It seems doubtful if this is true as the minority does have genuine grievances, especially economic ones. Recent elections have seen candidates from Thrace elected to parliament in Athens running on an open 'Turkish' ticket, much to the chagrin of the Athens establishment which has attempted to enforce the old law which says that to call yourself a Turk is illegal. There were quite serious disturbances in Komotini and other parts of Thrace over this issue in 1990 and 1991 which led to local minority leaders being gaoled. The election of a new Patriarch in Istanbul in 1992 also led to various rows and conflicts. Accusations of Greek discrimination against the Thracian Moslems were made in Istanbul in what appears to have been an anti-Greek press campaign instigated by the Turkish government.

But in one sense it hardly matters in international relations terms. However bad relations between Greece and Turkey have been, no Greek government has been tempted to emulate Ankara in the 1950s and play politics with the lives of a minority. Most impartial observers believe that the anti-Greek riots in Turkey in 1955 were instigated at the highest level of the Ankara government as a policy initiative against Greece in the Cyprus crisis then. Cynics sometimes observe that the running sore actually helps both governments by providing a safety-valve for feelings that in some instances could have led both NATO allies towards full-scale war. But it is difficult to believe, quiet as Thrace is compared with the other areas of Balkan conflict, that it can remain free of the tensions spreading elsewhere. The impetus has always been for neighbouring states to integrate their compatriot minorities, and the Treaty of Lausanne was written an awfully long time ago. It would not take very much in the way of militancy from the Moslems in the direction of closer integration with Turkey for Greece to be faced with yet another major confrontation with its larger neighbour.

Cyprus, on the contrary, tends to illustrate the opposite facet of Greek–Turkish relations and differences there do tend to be taken to extremes. There is still enormous Greek bitterness over the 1974 Turkish invasion and the accompanying disappearance of thousands of innocent people with the loss of millions of pounds-worth of Greek property. But the Greek attitude to Cyprus is very complex and appears to have changed a good deal over recent years. In particular, there is no longer present in mainstream Greek politics any significant body of support for the old irredentist and nationalist Right – the forces represented by General Grivas who, however misguidedly, saw the redemption of Cyprus as a national duty and was not afraid to advocate military methods. And Greek public opinion has many ambivalences.

I remember on the bus between Kalamata and Cambos, the elderly middle-class Greek lady who was looking out of the window and musing about the number of Greek-Cypriot refugees in London that I had put a figure to. 'A quarter of a million? No! . . . So many?' I said I thought that was about the number of refugees and established settlers, remembering my favourite vegetable shop in Green Lanes and the incomparable Chris Milia's in Camden Town, an oasis for London's retsina drinkers. She paused a moment and watched a speedboat cross the bay of Messenia – a white spreading V of foam and froth hitting the beach – then her voice quietened, became gentle, almost conspiratorial. 'So many shifty people in *one* place.'

Although the fate of the Greeks on Cyprus has brought Turkey and Greece close to war more than once and has proved as obstructive and difficult as any issue in international relations since the War, the average Greek, particularly in the better-off classes, does not admire the Greek Cypriot at a personal level. They are seen as wanting to be Greek when it suits them, Cypriot when it does not. Greeks are also fond of pointing out that, despite the ruination of the island after the Turkish invasion in 1974, Greek Cypriots enjoy one of the highest standards of living in the Mediterranean, higher than the four poorest EC members, including Greece itself. Success brings envy, in Greece as elsewhere. It is not the way to win Greek friends and influence people to point out that Cypriots work much harder than many Greeks and that, at a practical level, things function in Cyprus that somehow never quite seem to in Greece. But these feelings quickly disappear if a Greek

Cypriot is victim of Turkish policy and mainland Greeks raised a great deal of money for refugees after 1974, extending the hand of friendship to those in need. However logjammed the peace process seems to be, it is of central importance in terms of the regional politics of the eastern Mediterranean. This impasse prevents many potentially good things happening between Greece and Turkey and is a major obstacle to Turkish European Community entry.

It is a long way from Athens to Nicosia, the divided capital of the island with its medieval walls, Ottoman *hans*, mosques and churches – all under the Pendedactylos, the five-peaked mountain, five fingers of rock sticking up into the blue sky from behind the town on the Turkish side. The Greek side is a strange mixture, half Greek, with a little of the atmosphere of an English garrison town but it has also more than a touch of the flash and glitz of a prosperous Middle East city with many stretch limo Mercedes Benz in evidence. Cypriots love to spend as well as make money and after the privations of the last two generations they are not slow to enjoy themselves. To more conservative mainland Greeks, they often seem unbearably vulgar and ostentatious, rather as some Americans look to the more traditionally minded English. A wedding at the Nicosia Hilton is, well, quite a wedding, with more huge flower displays than at an East End gangland funeral. It is a world apart from the lonely villages in the Troodos mountains which are profoundly Greek. In Cyprus, as elsewhere in the Ottoman Empire, the Turks took the lowlands in cultural terms but never really exerted much effective control over the mountains. When Archbishop Makarios fled to Paphos and then into the mountains after the attempt on his life failed during the 1974 turmoil, he was also making a symbolic journey.

Cyprus is a jewel, as Lawrence Durrell and others have written, with a wealth of monuments from different cultures, but with a bloody and tragic history. The Turkish invasion in 1974 has been the only successful attempt in Europe to change borders by armed force since the end of the Second World War. It was the culmination of a long and complex series of events and partly the failure of Cyprus to be fully included in the British decolonization process. Many, such as the historian C. M. Woodhouse, feel that if Cyprus had been given to the Greeks originally, with proper safeguards for the Turkish minority, the whole terrible and bloody mess could have been avoided. Instead the island is effectively partitioned and, with minimal contact between the two communities, it seems very difficult to see how even the most carefully conceived form of federation or confederation can 'solve' the problem.

Despite poverty, international condemnation and lack of real independence from Turkey itself, Rauf Denktash's little 'republic' on the northern side of the island has struggled on since 1974. All efforts to find an international solution have failed and the Cyprus problem has become one of the hoariest chestnuts at the United Nations, the twentieth-century equivalent, perhaps, of the Schleswig-Holstein conundrum that so baffled Palmerston and his nineteenth-century contemporaries. And with the end of the Cold War, the pressure for a solution has eased somewhat, in terms of international *realpolitik*. At one stage, the Cyprus crisis may have led to a major regional, or even world, war but it is extremely difficult to conceive of that now and the ersatz Berlin Wall that crosses the island with its sad panoply of trees and bushes growing up through barbed wire is doomed to remain for some while yet.

In essence, the Greek case is that the invasion was an illegal act, a violation of international law. They demand a withdrawal of the Turkish army from the occupied territory and compensation for those who lost both family and property during the invasion. Turkey and the Turkish Cypriots, or most of them, want the status quo to continue, as far as territory goes, and some form of federation or confederation.

'They want our money, that's all.' The Greek-Cypriot taxi-driver in Nicosia spat into the gutter at the prospect of reunification. The problem for Greek-Cypriot political leaders is that after the heroic material effort to rebuild Cyprus after the invasion, and now with a booming economy that acts as a magnet for investors from Europe and the Middle East, there is some popular support in the Greek community for the status quo – or at least a tacit acceptance of it. The Turkish part of the island, though beautiful and maintaining more of the traditional way of life, is pitifully starved of capital, a problem not helped by the demise of the Polly Peck business empire of Mr Asil Nadir based in northern Cyprus.

Some Greeks regret his fall, just as others admired his potential to become a bridge-building force between the two communities. Nadir's father was a mine supervisor where many of the workers were Greek Cypriots and Nadir grew up speaking fluent Greek – a rare quality among Turkish Cypriots these days. Some of the businesses in the Polly Peck empire, for example, citrus fruit, would have dovetailed nicely with parallel industries on the Greek side of the fence. Another loser in the affair was Denktash himself. The Turkish-Cypriot leader depends for his position on a network of patronage and clientism, and Polly Peck money was of considerable assistance in his election campaigns. Ironically, the lack of help from the mainland Turkish business community when Nadir was in trouble was seen by most Cypriots in both communities as the Turkish equivalent of anti-Cypriot prejudice that they find in some quarters on the Greek mainland.

The difficulty of envisaging a settlement can in many ways be best understood by listening to Mr Denktash himself. One of the longest survivors among politicians, he was a prominent leader of the Turkish Cypriots as a brilliant barrister in London in the 1950s, years before independence. In many ways his political attitudes are stuck in the early years of the Cold War when Greek Cypriots were suspected of being pro-Communist by the United States, and Turkey was seen as a bulwark against the Soviet Union. In Denktash's view the expansionist Greeks oppressed the Turkish-Cypriot 20 per cent of the population after independence in 1961 and the Turkish army invasion in 1974 was essential to protect them against Greek proposals for *enosis*, union with Greece.

Denktash's conversation is formulaic and the end of the Cold War has brought no change in his outlook. The Greeks are still seen as a potential security threat to the West, although it is never explained quite how. AKEL, the Greek-Cypriot Communist Party, has played the democratic game entirely properly for many years and with its 20 per cent or so of the vote it has taken part in normal parliamentary democracy but Mr Denktash sees enemies everywhere, as do many Greek Cypriots – sometimes for good reason. There are many Cypriots with bitter recent grievances and it is not difficult to believe that some would be willing to murder their enemies, given the chance.

In her dark bar near the port entrance in Larnaca, Fari pours a whisky and muses over lost grandeur, a little like one of Christopher Isherwood's deprived middle classes in pre-Hitler Berlin. Now she keeps a small bar but before the invasion she and her husband owned two of the largest hotels in Famagusta, wrenched from them. Famagusta, or most of it, has in effect been a closed city since the Turkish military intervention in 1974 and very difficult for journalists to visit, as are substantial other areas of northern Cyprus classified as military zones. Fari, like all Greek Cypriots, is certainly not allowed to visit her old property. In politics she is an admirer of the quasi-fascist Nikos Sampson, imprisoned for his part in the military coup against Archbishop Makarios in 1974. She would happily see the Turks and Turkish settlers driven into the sea or, as she said with an eye to the inherent symbolism of events in Greek history, evacuated on ships back to Izmir, now a major port for the Turkish navy but once Greek Smyrna.

Speaking to her, or to anyone who has lost substantial amounts of property and status as a result of the invasion, it is difficult to believe that there would not be a bloodbath if the UN withdrew and the Green Line separating the two communities was removed. Revenge might seem, as the Jacobean playwright wrote, a kind of wild justice, given the appalling record of destruction and human rights violations of the Turkish army, and the continual immigration of Turkish settlers from the mainland, particularly to the northern coast.

It is almost impossible to find anyone who really believes that the old system on the island can be put together again. Many older Turkish Cypriots also lost property in the 1974 events, such as Hassan, a taxi-driver in Lefkosia, as the Turks now call Nicosia. A gentle, dignified man, he was a British government chauffeur under colonial rule, days he looks back on with affection. For him, as a member of a very small Turkish minority in a Greek village, 1974 meant that his mother's house was burnt down. His own survived and he is profoundly grateful that he has not had to live with Greek Cypriots, even if it means that he only has a small flat, a very old car and is a good deal poorer than he would otherwise be. Like the Greek Cypriots displaced by the invasion, he has received no property compensation.

'They never gave us a fair chance. When the British were here, it was fairer. A Turkish Cypriot could get a government job. But not after independence; the Greeks took everything.'

He smiles and breathes his cigarette smoke into the sunny air of Kyrenia harbour below the Venetian fortifications, at peace with his small claustrophobic world. But how long it can continue must be a very open question. Despite Mr

Denktash's propaganda, the Turkish republic of northern Cyprus has not achieved any non-Turkish recognition in its years of existence and to all intents and purposes seems to be part of Turkey. Most Greek Cypriots regard the Denktash regime as a puppet animated from Ankara, without any independent life. Perhaps the single most important aspect is the arrival of the large number of mainland Turkish settlers who have taken over ex-Greek-Cypriot property and land. They will be very difficult to dislodge in the event of any peace settlement. There are still large numbers of Turkish troops stationed on the island, mostly in the north-west Karpas peninsula. Ankara claims they are there to prevent a bloodbath should the Greek Cypriots ever try to take revenge across the Green Line, but in reality they are part of the mechanism of the Turkish takeover.

On the other hand, Cyprus costs Ankara a good deal of money, likely to increase following the collapse of Polly Peck. The company was a serious player in the world economy and was able to ease the cultural and political isolation of inhabitants in small but significant ways. For instance, few international sporting organizations would allow a team from the Turkish republic to enter, but there was nothing stopping a Polly Peck team of exactly the same players competing abroad. The fortunes of the island's potentially lucrative tourist industry were closely linked to Polly Peck, with some of the most famous hotels owned by the company. Mr Asil Nadir himself was an important political voice for Cyprus in Ankara and was personally close to the then Turkish Prime Minister, Turgut Ozal, who made efforts to rescue the empire that foundered in the face of opposition from anti-Nadir elements in the Turkish business establishment. In many ways the atmosphere in the northern sector of the island is profoundly reminiscent of that in some parts of Eastern Europe before the demise of Communism. There is a mildly repressive one-party state built around an ageing leader, and considerable dis-satisfaction, particularly at their cultural isolation, expressed by the younger generation. The economy is creaking and inefficient with many state 'enterprises' that ought, on any rational economic criteria, to be closed down but are kept going because of political clientism. The whole caboodle depends ultimately on support from a large outside power, in this instance Turkey rather than the Soviet Union, which finds it necessary to keep the edifice in being because of its wider strategic interests. It is hard to avoid the conclusion that northern Cyprus in its present form has no more future than the satellite states of old-style Eastern Europe but it would be a brave person to put a date on its collapse. Mr Denktash's death, though, is obviously going to present a serious problem for the Turkish Cypriots and Ankara. There is no obvious successor with his blend of charisma, intelligence, cunning and chauvinist ideology, and the inevitable succession struggle is bound to put great strain on the fabric of the 'statelet'.

Undoubtedly, the prospects for any real progress towards a settlement will depend largely on what happens with many outside powers. The picture is extraordinarily complex. For instance, the American administration is generally obliged to Turkey for its vital support during the Gulf War and it is very unlikely to oppose Turkish interests in Cyprus unless there is any risk of a repetition of the military activity and expansion-ism of the 1970s. The US also has more than enough to cope with in trying to bring about a peace settlement between the Arabs and Israel, and in that context the inertia in Cyprus does not really matter as long as nobody is actually getting killed. The traditional arguments that found favour in many sections of the State Department in favour of building up Turkey as a strong regional policeman continue to attract many US diplomats, although it would seem that the end of the Cold War disposed of their rationale. The defenders of this theory claim that general regional disorder is as much a threat to US strategic interests as Communism was and that Turkey has a vital peacekeeping role. The Soviet Union used to be a firm backer of the Greek-Cypriot position but has now all but disappeared from the scene. Britain, which still has the Sovereign Base Areas on the island and a number of political responsibilities arising from past treaties and international agreements, has not been willing to take an active policy, many commentators would say, since the craven surrender of the Callaghan Labour government to American pressure over the original invasion in 1974. A major long-term development is the increasing role of Arab money on the island, which may come close to threatening Cypriot financial independence. It is impossible to avoid the impression that some of the ruling families in the Gulf are preparing Cyprus as a potential future bolthole if their regimes have a limited shelf-life. A grandiose scheme to build a kind of housing estate for sheikhs near Paphos, costing over three billion pounds, was thrown out by the Nicosia planners in 1991, but it is doubtful how long these and similar Arab financial and cultural pressures can be resisted. The island is, as ever, a pawn between mighty neighbours and international interests and the best hope may be for the Greek and Turkish Cypriots to be left to themselves to sort out their destiny.

This certainly seems to be the best principle in other areas of Greek–Turkish relations. Although inter-governmental relations are usually tense, punctuated by occasional meetings between heads of state on a bilateral basis that always produce well-meaning communiqués, many people can detect a perceptible improvement at local level. Mutual tourist exchanges are increasing with over fifty thousand Greeks visiting Turkey for their holidays in 1990, attracted by the cheapness of the Turkish resorts. The difficulties of the early 1980s about oil-drilling rights in the Aegean have been sorted out, and a crisis management procedure has been set up to try to avoid the rapid drift towards a potential war situation as in the past when national interests clashed over some relatively minor issue. A Greek–Turkish friendship association, set up by the distinguished composer Theodorakis, has a programme of cultural exchanges and a Greek–Turkish Business Council is chaired by a personal friend of ex-Prime Minister Constantine Mitsotakis, Rahim Kots. It is to be hoped that this is the direction in which things will go, as good relations with Turkey could provide Greece with an invaluable bridge towards the markets of the Middle East. But, as in so many areas of Greek political and diplomatic life, the Balkan crisis is casting a shadow over the future – just as relationships in the Mediterranean were beginning to show some sign of improvement. Both countries are struggling to establish legitimate spheres of influence – the Turks with the Albanians and the Moslems in Bosnia, which Greece sees as a threat. It is difficult to envisage the necessary goodwill developing to improve relations further if this is the dominant political background in the region. There is, ultimately, a great danger of Cyprus simply being forgotten by the international community.

17. The Macedonian Question

The Internal Macedonian Revolutionary Organization has changed its skin. It is now a hidden retreat
of terrorists – from the skin of a lion it has changed
into the skin of a wolf.

– Albert Londres, *Terror in the Balkans*

Zivko Stefanouski is a post office manager in Skopje, the
largest town in the most southerly republic that has emerged
from the ruins of Yugoslavia. The republic follows a long
border with northern Greece from Lake Ochrid in the west to
the Rhodope mountains and Bulgaria in the east. Until very
recently the existence of a country called Macedonia would
have been unthinkable in Athens; now it has reopened what is
perhaps the bloodiest and most intractable Balkan dispute of
all, in which Greece is inextricably involved, the Macedonian
question.

Zivko's office is a dark room in the old Turkish *han*. These
inns were built by the Ottomans for dusty and weary
merchants travelling the Sublime Porte's roads on their business in the vast, ramshackle, theocratic empire ruled for
hundreds of years from Constantinople. Thirty or forty
languages would have been spoken inside its grey stone walls.

But on the wall now is a red-and-black poster, the colours
of the new Macedonian flag, with one word: *Da* (Yes). Like
the 93 per cent of those who voted here in the independence
referendum in September 1991, Zivko said Yes. He is for an

independent Macedonian state and thinks that multicultural-ism is as dead as the dodo. But the referendum was the easy part for about 25 per cent did not vote at all: the minorities of Turks, Serbs, Albanians, gypsies, Greeks, Vlachs and Pomaks who made this endlessly complex republic give the name *Macedoine* to a French salad – a mixture indeed.

'If we had stayed in Yugoslavia, we would have been taken over by the Serbs. There is no doubt about it. We had no alternative. But to be on our own ... What are we going to build a state from? Tobacco plants? I don't know.' Zivko shrugs and there is a strange echo of Clint Eastwood about him. He has the tall, angular good looks of many Macedonian men, a gentle, puzzled smile, a long, straggly brown moustache, a wave of the hand at the prospect of trying to be an independent country. Macedonia is, so far, largely free of the wild Ramboism of parts of Serbia and Croatia, where a man is not a man until he can use a machine-gun, where music is belligerent nationalist pop songs and poetry a xenophobic slogan sewn on to your combat jacket.

But Zivko has his views on the minorities, none the less, the Albanian minority particularly, much the most numerous at about twenty-odd per cent of the population. 'I have one child. My friends, they have two, three children. But the Albanians, they have six, ten ...' He clenches his fist by his small blue coffee cup.

The regional history is worse than that of northern ex-Yugoslavia, if less immediate than the horrors of Croatian fascists presenting babies' eyes to their mothers or Serbian revenge executions. Macedonia has always been the most contentious, complex issue in foreign countries' claims on Yugoslav territory – the Four Wolves of Greece, Albania, Bulgaria and Serbia. Now it is back with us – the referendum has let the bloodstained, spitting old cat out of the bag, spoiling for yet another fight.

The people are well aware that they are playing with fire. Konstantin is a Skopje taxi-driver, a complete contrast to his London opposite numbers with immediate views on every question. He is taciturn and pretends at first not to speak Greek. He admits, eventually, that he is an ethnic Greek, born in Macedonia in the aftermath of the Greek Civil War and that he hates nationalism and abstained in the referendum. But he refuses to reveal his surname and knows that he is living on a dangerous crossroads.

The Macedonian question has echoes of Disraeli and Bismarck and of the languid nineteenth-century political conferences that lasted weeks, with breaks for shooting-parties and elegant balls. It originated in the web of treaties drawn up in the nineteenth century when the Powers were trying to decide what to do about the Sick Man of Europe, the decaying Ottoman Empire. The different nationalities of Serbs, Albanians, Bulgarians and others were trying to establish independent states within the ruins of the Ottoman *millet* system of government which divided subject people on the basis of religious affiliation rather than on language.

From this stemmed much of the succeeding chaos and violent conflict. Assassination has been a Macedonian speciality; the most theatrical was the violent demise of King Alexander of Yugoslavia in Marseilles in 1934. If the Archduke fell to a Serbian hand at Sarajevo, elsewhere Macedonians were energetic wielders of knife, pistol and bomb.

The most important dates for the region were the Treaty of San Stefano in March 1878 and the Congress of Berlin in June and July of that year. San Stefano gave much of Macedonia to a Greater Bulgaria which would have dominated the whole region but the Powers, particularly Britain and Austro-Hungary, feared it would become a client state of Russia and so forced its abandonment and replacement by a dismembered Bulgaria at the Treaty of Berlin.

As a result Bulgarian irredentists were able to play on a sense of national grievance for many years, culminating in the vicious fighting in the early years of this century between armed bands of Bulgarians, Serbs and Greeks. The Macedonian Internal Revolutionary Organization (IMRO) was set up in 1893 and favoured initially a south Slav federation of Serbs, Bulgarians and Macedonians. It won wide support and made plans for an armed uprising.

But vast numbers had fled to Bulgaria after the failure of Greater Bulgaria and the San Stefano débâcle. A rival organization to IMRO, the External Organization of Supremacists, was set up in Sofia in 1895 and aimed at the absorption of Macedonia by Bulgaria. Thus, from the outset, the Macedonian nationalist movement was fatally split between those who wanted an independent Macedonia and those who wanted to be part of Bulgaria.

One way of trying to understand the issue is to pore over tomes in libraries, some with medical-sounding titles such as *The Acute Phase of the Macedonian Question*. Another is to have a conversation with Gotse who sells T-shirts at the end of the old Turkish stone bridge across the river Vardar that bisects Skopje. The river, rushing down from the Suva mountains through the city over pebbles, is fresh and clear. Wading birds prod the mud in reed-beds along its banks and it is difficult to believe anything important could, or did, ever happen here. A great question asked *here*?

Even in Shakespeare's time people were a little vague about Macedonia, as witness Fluellen in *Henry V*:

I think it is in Macedon where Alexander is porn. I tell you, Captain, if you look in the maps of the 'orld, I warrant you sall find, in the comparisons between Macedon and Monmouth, that the situations, look you, is both alike. There is a river in Macedon, and there is also moreover a river at Monmouth . . .

But standing by the Vardar river Gotse is not vague, to put it mildly. He holds up a T-shirt and points to the three arrows under the slogan with EGEJ, VARDAR and PIRIN, the rivers of the region, written inside them: 'Our new country. We will make the Bulgars give us Pirin back. And if the Albanians want to go off to Albania, good luck to them. It will take time. But we will have all our people together.'

The political leader who gives clearest expression to this sort of fundamentalist nationalism is Ljupco Georgievski, the oddly titled Vice-President of the President of Macedonia. He is a firebrand of twenty-six, long-haired and wild-eyed, in appearance a cross between hippie and priest. His outlook has the increasingly familiar, some would say lethal, mix of mysticism and politics found elsewhere in the new Balkans. His favourite food is said to be honey eaten straight from the hive.

What is important is that Georgievski is leader of the descendants of the IMRO of 1893, the VMRO-DPMNE, now the strongest party in the Skopje parliament. (Adoring followers shouted the party initials rhythmically to the tune of the Beatles 'Yellow Submarine'.) As a Bulgarophile and Greek and Serbophobe, Georgievski is probably more responsible than any other individual for the overwhelming Yes vote to independence in the referendum.

Like Gotse, he has few doubts about the world or the place of an enlarged country in it. Party posters show a 'Macedonia' including tracts of territory that are now Greek, Bulgarian and Serbian – huge areas of northern Greece. Opponents claim Georgievski is an agent for Bulgarians trying to recover what was lost at San Stefano, the opening to the Aegean and Thessaloniki. He claimed in a speech in June 1991 that 51 per cent of 'Macedonia's' people lived in Greece and should join a united 'Macedonian' state under his leadership.

So it is primarily Greeks who will be asked the question in the next few years – or possibly sooner at the speed events are moving. It is an awesome prospect. Despite Greece being firmly anchored in the West in security and economic terms, it should not be forgotten that the greatest Greek of all in popular imagination, Alexander the Great, ruled in Macedon. Yet Greece does not recognize the Macedonian language, seeing it as an ersatz dialect of Bulgarian, and it has been the official policy of all Greek governments to regard their 'nationality' as an invention of the 'Slav-Communist bloc', as Greek President Karamanlis once put it. Greek scholars reject Slav claims that ancient Macedonia was only partly Greek, or that a Greek-speaking ruling class, to which Alexander and Philip of Macedon belonged, ruled over a mass of Slav-speaking peasants. In more contemporary terms, the issue is likely to reopen deep fissures in Greek political life going back to the wounds of the Axis Occupation and Civil War. By 1949 at least 50 per cent of the troops in the Communist army in the Greek Civil War were Slav-Macedonians. Taxi-driver Konstantin's father was almost certainly among them. Most mainstream Greek history of the Civil War purports to show it, especially in the latter stages, as something of a conspiracy against an ethnically pure and anti-Communist Greece.

Greece faces some very difficult decisions over this issue. Policy until now has been dominated by two main phases. The first was to try to keep Yugoslavia as an entity, even if this meant going out on a limb, in European terms, during the war between Croatia and Serbia by assisting Serbia, a fellow Orthodox country and Greece's most traditional Balkan ally from early struggles against the Turks. When this policy failed, with the open and irreversible disintegration of Yugoslavia and the irresistible force of German diplomatic backing for an independent Croatia, the focus changed to the prevention of EC recognition. To date Athens diplomacy has been more successful here with an effective non-recognition of anything called 'Macedonia': the new state was not recognized along with Croatia and Slovenia on 15 January 1992. This delay has allowed a joint Serbian–Greek stranglehold to develop on Skopje. But it has also threatened the future of New Democracy with the sacking of Mr Antonis Samaras, the Foreign Minister, in March 1992 for his outspoken position against recognition, and an enforced vote of confidence in parliament that Mr Mitsotakis only narrowly survived and, as events developed, later led directly to the downfall of his government in 1993. But the Prime Minister's room for manoeuvre was limited; he depended on the votes, among others, of MPs from northern constituencies, and their constituents did not welcome any weakening on the border recognition issue. Mr Mitsotakis's position was strengthened by the decision of the EC Foreign Ministers to support the Greek position on the name issue at their meeting in Lisbon in July 1992.

But although this line has some short-term viability, it is difficult to see how it can contribute to a reassertion of stability in the southern Balkans. The salient fact about the ex-Yugoslav republic is its extreme economic weakness. It has, apart from its problems with agriculture and industry, almost no foreign exchange reserves and although the Yugoslav dinar continues to circulate in the region, it has become almost worthless, given spiralling inflation approaching 5,000 per cent at the time of writing. Without monetary stabilization the region is heading for economic collapse. There is little prospect of a stable and viable Macedonian currency appearing in the foreseeable future, although a new dinar has been printed. In this situation, there are already signs of a disturbing tendency in Macedonia for all important economic transactions to be conducted in the currencies of neighbouring states, so that, say, the inhabitants of the Pirin area adjoining Bulgaria are already beginning to use Bulgarian currency, if they can, in the absence of any stable Macedonian alternative.

If the same tendency starts in areas adjoining the Greek

border – which is very likely, given the number of natural economic links across the borders – the new state risks being 'Balkanized' itself, with different currencies circulating, giving the progenitors of the currencies political power over different parts of Macedonia. Although the Greek response to the crisis may seem exaggerated in many northern European eyes, at what at first sight may appear a sentimental issue of whether the new state is called Macedonia or not, it does conceal a political issue of major substance.

It may be correct to say that the new phase of the Macedonian question differs from the old in that the governments of Bulgaria, Greece, Albania and Serbia have said that they do not have any designs on Macedonian territory. This should give grounds for optimism but it does not take into account the extreme economic weakness of the new state or the fact that in Serbia, Albania and Bulgaria there are major political parties which either do have specific designs on areas of Macedonian territory or who seek a major revision in the position of their compatriot minorities within Macedonia that would lead to profound destabilization.

Perhaps the clearest example is that of the Albanian inhabitants of western Macedonia, wild and underdeveloped, who boycotted the original independence referendum in the autumn of 1991 and who voted overwhelmingly in their own referendum for a form of autonomy. But, given the weakness of authority in Skopje, this would mean a *de facto* unity with neighbouring Albania – and a new Greater Albania on Greece's northern border.

Similar pressures exist with the other neighbours. Serbia at the moment is too weak with its military commitment in Bosnia to attempt to follow a forward policy but Serbian President Slobodan Milosevic has in the past allied himself with the expansionist Right in Belgrade who hold to the pre-Balkan War position that much of Macedonia is in fact south

Serbia and should be integrated with Belgrade. Other Serbian leaders have argued that there should be a partition of Macedonia, mainly between Bulgaria and Serbia, with Albania getting one or two little bits, mainly the Albanian 'capital' of Tetovo with its Moslem traditions exemplified by the Dervish *teke*.

Bulgaria was the first country to recognize the independence of Macedonia, before Russia and Turkey, and clearly intends to play an influential part in its affairs. But the current Macedonian state is very far from what the nineteenth-century Bulgarian irredentists sought. Then, the impetus of Bulgarian territorial revisionism was the *Drang nach Saloniki*, where all the territories of 'Aegean Macedonia' would be taken by Bulgaria to form a Greater Bulgaria with a major port, Thessaloniki, to give the country its long-sought opening to the Aegean and transform its economic prospects and political standing. This ambition is perhaps the source of the deepest Greek fears about the future. These territories were won by the shedding of Greek blood against the Turks and subsequently fought over just as bitterly in the last War, when many Bulgarians took part in the puppet regime set up by the Germans that ruled northern Greece with such ferocity and violations of human rights that eventually the Gestapo high command in Thessaloniki had to dismantle it. Any suggestion of a revival of Bulgarian designs on Greek territory would guarantee a major war and it has been claimed by reliable sources in Athens that the Bulgarians would face not only the Greek army but those from NATO and the West European Union – to which Greece has only recently been admitted. How realistic this appalling scenario is, is difficult to say, although Greek hopes of allied assistance may not be well founded, given the traditional reluctance of outside powers to involve themselves in Balkan disputes. But if what is now Macedonia collapses, as is likely without substantial outside assistance, the political vacuum will undoubtedly be filled, and the Greeks can have no certainty that an expansionist Bulgaria, sensing an opportunity to gain territory as well as a sphere of influence, will not emerge.

So the current Greek policy implies considerable risks in that if Athens and Belgrade are seen by the present moderate government in Skopje to be involved in a pincer movement to snuff out the new state, Macedonia's leaders will be forced to seek new allies. The only possible candidates with adjoining borders, or close borders, are Albania, Bulgaria or Turkey. None of these alliances can be welcome in Athens, particularly the last. Up until now Turkey has only recognized Macedonia but has taken little active role in developments. That could easily change if the large Islamic minority of Albanians, gypsies and the sixty thousand or so ethnic Turks were threatened. These were the residue of Ottoman attempts to import settlers, given land as peasants in an attempt to increase the Turkish element in the region. Albania is at present too weak and preoccupied with its internal chaos to present any threat, but in any foreseeable quarrel it would probably take the side opposite to Greece, thanks to the current deterioration in relations over the future of the Greek minority in Albania.

So it is a gloomy outlook on the northern border, seen from the Foreign Ministry in Zolocastra Street, Athens. An important setback to Greek foreign policy objectives in August 1992 was the recognition of Macedonia by the Russian leadership. President Yeltsin appeared to be taking a direction influenced by pan-Slavist advisers, an ominous development in view of Balkan history. The Russian assumption must be that the new Macedonia will collapse economically, but in a reasonably orderly way, so that it will be forced to join some sort of revived 'Yugoslav' federation, or confederation, under the effective domination of Serbia. But how likely is that? The Slavonic majority have pride in being independent and Macedonian and it seems very unlikely that they will easily give this up, particularly if the alternative is effective union with a profoundly undemocratic and nearly bankrupt Serbia with an old-fashioned Communist ethos – even if the party organization has more or less disintegrated and where the leadership has recently lost an important war. Much more likely is a breakdown of the border and any semblance of law and order in these areas, putting an increasing strain on Greek military resources.

Perhaps it is time that the politicians thought again about a kind of Balkan federation to solve the Macedonian problem. In the inter-war period federation was supported by great independent thinkers such as Albert Einstein. One of the underlying ironies is how much the prosperity of northern Greece would be improved by good economic relations with a hinterland at the moment within the new Macedonian state. Greece has far too many small Aegean ports for the limited hinterland behind them and the trade of the smallest, like Kavala, is dying. With the right kind of European investment in Macedonian agriculture, goods could be produced for the growing markets of the Middle East and North Africa, and the economy of the region would be transformed. But this, at the moment, is a distant and unlikely prospect.

In the meantime, the political and security situation continues to deteriorate. There have been violent clashes between ethnic Albanians and Macedonians in Skopje, and IMRO has begun to form 'protection committees' – armed militias of militant Macedonian nationalists who act in parallel to the police and state security forces in the cities. Members of these groups have been arrested trying to blow up Albanian mosques. It must only be a matter of time before President Gligorov's moderate government, based on an unstable coalition of the Albanian and Social Democrat parties, falls, and some of the worst fears of the Greek leaders may be borne out. From cities like Tetovo in the Albanian heartlands in the western mountains, there is already great pressure on the Albanians to bring down the government. Ethnic Albanians there feel that their participation in the government is pointless if their human-rights grievances are not remedied and the constitution changed to guarantee their position. The question of the name of the area, and the internal controversies within the European Community over the issue, may well become irrelevant if the politics of intimidation and ethnic cleansing take over at street level. At the moment the Macedonian militias are in an early state of development with only light arms, and it appears that these will be directed at the Albanian minority rather than used to launch the much-feared terrorist campaign in Greece. But if violence begins in the ex-Yugoslav republic, it is bound to spread in some way, sooner or later, to the northern border of Greece. The severely stretched Greek army will need reinforcement, and an extension of the period of compulsory military conscription looks a distinct possibility. In turn this will have very serious economic implications. The most difficult time for the Greek economy recently was as a result of the Cyprus-crisis-inspired military mobilizations of the mid Seventies.

18. The Diaspora

> At that time Christians were great sinners, for that
> reason alone God sent the Turks and they came to
> take first the City, the great capital. Later they also
> took Trebizond and all of Romania was lost. But
> the time will come, he said, when we will take them
> back. He also sang:
>
> Romania is dead, Romania is taken:
> If Romania has died it will blossom and bear again.
>
> – Akoglous, *O Akritas*

Quite recently the leader of the Greek community in South
Africa addressed a large conference in Athens on business
developments in Greece. His speech, widely reported in the
business press, expressed disappointment that trade relations
with emigré Greeks were not closer and he added that he
hoped the 85,000 Greeks in South Africa would be able to
play an important role in the economic revival Greece needed.
In all probability most people who read these reports, even the
well informed, would have had little idea that there were so
many Greeks in South Africa, let alone ever considered whether
trading relationships with them would be useful. And they
may in this case, understandably, have felt that it was a bit of
special pleading as the Greek community was mostly firmly
behind apartheid. In a 'poor white' economic and social
position and loyal to the Nationalist party, they had suffered
in business terms from South Africa's isolation.

Generally speaking, it is the same story worldwide.
Although within the family there are tight links at every level
– and bonds with Greeks stretch across oceans as easily as
across a village street – formal business relationships are
uncommon. The Greeks of Astoria district in New York, say,
obviously provide a ready market for imported Greek food
and drink, icons, the travel business, and so on, but there are
not many Greek-American businesses of any size in important
areas of the economy. This was not always so. The whole
economy of one important Greek city, Kastoria in the north,
was based on fur trading. A business relationship was
established in the early years of this century where offcuts
from mink and other furs in the New York workshops were
shipped to Greece to be expertly sewed into the cheaper coats
sold and worn in Athens. This still continues, as the anti-fur-
trade lobby has yet to fully establish itself in Greece, but it is
difficult to think of other modern examples.

In the past, and to a large extent the pattern still persists,
three types of Greeks made up the diaspora: the very poor, the
very rich and the political exile. The last category has more or
less vanished, thankfully, although it does still include the ex-
monarch and his family. The stream of the very poor who
flocked to the United States and Canada in the last years of
the nineteenth century has also dried up as work permits are
no longer available and traditional rural poverty in Greece has
come to an end.

The very rich are those who in many cases have been in the
diaspora longest. Some of the most prominent names in the
London Greek business community left islands such as Chios
at various stages during the last century. Then, London was
becoming the centre of all international trade, especially shipping and marine insurance, and it was essential for a Greek
family firm based in Athens, Alexandria, or wherever, to have
a branch office there. All too commonly, the branch office

under the guiding hand of the younger son soon outgrew the parent, and in no time the basis was being laid for modern dynasties with names like Kulukundis, Hadjipateras, Nomikos, Leventis and Embirícos that echo through the pages of Lloyd's List like the sound of ships' bells. The names also echo through the halls of art galleries, churches, schools and museums as generous patrons of the arts, active in good causes, and great assets to both Greece and Britain. A typically generous and useful recent benefaction in Greece has been the Nomikos Foundation gift of a cable car up the steep cliff of Santorini. Perhaps significantly, it is plastered with signs stressing its Austrian manufacture and its Swiss electrical machinery as many Greeks would not trust their own compatriots to construct a cable car properly.

Many Greeks took jobs within the British Empire and through their toughness and adaptability were often chosen to run branch offices of the London-based firms. The significant Greek and Cypriot community along the coast of West Africa grew up in this way and the Greeks of Egypt flourished under British rule there. The Egyptian census in 1906 showed a population of 97,000 Greeks, with a substantial additional number who were Orthodox but not of Greek nationality. Some parts of northern central Greece had strong Egyptian connections. Its emigrants were, of course, usually able to find an existing Greek community and soon churches were being built and newspapers published. Long complex arguments about what Primo Levi calls the great Greek themes of life, death and the effects of fate were held in the new kafenia after work.

I remember travelling by car high in the Pindus and stopping for a coffee and to consult the map. In the tiny dark bar on this wet autumn night, a fellow refugee from the weather noticed the English text and, in an accent like John F. Kennedy's, offered to help. Soon there was a small group round the table, each with a similar accent, as all had worked in the same shoe factory in Boston, Massachusetts. My companion was unusual in speaking English reasonably well but one old man there who had spent nine years in the States could hardly speak a word of the language as he had stayed exclusively in a monocultural Greek world. Although this was a right-wing village, their views of the United States were poor and all were glad to be back home with little nest eggs of dollars. In most cases these seemed to be more an insurance against misfortune than for anything else – disproving the old myth that emigré dollars would enable the Greek economy to revive through the investment of remittances.

'Americans are stupid. And Greeks, if they stay too long in America, they get stupid too.' My friend extended his arms as if this was a self-evident truth. I asked why. 'The weather. The weather makes people stupid there.'

At this point the bar owner appeared clutching a battered old *tavli* board. He turned out to be the only Communist in the village for he had got involved with ELAS as a young man, spending a short time in exile in Romania. However bad America was, he said, it had to be better than Romania. Greeks are not slow to point out the faults of other nations or races in terms that do not usually embody the liberal doubts or euphemisms that the race relations bodies in Britain have brought into being. A lengthy philosophical analysis began as to why America made good Greeks stupid. At this juncture I made my excuses and went out into the sheeting black rain.

It is a long way to another 'Greek' village near Geneva in Switzerland. It is perched on the side of a hill and almost all its inhabitants seem to be Greek, with most cars bearing Greek numberplates. It is the other Greece – with a vengeance. The general image is of the very rich having Swiss bank accounts, but for them actually to *inhabit* part, even a little part, of Switzerland is something else. Although, needless to say, there are no figures available, the Greeks are believed to be one of the richest communities in Switzerland. There is the usual mixture of reasons for being there. The art market, particularly for classical antiquities, is important and some shipping companies use Swiss banks as a basis for their financial organization, and so on. But most residents are professionals, doctors or dentists, and tax avoidance is the name of the game. Whereas the little nest eggs of hard currency saved up after long work in exile are lovingly brought home to the northern villages, here as much money as possible leaves Athens to find a home outside the country. Although there is an elaborate mechanism of currency declarations for residents at Greek ports and airports, in practice there is little actual control over what leaves the country. The very rich nearly always have a boat to cruise the Mediterranean in summer and call at ports where there are branches of foreign banks. There is nothing to stop one making the fairly short trip to Italy, say, or to Cyprus, where these operations can be conducted with complete discretion. There is not a single branch of any Swiss bank in Athens though – perhaps significant in itself. It has been a demand of the Greek Left that legislation similar to that of the United States should be introduced to limit Greek citizens' right to invest in Switzerland or elsewhere abroad. But the proposal has always run into the sand of the realities of the operations of the shipping industry. These need complex international financial services, and as so many shipping and associated companies are in essence private family businesses, rather than public companies with automatic financial disclosure laws, the investors would simply leave Greece altogether if the government tried to inhibit their practices.

Another of the diasporas is an intellectual one. In virtually every research institute or academic institution in the West, there will be Greek teachers, researchers, or expert technicians. One or two of the major multinational companies, like the immensely successful British-based pharmaceutical giant Glaxo, seem to have made a speciality of recruiting Greek and Greek-Cypriot chemists. The simple explanation would be that Greeks are often very clever people, in demand internationally. But in many cases their career patterns have not been dictated by headhunting or the normal intellectual exchanges between different countries. They reflect the crisis in Greek higher education where, mainly in the sciences, it is impossible to study for many graduate degrees in Greece itself, and so study abroad is essential. Once a bright student begins to work in a foreign country and gets noticed, he or she rarely returns to Greece. There are exceptions, of course, but one of the main problems for the wider Greek economy is this brain drain. Its undoubted existence is one of the strongest arguments to support the PASOK view of Greece as in many senses having more in common with the underdeveloped world rather than with mainstream Europe.

But, as in so much Greek life, patterns of behaviour among intellectuals have much older roots than may seem evident. In ancient Greece philosophers frequently wandered the country to teach and some of the most powerful intellects existed in exile from Athens and sometimes from Greece altogether. The popular image is of Plato and his pupils walking among the olive trees in the Academy, not far from the centre of the old city, with intellectual life at its heart and in harmony with it. An equally strong and characteristic image is of Socrates drinking hemlock to escape his persecutors in a noble and dignified death.

It is very difficult to be an intellectual in Greece, in ways that some outsiders find hard to understand. But it is a small country with many clever people in its universities and laboratories, and jobs are so scarce and rivalries for them so intense that competition for available posts often entails political or other clientism and is not conducted according to the rules of cricket. There is also the legacy of an ancient heritage. It is very difficult, in any objective sense, to think of anyone becoming a 'better' philosopher than Plato or Aristotle, in the same way that many English dramatists do not measure up to Shakespeare. The classical and ancient past can become a burden as much as an inspiration, and it is perhaps not surprising that many of the brightest young students tend these days to favour the scientific disciplines. Work abroad removes the intellectual from the intensity of Athens which, in the exceptionally centralized world of the Greek intelligentsia, is where all magazines are edited and where anybody who matters is to be found. Intellectuals abroad tend to go native in a way that most ordinary Greek workers do not. Those who have studied in Paris or London seem to take on some of the characteristics of their adopted country. Under the junta in the Sixties and Seventies many students and teachers involved in the underground struggle had to go into exile to escape torture and imprisonment and the existing exiles provided shelter and money for new arrivals. Many of the most important movements in Greek history were started in exile. In some ways the struggle for national independence has at several different times depended as much on what happened in London as anywhere else, and the development of the Left in Greece since the end of the Civil War has been deeply influenced by the pattern of the diaspora of Greek Leftists, those going to the former Soviet Union tending to remain politically conservative, while those who went to Western Europe did not.

Then there is the deeper element in history, stemming ultimately from the fall of Constantinople in 1453 and with it the end of the Byzantine world. If someone is a 'real' Greek they will often say they are *Romios*, that is belonging to the new Rome, which the Greek-speaking Byzantine Empire represented. In a certain sense, all Greeks are exiles now. Even the inhabitant of the most central Athens flat is part of a diaspora because the real centre of the Greek world is not Athens at all but the lost capital of Constantinople, *I Polis*, The City itself. This may seem a fanciful and romantic notion to many, or even an empty intellectual conceit, but it is a genuine and deeply felt intellectual and spiritual reality for many Greeks and by no means confined to right-wing religious conservatives. A close friend who is a feminist university teacher and member of a small left-wing group refers to *I Polis* with profound respect and with a real sense of loss, and she is not untypical. This is perhaps another background reason for some of the unresolved intellectual and political dilemmas of contemporary Greek governments and why, contrary to the image, many Greeks do not feel really at home in their own society, and why Marxist theories of social alienation have become so influential in Greek intellectual life, even among the majority of non-Marxists.

So the ordinary exile is not perhaps an admired figure, in the Irish sense, but he or she is certainly someone who is understood and sympathized with. The fact of exile may be regretted but in itself is not controversial, whereas if a person neglects their responsibility towards family and village and doesn't bother to come home for Easter, *that* is a serious matter.

The pattern of religion is very much influenced by the notion of pilgrimage, as anyone knows who has attended a saint's day festival or walked the Sacred Way to the Acropolis or the long, crowded path up to the theatre at Epidauros. And the centralization of life in Athens means that many journeys have to be made there which would not be necessary in other countries.

Most powerful of all, of course, is the classical model. The obvious image that springs to mind is the wandering Odysseus in Homer, the hero who is wily and adaptable, and manages to come home to rescue his wife from unwanted suitors after long years overseas. Although this image matters very much, equal, if not more powerful, is that of Alexander the Great and his army who conquered the known world from Macedonia. Alexander did not return and so symbolizes the ultimate universality of Hellenism, that in the last analysis it does not really matter if your bones rest in some suburban burial ground in Melbourne provided you lived a good Greek Christian life on earth.

So, when thinking about Greeks abroad, it is helpful to forget any notion of a Greek nation in the western sense. The idea of nationalism is quite foreign to Byzantium, a universal empire with access to all, in the eyes of believing Christians. But a tragedy remains none the less. So many Greeks leave the country with a sense of bitterness and unfulfilled ambition and this is perhaps why the kind of appeal made by the South African business leader could fall on deaf ears. Emigré Greeks, when successful, tend to run Greece down in the same way as many ex-English in Australia or ex-Irish in America do. If money is made, it will tend to stay invested abroad rather than return to Greece.

There are often immense pressures in terms of culture in the diaspora. The problem is worst in America with the uncertain survival of the Greek language there. Even at the level of a modest amount of passive understanding, it is under threat among second- and third-generation Greek-Americans. The pull of American mass culture is intense and Greekness is best preserved abroad among some of the odder and smaller out-of-the-way communities. The returnees from Russia, scattering their way through the Athens street markets and setting up new communities at places like Lavrion in Attica, are profoundly Greek with a rich oral culture, unique dances and a vocabulary incorporating many medieval words that Athenians find hard to understand.

Ultimately, many of the diaspora experiences have been better captured by poets and writers than by anyone else, whether in the brilliant clarity of vision of Greece embodied in George Seferis's work – a man coming back from the old diaspora because of the political and human catastrophe of Smyrna in 1922 – or, perhaps more typically, in the work of the increasingly highly regarded Dimitris Tsaloumas. He was born on Leros but emigrated with his family to Melbourne in 1952 for political reasons. In 'The Approval' he writes:

> Your letter says that you've a mind to send
>   your son to foreign parts. Well send him then,
> just so they give him the right grounding
>   in the schools. For in the heart of Australia
> no woodworms have dug labyrinths in which
>   the Siren's songs can find themselves a nest,
> instead the mastery belongs to such vast deserts that
>   a skin filled tight with water won't suffice
> your crossing. No camels here, no comforts. Only
>   you, alone, where fevers crack the earth
> and prone the skeletons snort as the crow
>   laughs into the mirror of the heat,
> and you become blind to your homeland's faults,
>   and the labours of your loneliness are wasted.

Another dominant voice is that of the refugee from Smyrna, often more fluent in Turkish than in Greek and bringing great distance to the view of Athens. The rembetika song goes:

> What is it to you where I come from
> from Karatasi, light of my life, or from Kordelio?

What is it to you that you keep asking me
what village I'm from, since you don't love me?

Where I come from they know how to love
they know how to hide their sorrow and how to enjoy themselves.

What is it to you that you keep asking me
since you've no pity for me, light of my life, and torment me?

I've come from Smyrna to find some comfort
to find in this Athens of ours a loving embrace.

The experience of the diaspora, of exile, is central to the modern Greek experience and many of the most interesting and distinguished Greeks have been through it in one form or another. But like the nature of Greek identity itself, it is ultimately elusive and indefinable, with mystery at its heart.

19. A Balkan or a European Future?

Εθώ δεν είναι παίζε
γέλαδε, εθώ είναι βαλκανία

This is not a place for laughing or playing games,
this is the Balkans

— Theophilus

Balkan is a Turkish word that means mountain. By all the
normal criteria, Greece is a profoundly Balkan country: its
geography, location, the hundreds of years of Ottoman government, its active participation in national liberation movements
against the Turks alongside neighbours like Serbia and
Bulgaria, and so on. Yet Greece is not Balkan in the political
sense — at least that is the prevailing wisdom in Athens now.
Not long ago a conference was organized in London, largely
to put the Greek point of view on the Yugoslav crisis, called
'Greece: A European Democracy between the Balkans and the
Middle East'. Although, at first, the title seems plausible
enough, in reality it should have provoked gales of laughter
among those invited to attend the conference. In the view of
the Athens government, European Community membership
has removed Greece from the Balkan imbroglio but the realities
of the situation do not support this view. The fact that the
conference was called at all is indicative of the very serious
crisis in Greek identity and political direction that has arisen
as a result of economic failure and the disintegration of
Yugoslavia.

Greece sees itself as the source of much European culture, and there was undoubtedly wholehearted assent to European Community entry among most intellectuals. But not all. Even at the high tide of optimism about European unity in the late 1970s, there was always a substantial minority of Greek public opinion against Europe, ranging from old-fashioned national- ists to the old KKE, to the old Byzantinists, to people who simply didn't like the idea of being mixed up in what seemed largely run by, and for, the French and Germans, at one level, or by what most Greeks see as nonentity nationalities like the Belgians at another. But other Greeks were very enthusiastic Europeans: western-looking modernists interviewed frequently on television and, increasingly, anyone seriously concerned with Greek finances from almost any party or viewpoint. But none the less doubts remained. Many Greeks saw the EC, correctly enough in some ways, as primarily the economic arm of NATO, an organization in which Greek membership was involved in endless national security issues, and where member- ship was necessary to balance the influence of Turkey in NATO and Washington. But the Community is not loved, in the way that it has a distinct hold on public opinion in a small country like Holland.

It should be borne in mind that the doubts were not all on one side. Without the overriding imperative to shore up Greek democracy after the colonels' regime, it is more than possible that Greece would never have been allowed to join. In 1976 the Commission in Brussels had written a long internal report on the merits and demerits of Greek membership, and had come to the initial conclusion that membership should be delayed as it could drag the EC into the complicated and sometimes lethal quarrels of eastern Mediterranean countries, and that some sort of settlement with Turkey should be a condition of full membership. But these doubts in the highest reaches of the bureaucracy were overcome by politicians such as the French leader of that time, Mr Valéry Giscard d'Estaing, a keen Philhellene, who put the stabilization of Greek democracy at the top of his list of priorities. He was supported by the German Foreign Minister Hans-Dietrich Genscher – and Britain and the smaller members fell into line. Mr Genscher is also a keen admirer of Greek culture and frequently holidays with German friends at their house on the island of Skiathos.

But all these deliberations took place in a world where Greece was seen as an island of potential western influence in the Balkans, where countries like Bulgaria, Albania and Yugoslavia were all ruled by more or less entrenched and hostile Communist systems. There was no doubt that Greece needed the Community very much, in terms of finance and a source of loan capital to replace declining American subventions, but at that time the Community needed Greece as well – and NATO and the United States needed it even more. The most graphic illustration is the existence of United States bases in Greece and the role that country has played in the various Middle East crises and military confrontations over the years, from the Six-Day War between the Arabs and Israel that so enhanced the status of the junta in Washington to the Gulf War in 1991.

But the collapse of Communism and the fundamental, and what appear to be irreversible, changes in Eastern Europe over the last two or three years have altered Greece's position dramatically. The country no longer appears to be a democratic enclave set in a mountainous landscape full of totalitarians but rather just one more small state in the Balkans as quarrelsome and difficult as the rest but with the very serious additional disadvantage, from the EC point of view, of being extremely expensive. In March 1992 the European Commission sent a damning report to the Community's monetary committee. It pointed out that the GDP per person in Greece fell from 52 per cent of the EC average in 1983–5 to 48 per cent in 1988–90, and that ever larger sums of EC aid – 7 billion ECUs in 1989–93 – have failed to change the situation. Depending on how the figures are analysed, Greek government debt totals 135–40 per cent of GDP and the number of civil servants is still rising by an annual 4.4 per cent. The EC called for spending cuts of 300 billion drachmas in 1992 and 500 billion in 1993.

But with a parliamentary majority of two the only result of Mr Mitsotakis trying to implement such a policy has been to bring down his government and to have it replaced by what is likely to be a militantly nationalist PASOK. Whatever the disciples of financial orthodoxy may hope, the reality for many Greeks is that the kind of economic policies designed to allow Greece to integrate with the Single European Market, and the process towards monetary union envisaged in the Maastricht treaty, have driven up the prices of many necessities while wages have been held down, particularly in the public sector, as a result of EC dictats. A bone of contention has been the dramatic increase in the price of spirits, ouzo especially. Seen from Brussels, Greek governments recently have been regarded as irresponsible and difficult, but there are limits to what Greek public opinion will take, moreover, as there is no perceived enthusiasm for European unity as such in most of Greece. Although a majority of the people would probably favour continuation of EC membership if the question was put to them, there are very few federalists in Greece. From the point of view of diplomatic effectiveness and general political influence, the ideal for Greece is a Europe of nations, where the skill and intelligence of Greek diplomats could wield a disproportionate influence. The kind of increase in centralization proposed under the original version of Maastricht would mean a marked diminution in the role of the smaller countries. At the time of writing, following the

Danish referendum rejection of Maastricht, it is very uncertain what direction the Community will take, and the rejection of Mr Jacques Delors' ambitious plans to transfer large sums under the new EC budgetary arrangements to the poorer EC countries augurs badly for Greek government finances. But although money and *realpolitik* mean that the Mitsotakis government had to toe the general EC line, it should not be assumed that in the event of a showdown between the Community and Athens over Macedonia and/or the Greek financial crisis, the majority of Greek people would necessarily back European-Community-imposed positions. The prolonged rows over Macedonian recognition have affected Greek public perceptions of Europe in fundamental ways. The idea of a Europe without borders is not attractive, given the deepening security crisis in northern Greece with Albania and Macedonia. Here, as always, the attitudes and psychology of the small Benelux countries seem to be the tail wagging the European dog. Relations have reached a very serious stage and the increasingly urgent attempts in Athens to bang the European drum have an empty ring.

At the heart of the crisis is the problem of the economy. In the report of the EC Commission on the Greek economy in March 1992, it was made clear that the financial stabilization programme of the previous two years had not brought any of the changes that were expected in Brussels. As a result, very large tax increases have been proposed but a majority in the Greek government has not supported them. A prominent exception was the Industry Minister Mr Andreas Andrianopoulos who said in April 1992 that the public sector deficit had 'taken on explosive proportions' and threatened to undermine Greece's efforts to join the United Europe. But he was against any further tax increases, saying that the only solution was the immediate privatization of all state-owned industries. The general outlook of the EC officials and Council of Ministers is bound to be shared by the International Monetary Fund officials also in Athens.

Against this background, serious discussion or analysis of what Greece's role might be in the process of further European integration is beginning to seem increasingly abstracted from reality. If there is no sign of Greek governments being able to solve the long-running and intractable economic problems with the benefit of large capital transfers of the kind that have been organized in the last few years, then it is really very difficult to see the richer northern states, such as Germany and Britain, the Community paymasters, being willing to go through with the substantial increases in the EC budget needed to finance Greek integration – or that of other poor, small countries like Ireland. In particular, given the level of Greek interest rates and the weakness of the drachma, it is very difficult indeed to see how a single currency based on the existing ECU would operate in Greece if monetary union goes ahead as envisaged under Maastricht.

So perhaps reality will mean a position for Greece in a kind of two-stage Europe – or something of the kind. But the depth of the crisis with Brussels should not be underestimated. There is no doubt at all that if the EC had a procedure to expel members of the Community, Greece would have been threatened with expulsion during the spring of 1992 in the disputes over Macedonian recognition. At the meeting of EC Foreign Ministers in Lisbon in May 1992, apart from bitter exchanges over Macedonia, Greece continued to block EC aid to Turkey worth 600 million ECUs, despite British and French arguments that Turkey's pivotal role in Central Asia required the Community to assist the Turkish economy.

So with problems of this kind in the wider Europe, new diplomatic initiatives have been taken to secure friends nearer home. Of these, undoubtedly the most controversial has been the connection with Serbia. The visit of Serbian leader Slobodan Milosevic to Athens in March 1992 was designed principally to synchronize policy over Macedonian recognition – or the lack of it – and close links have also been built up with Romania, partly for the same reason. Romanian President Iliescu had long meetings with Greek Prime Minister Mitsotakis on the subject in February 1992. Although it is obviously natural for Greece to forge local diplomatic links in the Balkans, it has been unfortunate from the point of view of international opinion, especially with the administration in Washington, that Greece's two closest friends in the Balkans are Serbia, a state cast in the role of general pariah after the war in Croatia and Bosnia, and Romania, a state with a doubtful transition from Communism and where many observers feel prominent members of the old regime are still in positions of power, with limited progress towards a market economy. But Greece, otherwise, faces increasing isolation and if the political and military situation in the Balkans continues to worsen, it will need all the friends it can find, especially those close to home. Relations with the Bulgarian government appear to be improving somewhat after the dramatic setback earlier this year when Bulgaria recognized Macedonia, and a joint programme of military training has been agreed. Trade links with Sofia are also flourishing: it takes five hours to drive from Thessaloniki to Athens, but only three to reach the Bulgarian capital. Over two hundred Greek–Bulgarian joint ventures have been established since Bulgaria started its move to a market economy. Greek consumer goods, such as ice-cream, trainers and jeans, are in great demand. Behind all this economic activity, the shadow of the Macedonian crisis looms. Greece cannot afford bad relations with Bulgaria: if war does break out in ex-Yugoslav Macedonia, Greece's only overland route to Western Europe will lie through Bulgaria. This appears to be a case of your enemy's enemy being your friend, as a central concern of

Bulgaria's, like that of Greece, is the position of the country *vis-à-vis* Turkey. Bulgaria has a large Turkish minority, living mostly in the south of the country adjoining Turkey, who were persecuted under the last years of Todor Zhivkov, the Stalinist leader of the Bulgarian Communists, and this gave rise to the refugee crisis of 1989–90 in Turkey. This problem ended with democracy and pluralism, but the Turks have their own political party in Bulgaria and could hold the balance of power in a future government. A Greek–Bulgarian alliance makes sense if the attentions of Ankara extend further into creating a sphere of influence in the Balkans.

The future for Greece looks very difficult. The opportunities offered by European Community membership have not really been taken and on every side, seen from Athens, there are problems. For the West, the role of Greece in the new Europe is far from clear. It does not look as if integration into a Single Market and the Maastricht arrangements are going to work – whatever develops on that front in the next year or so. To the north is a rapid and spreading crisis in the Balkans, poor relations with Albania over illegal immigration and the Vorio Epirus question, and the conflict over Macedonia. To the east and north-east lie the always antagonistic interests of Turkey, and the unpredictable pattern of development of the ex-Communist states of Eastern Europe and the Commonwealth of Independent States. A little further round the clock, as it were, lies Cyprus, and the possibility of some future crisis over that troubled island. Only to the south lies calm, in the form of the waves and changing colours of the Mediterranean. And even there, peace of mind should perhaps be regarded critically as the possibility of ecological disaster is always present with major oil tankers plying the busy shipping lanes. An accident could ruin the tourist industry – as could a single attack from Macedonian terrorists. So the 1990s for Greece will mean, in all probability, the rediscovery of itself as a

Balkan country and a process of greater distancing from northern Europe. Such a perspective is not without hope, however uncomfortable it may appear to the softer members of the élite in Athens who have seen the lost Holy Grail of Greek prosperity in Brussels. The twin sides of the Greek national and personal character have always co-existed: the western-looking rationalist side – the thinking that gave rise to philosophy and mathematics as peculiarly Greek creations – and the mystical Eastern side, which finds its roots in Byzantium and Orthodoxy, not really sure whether a national identity based on Athens is at heart Greek. The last years have been dominated by the rationalist side but if the problems of the Balkans are going to dominate the agenda the political skills and mentality of the East will be much more important. However unpleasant and difficult Balkan conflicts appear to be, the perceived superiority of ancient Greek culture was responsible for the existence of so many small states, where the Roman conquerors respected local boundaries as they did not elsewhere. It may seem strange but in a real sense Greece is the regional superpower. To be a Balkan, not a European, country, in the sense of being part of a potential federal Europe, must be a likely destiny for Greece. In cultural terms, if this means the reaffirmation of many features of traditional Greek life at risk from an increasingly technocratic and conformist culture emanating from the United States and Brussels, it must be a welcome development.

Epilogue

The new Balkans often seem to be only about the revival of the past. Borders, frontiers, men in ill-fitting uniforms staring down at filthy old desks covered in passports. Ramboism, xenophobia, militarism, hunting-club members turned murderers, drunk on slivowitz and shooting up the town, the hasty search for arms in the boot of the car. But here in the Epirus mountains, an Albanian refugee is gazing at a prosperous-looking Greek businessman standing in the dust and amidst piles of rubbish – old squashed cardboard boxes and half-eaten meals abandoned when the bus to Yannina comes unexpectedly early. This is high Epirus. Behind the two men is a thickly forested hillside with houses of one of the most remote villages in Greece just visible as the trees march around the edge of the scree, countless green soldiers in heavy uniforms of leaves, rising above the dense undergrowth. Nikos is looking at the border, adjusting his blazer buttons. His grey flannels are well creased and he could have just emerged from Harrods men's department rather than standing here, staring north at the majestic Alpine scale of the Buret mountains in southern Albania. A Golden eagle sweeps and loops overhead, oblivious on its thermals to border distinctions or political systems. The sun picks up the river Dropull – or Drin as the Albanians call it – rushing over the limestone pebbles far below. Nikos is about forty, with a successful business trading in chemicals in Piraeus. He normally lives in a world of telex and fax messages, and his great love, his boat, is kept at Glifada, the Athenian marina. Business takes him to Albania where his father, as a retreating Democratic Army soldier, had struggled over the frontier at the end of the Greek Civil War to be demobbed at the Albanian industrial city of Elbasan. He had then returned to Thessaly, to the family home, not as bad for reprisals as many areas. He had not been physically threatened but no one would use his grocer's shop, so the family abandoned home and went to Piraeus. The old man moved chemicals, pushing tin drums across the factory floor. His son Nikos now moves them in airplanes and ships across the world. He has a public position as a member of the PASOK committee on the environment.

As the sun crosses the valley, a green and black lizard streaks over the road and the Albanian refugee fiddles with his broken glasses, trying to wedge a lens back in with a tiny piece of wood. Nikos reflects on his country and countrymen: 'I am very pessimistic. I think things look black for Greece now, *polli mavro*. But for the Greeks – for us – yes, I am very optimistic. Very optimistic.'

In the distance, down the valley, a speck moves on the road. The bus to Yannina is coming and the refugee stands up, clutching his precious passport. Soon he will be sweating in the sun at Arta, not for very many drachmas a day picking many oranges – thousands of boxes to load the container lorries for Dutch and German supermarkets.

As in Ottoman days, the mountains lose their men. The city is waiting. The cover will soon be taken off the lanterna in the taverna in Panormou Street, the squid will be cooking. Up here, the sun will go down over the mountains, the road will be deserted. The ghosts of dead soldiers will remain as in the andartes song:

> What is the matter with the mountains of Epirus,
>   my poor Nikos Pakos
> that they are shrouded so, Nikos Pakos, my brave man.

Perhaps they're lashed with hail, perhaps they're
   whipped with rain.

It's not that they're lashed with hail, nor that they're
   whipped with rain.

They're weeping for their *kapetanios* who has been
   killed.

Index

(*Historical sub-entries in chronological order precede the subjective sub-entries in alphabetical sequence*)

STOCKPORT GRAMMAR SCHOOL
LIBRARY